SCHOL CHANGE

and the

MicroSociety® Program

*To Seymour B. Sarason, teacher, mentor, guide,
and friend; and to the memory of George Richmond,
a creative visionary who gave so much to so many*

SCHOOL CHANGE

and the

MicroSociety®

Program

CARY CHERNISS
Foreword by
Roland S. Barth

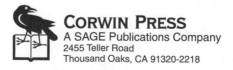

CORWIN PRESS
A SAGE Publications Company
2455 Teller Road
Thousand Oaks, CA 91320-2218

For information:

Corwin Press
A Sage Publications Company
2455 Teller Road
Thousand Oaks, California 91320
www.corwinpress.com

Sage Publications Ltd.
1 Oliver's Yard
55 City Road
London EC1Y 1SP
United Kingdom

Sage Publications India Pvt. Ltd.
B-42, Panchsheel Enclave
Post Box 4109
New Delhi 110 017 India

Printed in the United States of America

Library of Congress Cataloging-in-Publication Data

Cherniss, Cary.
School change and the *MicroSociety*® Program/Cary Cherniss.
    p. cm.
Includes bibliographical references and index.
ISBN 1–4129–1760–3 (cloth)—ISBN 1–4129–1761–1 (pbk.)
    1. School improvement programs—United States.
2. School management and organization—United States. 3. Educational change—United States. I. Title.
LB2822.82.C44 2006
371.2'00973—dc22   2005009586

This book is printed on acid-free paper.

05   06   07   08   09   10   9   8   7   6   5   4   3   2   1

Acquisitions Editor:	Elizabeth Brenkus
Editorial Assistant:	Candice L. Ling
Production Editor:	Beth A. Bernstein
Copy Editor:	Carla Freeman
Typesetter:	C&M Digitals (P) Ltd.
Proofreader:	Colleen Brennan
Indexer:	Judy Hunt
Cover Designer:	Anthony Paular
Graphic Designer:	Scott Van Atta

Contents

Foreword   ix
   Roland S. Barth

Preface   xv

Acknowledgements   xxiv

About the Author   xxvii

PART I: OVERVIEW OF THE PROGRAM   1

1. The MicroSociety® Program   3
    A Day in the Life of a *MicroSociety*® Program School   3
       Life in the Classroom   4
       Micro Begins   5
       Crime and Punishment   6
    The Origins of the *MicroSociety*® Program   7
    The *MicroSociety*® Idea Spreads   9
    The Guiding Philosophy
      Behind the *MicroSociety*® Program   10
    Basic Elements of the Program   12
       The Economic System   13
       The Political System   14
       Adult Roles   15
    MicroSociety® Program
      Outcomes: What the Research Shows   17
       Impact on Academic Skills   17
       Nonacademic Outcomes   19
    The Problem of Implementation   21
    Conclusion   21

2. Challenges Encountered in Implementing the Program   23
    Lack of Teacher Buy-In   24
    Excessive Time and Work Demands   25

Making Links Between
    the *MicroSociety*® Program and the Core Curriculum   30
What to Do With "Problem" Students?   34
The Problem of Staff Conflict   37
The "Fog of Change"   39
Threats to Sustainability   40
Conclusion   42

PART II: GUIDELINES FOR SUCCESSFUL IMPLEMENTATION   **45**

3. **Creating a Favorable Context**   **47**
    Guideline 1: Relationships Among Teachers and Principal   48
    Guideline 2: Goodness of Fit   51
    Guideline 3: Parent and Community Involvement   53
    Guideline 4: Principal Support   56

4. **Introducing the Program to the School**   **59**
    Guideline 5: Giving Teachers a Meaningful Voice   59
    Guideline 6: Planning Before the Program Begins   65
    Guideline 7: Securing Additional Funding   71
    Guideline 8: Matching Teachers With Ventures   73
    Guideline 9: Realistic Goals and Time Perspectives   74
    Conclusion   77

5. **Keeping It Running**   **79**
    Guideline 10: Expand Student Responsibility   79
    Guideline 11: Seek Out Additional Resources   82
    Guideline 12: Create a Culture of Experimentation   87
    Guideline 13: Continue to Set Aside Time for Planning   90
    Guideline 14: Create an Open and
        Flexible Decision-Making Structure   94
    Conclusion   97

6. **Leadership: The Critical Ingredient**   **99**
    Guideline 15: The Principal as Advocate   100
    Guideline 16: Emotionally Intelligent Leadership   103
    Conclusion   108

PART III: CASE STUDIES IN IMPLEMENTATION   **109**

7. **A Successful Replication: Mesquite Elementary School**   **111**
    Before-the-Beginning: Providing a Favorable Context   114
    Introducing the Program to the School   116

Making It Work: The Management Team,
    Coordinator, and Consultant   121
        The Management Team   122
        The *MicroSociety* Program Coordinator   123
        The External Consultant   123
Maintaining Teacher Commitment
    Through Decision Making, Planning, and Training   124
Seeking Out and Using Resources   126
A Supportive Principal and Organizational Climate   128
The Principal's Social Capital and Emotional Intelligence   131
Conclusion   132

8. **Wellfleet Elementary: Everything That Can Go Wrong . . .**   **135**
The School and Its History With the Program   135
What Went Wrong? The Before-the-Beginning Phase   138
Sowing the Seeds of Trouble:
    Introducing the Program to the School   140
Becoming Operational: Trying to Cope With Chaos   142
The Organizational Context:
    Weak Leadership and a Negative Climate   146

9. **The Challenge of Sustainability:**
Montgomery Middle School   **153**
The School and Its Community   154
Introducing the Program to the School:
    The Principal Takes the Lead   156
Becoming Operational: The Teachers Confront Reality   160
The Problem of Resources   162
Insufficient Training and Planning Time   164
Lack of Teacher Voice in Decision Making   165
An Effective Coordinator   166
The Organizational Context: A Supportive Principal   167
The Program Ends   171

**PART IV: SUSTAINING SCHOOL
CHANGE IN AN EVER-CHANGING WORLD**   **173**

10. **Implications for Research, Policy, and Practice**   **175**
Implementing Change Versus Sustaining It   175
Two Central Lessons That Emerge From the Study   179
A First Step: The Selection and Training of Educators   184
The Role of the External Environment   185
Conclusion   188

Resource A: A Description of the Study   189

Resource B: The Implementation Guidelines   195

References   197

Index   200

Foreword

Few issues in our society are more vital than creating good schools. And few are more elusive and intractable. Indeed, the history of American education is littered with remnants of disappointing efforts to improve schools.

Limited success in making schools hospitable to human learning is not for lack of effort. Indeed, hosts of change agents heroically try to make a difference from their distinctive positions. For instance, it is believed that schools can be improved by:

Improving teacher preparation and selection

Providing preservice and inservice leadership development

Improving the curriculum

Involving parents

Central office mandates

Deployment of funds by private foundations

State and federal legislation

Rigorous and frequent standardized testing

Yet all too often, the impact of these efforts is marginalized because each sees and latches onto only the trunk, leg, or tail of the elephant.

Enter the "comprehensive school reform" movement. The rationale is straightforward and compelling: Schools will change only through coherent, systemic, and systematic efforts in which the entire school focuses upon a particular educational philosophy and a particular methodology. Things happen only when the entire elephant is comprehended and grasped!

The *MicroSociety*® program is one of many whole-school reform efforts proliferating throughout the country over the past decade or so. The pages you are about to encounter are about "Micro," its derivation, its underlying set of beliefs and practices, and its robust place in the life of more than 200 elementary and middle schools in America.

Yet the volume is much more. In many ways, it is about ALL attempts to improve schools. Micro may be but one idiosyncratic school reform effort. However, I find the conditions for change explicated here and the process of implementing and sustaining change to be generic.

Hence what you are about to encounter in the pages that follow can be approached along two parallel tracks: the learnings from the *MicroSociety* experience, on one hand, and what we can learn about the exquisitely treacherous and difficult work of improving a school, on the other.

Among the issues considered here—all too familiar to those of us who have or will ever attempt to improve a school—are:

Gaining teacher buy-in and commitment

Getting teachers and principals to relinquish "control"

Reconciling philosophical and pedagogical differences

Dealing with additional "add-ons" of time and effort

Curriculum development and articulation

Problem students who will not comply

Parental involvement

Leadership

Generating adequate resources

Sustaining change over time

George Richmond, the founder of *MicroSociety*, was my close friend for 40 years. Throughout my career, I have also been a close friend of imaginative, experiential education, of which Micro is an example. I serve on the Board of MicroSociety, Inc. And I have been an enthusiastic member of the cheering section for this book in its various stages of development. So let me be frank to point out that I am heavily biased in favor of the innovator, the innovation, and the scribe.

Fortunately, Cary Cherniss, who writes with welcome clarity and insight, is far more objective, independent, rigorous, and scholarly in his treatment of *MicroSociety*—although he too, in the end, becomes converted by the power of this compelling idea for improving schools.

Over the years, I have visited several *MicroSociety* Schools. I like what I see. It feels right. It 's "working." Easy to see and to say, but oh so difficult to capture in words. Let me try to articulate why I feel *MicroSociety* offers such a promising road to fundamental school reform. There are several reasons:

1. We often read in curriculum guides some version of this sentence: "The purpose of education is to prepare students to prepare for and live successfully within our democratic society." A noble goal indeed. Yet why is it that the governance of most schools and classrooms resembles far more a South American dictatorship than a New England town meeting? I fear that our schools are succeeding in teaching that democracy is a fraud.

   Students will come to fill their places in a democratic society not by taking civics classes, but by being immersed in a working democracy. *MicroSociety* provides just such a setting. In the Micro schools I have visited, it is clear that students know what a vibrant democracy is all about. They know what a democracy can do for them and what they can do for a democracy. And they come to demand it outside of school as well as in.

2. Most of what goes on in schools is problem solving, those posed by teachers to students. Youngsters solve algebra problems. They find the causes of the War of 1812. They answer the questions the teacher poses for a reading assignment. To be sure, there are plenty of times that addressing the teachers' problems is important, even essential, for a student's well-being.

   Yet the learning potential in students responding to teachers' problems is limited. It is the problems that we humans pose for ourselves, care deeply about, and in which we are motivated to engage and find meaning that harbor the greatest learning . . . in the short run while in school, and in the longer run beyond school. Consequently, I believe learning in schools will become energized and likely to spread to out of school time only when youngsters have as many opportunities to pose and address their own problems as teachers pose for them.

   No one sums it up better than George Bernard Shaw: "What we want to see is the child in pursuit of knowledge, not knowledge in pursuit of the child."

   I see in *MicroSociety* an elegant, comprehensive structure that enables teachers and students to achieve a balance of the problems posed by each. Here students (and teachers!) learn how to pose and sharpen problems and questions and invest themselves in marshalling resources to address and resolve them. Here, we see the child in pursuit of knowledge.

3. The predominant sound within the schoolhouse is the voice of the teacher. It has been estimated that about 85% of what goes on in schools is teacher-directed, didactic instruction. This is a transmission

of information from the teacher (who presumably has it) to the student (who presumably does not); 15% is something else.

Unfortunately, ample research suggests that a person retains a few weeks later perhaps 5% of what he or she is told. A weak treatment. This, despite the fact that current brain research suggests the length of time a teacher talks to students should not exceed in minutes the age of the student in years. So, for instance: didactic instruction no longer than 10 minutes for fourth graders who are 10 years old.

If I could do one thing to reform schools in this country it would be to shift the ratio to 15% didactic instruction, 85% something else.

"But what do I do for 85% of the time if I don't 'instruct' the students?" a teacher asks. It is when we ask, "How can I promote profound levels of human learning besides talking?" that I believe we really become educators.

MicroSociety finds a way to reduce the formal teacher instruction way below 85% and introduces a yeasty repertoire of "something else." How? By creating within the schoolhouse a miniature but genuine community of businesses, banks, courts, and law enforcement systems in which students play real and essential roles. To play those roles, they must, of course, learn. They learn about taxes, banking, law enforcement, the judiciary, about politics and an economic system. And in so doing, as both Cherniss and research suggest (even though Micro does not teach to the test), their literacy skills rise, their test scores rise, their attendance rises, and parent and teacher satisfaction rises.

4. I believe schools will succeed in promoting learning when students find on a regular basis in their school experiences both pleasure and success. Not all the time, of course. Not all learning is pleasant. Much learning comes from difficulty, even failure. But students must experience pleasure and success often enough so that they will feel absorbed, committed, and satisfied in their learning. Unfortunately, this is not the case for many students in many schools.

How to ensure that each day each student will experience times of pleasure and success in learning, then, is a crucial challenge for the educator. Those immersed in *MicroSociety* are finding success in meeting this challenge.

So in Micro, one finds nothing less than a democratic vehicle for empowering students in their own education, a framework that enables teachers to be facilitators of students' learning as well as transmitters of knowledge, a continuing source of satisfaction, accomplishment, and joy for students . . . and a holistic conception that enables the principal to hold it all together. That's a lot!

It's been said, "The only person who welcomes change is a wet baby." Cherniss forthrightly points out a sobering side to the *MicroSociety* story: The work of changing schools is not for the faint of heart. Impediments abound from within the school and from without. For all of the benefits Micro offers, it's not easy going. Indeed, as one case study of a school's failed attempt to adopt *MicroSociety* attests all too well, for this (or any) innovation to take root, a daunting array of conditions must be in place.

As much as he admires the *MicroSociety* model, Cary Cherniss warns us that a good model is not enough. Change agents need effective strategies for implementing and *sustaining* that model.

In this thoughtful "users' manual," school reformers, teachers, principals, central office officials, and scholars will find an approachable and immensely helpful guide full of strategies for walking that treacherous path toward school improvement.

I wish I had had this volume during my years as a principal!

Preface

Many Americans now believe that their schools should be better. Too many students leave school without mastery of the basic skills and knowledge that are critical for healthy and happy lives. The problem is especially severe for low-income and ethnic minority students who live in large cities. In the United States, only about 40% of students in urban schools score at a basic level on reading, mathematics, and science tests (Olson & Jerald, 1998). In addition, violence is an almost daily occurrence in such schools, and worn-out teachers often leave after teaching for only 2 or 3 years. Some of the most promising young teachers do not even survive the first year.

The situation usually is better in suburban schools serving middle-class communities, but even here, the picture is not bright. More students in nonurban schools manage to pass standardized tests, but only 65% score at a basic level or above on standardized tests (Olson & Jerald, 1998). Violence is less prevalent in these schools, but incidents like the one at Columbine High School in Colorado show that it does occur. Moreover, even though most students come to school and sit at their desks for most of the school day, too many of them tune out. As they pass through the system, the enthusiasm they once had for learning evaporates; they become disaffected not only from school but also from the learning process itself. Even students who emerge with strong academic records often lack basic knowledge about history, geography, and science; and they view reading, math, and writing as activities that they must do to get good grades or please adults. Few students emerge from the process of schooling with a sense that learning is intrinsically pleasurable.

A HISTORY OF REFORM EFFORTS

Dissatisfaction with the performance of our schools is not a new phenomenon. Our public education system's disappointing results have led to a constant stream of reform efforts. Almost as long as we have had universal, mandatory public education in America, we have had reformers who have tried to make the system work better. However, during the last 40 years, both the degree of dissatisfaction and the pace of change have increased substantially (Fullan, 1993). Two historical factors triggered this period of ferment and change. One was the launching of the first space satellite by the Soviet Union in 1958. This accomplishment, occurring in the midst of the Cold War, led many Americans to demand that the nation's schools do a better job of producing well-trained scientists and engineers so that we could win the "space race." In response, the government began to invest significant amounts of money into national curriculum reform efforts, such as the New Math (Dow, 1991; Evans, 1996; Sarason, 1996).

The other factor that shaped the reform agenda of the 1960s involved the discovery of "the other America" and the civil rights movement. A number of books written by idealistic young educators described the plight of teachers and students in inner-city schools. Many of these works also pointed to methods that are more progressive as a way of rejuvenating such schools. These works led many schools to adopt educational innovations such as the "open classroom."

Unfortunately, both personal experience and a growing body of negative research findings led many educators to question the wisdom of these reform efforts, and in the late 1970s, a new approach to reform emerged, which promised to be more successful than the earlier efforts. Known as the "effective schools" movement, it focused on the qualities of schools that, according to empirical research, predicted greater student learning.

In the early 1980s, historical events once again intruded and led to another change in course. This time, the perceived threat to the nation was economic rather than political. A deep economic recession set in during this period, and a number of reports emerged from Japan suggesting that a country we had totally defeated in war less than 30 years before had overtaken us economically. In 1983, a presidential commission concluded that a large part of the problem was due to the sorry state of our educational system. The commission issued an influential report, titled *A Nation at Risk*, which led to a variety of governmental reform efforts.

The problem with many of these reform efforts was that schools did not implement them effectively. A number of studies, books, and articles pointed to the fact that no matter how good a new educational approach might seem to the academics or policymakers who proposed it, many of those charged with implementing it failed to do so in a consistent and effective way. As a result, there was growing dissatisfaction with the highly technical, top-down approach to change that seemed to ignore the "human side" and, in doing so, ensured that "The more things changed, the more they remained the same" (Firestone & Corbett, 1988; Louis, Toole, & Hargreaves, 1999; Sarason, 1996).

In response to this growing concern with the process of change, there emerged in the mid-1980s a new movement called "restructuring," which shifted the emphasis onto the way in which instruction is organized at the level of the school building. An important element of this new approach was to empower those at the bottom of the educational hierarchy, such as parents and teachers. "School-based management" was one of the best-known innovations to come out of this period of reform.

During the 1990s, there appeared a new approach called "whole-school reform." As the name implies, whole-school reform calls for the entire school to become mobilized around a particular educational philosophy and model. However, unlike some earlier reform movements, an underlying premise was that no single model is best for all schools.

Whole-school reform received a boost in 1991 when the New American Schools (NAS) Development Corporation embarked on an ambitious initiative, founded on the premise that educational reform had been unsuccessful because it was based on "multiple and unconnected approaches to address each area of school" (Berends, Bodilly, & Kirby, 2003, p. xv). A better approach was for schools to "integrate research-based practices into a coherent and mutually reinforcing set of effective approaches to teaching and learning for the entire school" (Berends et al., 2003, p. xv). This premise came in part from earlier research that had identified the qualities that the most effective schools had in common (Purkey & Smith, 1983). NAS funded the development and implementation of several different designs, and these NAS-sponsored designs spread to more than 4,000 schools by 2001.

Encouraged by the NAS efforts, the U.S. Congress passed the Comprehensive School Reform Demonstration (CSRD) Act (1998). The act targeted those schools that consistently failed to educate many of their students, and it provided the schools with financial incentives to undertake whole-school reform. Schools that qualified could receive substantial amounts of federal money to help them improve their performance. However, to receive the money, schools had to adopt a "whole-school reform model." Schools could choose from a number of different models, but the model had to be one that had been "backed by scientifically-based research" (Traub, 2002).

By the late 1990s, various national and state educational bodies had certified as many as 30 different models (Traub, 2002). The best-known include Theodore Sizer's Coalition of Essential Schools, Robert Slavin's Success for All (and its expanded version, called "Roots and Wings"), and James Comer's School Development Program. Two other popular models are Henry Levin's Accelerated Schools approach and E. D. Hirsch Jr.'s Core Knowledge.

There have been other reform movements along the way, such as "systemic reform" and "school-to-careers." However, the most recent effort has once again put school reform on the national agenda. With the No Child Left Behind Act, passed by the U.S. Congress and signed into law in 2001, we have returned to a period of increasing governmental activism. The focus once again is on accountability and results. Now, more than ever, the emphasis is on changing the organizational incentives in order to force schools to improve their teaching efforts. The goal is for children to perform better on standardized tests. The new initiative also places even greater emphasis on educational practices that have received empirical support.

Not all educational researchers, theorists, or policymakers have been enamored with the prospect of educational reform during the last 40 years. Two respected educational historians have argued that Americans tend to expect too much of their schools and of school reform. They wrote, "Sometimes preserving good practices in the face of challenges is a major achievement, and sometimes teachers have been wise to resist reforms that violated their professional judgment" (Tyack & Cuban, 1995, p. 5). They also pointed out that while "policy talk" has often been utopian, actual reforms have been "gradual and incremental" and that such "tinkering" often is more useful than more radical transformations (Tyack & Cuban, 1995, pp. 6–7).

Despite these cautions, Americans continue to seek ways of improving their schools. The rate of educational failure is too high, and the consequences of failure are too costly. When it comes to education, the status quo simply is not good enough.

THE PROBLEMS OF IMPLEMENTATION AND SUSTAINABILITY

Unfortunately, when it comes to educational reform, having a good model is not good enough. There are many examples in the past of effective ideas, models, and programs that have failed to live up to their potential when proponents attempted to disseminate them widely or "go to scale" (Elmore, 1996; Firestone & Corbett, 1988; Louis et al., 1999; McLaughlin, 1990; Schorr, 1997). An early example was the famous "Dewey School," based at the University of Chicago, created and initially directed by John Dewey, the founder of Progressive Education. Available accounts suggest that this school was a model of intellectual vitality and growth for students, parents, and teachers (Mayhew & Edwards, 1966). However, when the Progressive approach spread across the country during the next 30 years, the results rarely approached those obtained by Dewey and his staff.

The problem of disseminating effective models that closely adhere to the original continues to plague reformers, and it is especially salient for whole-school reform efforts. When the RAND Corporation studied the implementation process in NAS schools, they found that there were many barriers to implementation and that implementation was uneven both across schools and within schools (Berends et al., 2003).

However, equally vexing is the problem of sustainability. Even when a new educational practice is implemented in a school with high fidelity, it rarely can be sustained for long. Often it takes only a change in the principal for the new practice to disappear, often to be replaced by a new innovation. It is not surprising that veteran educators have become so cynical about educational reform when they have seen so many "break-the-mold" innovations come and go over the years.

Although researchers have studied educational reform for decades, they have begun to look at the problem of sustainability only recently. However, they already are identifying many of the factors that are most important for sustaining new practices. They are finding that the organizational and political realities and the ways in which change agents address these realities strongly influence the long-term viability of an innovation. Potentially worthwhile educational alternatives often fail to persist because those who try to implement them are not aware of the organizational problems or the strategies that successful schools have used to overcome them (Schwebel, 2003). This book is about the factors that work for or against sustainability of school change.

THE *MICROSOCIETY*®
PROGRAM AS AN EXEMPLAR

This book addresses the problem of sustainability by focusing on the implementation of one particular innovation: the *MicroSociety*® program. Educator George Richmond first developed the concept while he was teaching a fifth-grade class in Brooklyn, New York, in 1967. To engage an unruly group of students in the learning process, Richmond came up with the idea of creating a miniature society within the classroom. He reasoned that if the school's traditional structures for imposing control over the students did not work, perhaps giving the students some freedom and responsibility could. Eventually, his classroom-based society included a bank, a government, publishing enterprises, and various businesses created and operated by the students. The students immediately became engrossed in their "micro-society," and Richmond used the students' experiences to bring alive their lessons in math, social studies, English, and science. Richmond eventually wrote a book on the experiment (Richmond,

1973), and other educators began to develop their own versions of the concept. In 1981, the city of Lowell, Massachusetts, created an entire school based on the model. Today, about 200 schools across the country have adopted the program, and the government has certified the *MicroSociety* program as one of those whole-school reform models that schools may adopt as part of the Comprehensive School Reform initiative.

When I first learned about the *MicroSociety* program from my friend and colleague, Lew Gantwerk, I realized that it provided a good opportunity to study the problems associated with trying to implement and sustain promising educational models. Therefore I arranged to meet with George Richmond. Dr. Richmond and his wife, Carolynn King, formed MicroSociety, Inc. (MSI), a private, nonprofit organization devoted to promoting and disseminating the model. They were willing to support an independent study of the implementation process.

Eventually, I studied about a dozen different schools that had implemented the *MicroSociety* program, and I studied six of the schools in depth. (Detailed information about the research can be found in Resource A.) The schools were diverse on a number of dimensions. Some were elementary, and some were middle schools. Some were urban, and some were suburban or rural. The ethnicity, special needs, and language mix of the schools varied as well. Most important, however, some of the schools were more successful in implementing the program and sustaining it over time than were others.

By "successful," I mean the extent to which schools implemented the *MicroSociety* program as intended (sometimes referred to as the "fidelity" criterion), the extent to which the staff were committed and satisfied with it, and the extent to which the school was able to sustain the innovation over an extended period. Two of the schools selected for in-depth study met all of the criteria for success.

I spent 2 to 5 days in each school. Data came from multiple sources. In addition to individual and group interviews, I observed one or more *MicroSociety* program application sessions in each school. I also observed classrooms during periods of the day when the applications learning period of the *MicroSociety* program was not in operation, and I observed nonclassroom settings such as the cafeteria, playground, halls, media center or library, main office, and teachers' lounge. Data also came from observation of faculty planning meetings and study of archival materials (which included minutes of faculty planning meetings, principals' notes, grant proposals, newspaper articles, etc.).

In addition to studying specific schools, I also attended three of the national summer training conferences, during which I participated in several workshops and informally spoke with dozens of teachers and principals from other *MicroSociety* program schools. I also led several workshops that focused on organizational problems associated with implementation.

It should be noted that the schools I studied had created their *MicroSociety* programs with little guidance from MSI. In fact, when they were created, MSI had no staff or training model. Their main activity was to organize a summer training conference each year. Thus at most, the schools I studied had read George Richmond's book, sent some staff to the national training conference, and visited a few other *MicroSociety* programs. After I had completed my research, MSI developed a much larger and stronger organization, including a formal training program, a cadre of full-time trainers, and a wealth of training materials. Schools that have adopted the *MicroSociety* program after I completed my study typically receive much more training and other kinds of external support for their implementation efforts.

THE ROLE OF THE RESEARCHER

In research of this sort, the beliefs and biases of the investigator are always an important part of the research process, and readers need to consider these when they evaluate the findings. My own views about the *MicroSociety* program changed as the study progressed. In the beginning, the *MicroSociety* program intrigued me, and it seemed to incorporate many of my own educational values. Nevertheless, I tried to retain as much of a neutral stance as possible, and I think I was initially successful in doing so. Over time, however, my views toward the program became more positive, and I became less concerned about remaining neutral toward the program itself. On the other hand, I continued to try to maintain an objective stance toward the focus of the study, which was not whether the *MicroSociety* program was worthwhile, but rather the process of trying to implement and sustain it in different schools across the country.

At this point, my view is that the *MicroSociety* program is a valuable approach to making schools more interesting and productive places for both teachers and children. However, like any innovation, achieving the full impact of the program and sustaining it over time depend on the mind-sets and skills of the educators who implement it. In addition, it is not a panacea, and it is not for everyone. For some children and teachers, other approaches may well be more appropriate.

WHAT I LEARNED: A PREVIEW

In comparing the successful cases with the less successful ones, a number of lessons about implementation emerged. Some of the findings confirmed results that have emerged in previous research on school improvement. For instance, in the most successful cases, the school and school system provided a more receptive context for the program. Particularly important was the organizational climate, that is, the quality of relationships among the teachers and between the teachers and the principal in the school. If mistrust and conflict characterized these relationships, then the chances of successful implementation were slim at best. Also fateful was the extent to which the new program matched the school and school district's needs and priorities.

Some of the other findings help to refine certain principles on school improvement that have become almost axiomatic. For instance, many reformers now see "teacher buy-in" as an essential condition for successful reform. Thus it is not surprising that in every school I studied, the administration gave the teachers the opportunity to decide whether the school would adopt the program. However, a careful study of how teachers participated in this decision revealed important differences in the quality of participation. In the less successful cases, teacher participation was perfunctory. Many of the teachers did not have a very good understanding of what they were voting for, and some "went along" despite incomplete information or even reservations because "the principal wanted to do it" and they figured there was no point in standing in the way. The research helped to clarify what kind of adoption process is most likely to secure an informed and genuine commitment on the part of the teachers. It provided concrete, detailed models of effective teacher participation that can serve as guides for policy and practice in the future.

A few findings were unexpected and led to new insights about the implementation process. One of the most important of these insights is that the outcome will greatly depend on how well school leaders and change agents effectively manage and understand their own emotions and those of others throughout the difficult process of change, a set of abilities known as "emotional intelligence." Although a few writers on school reform have recognized that emotion plays an important role, this study adds to our understanding of this aspect of reform by exploring how emotional intelligence influences the outcome of the change process.

INTENDED AUDIENCE

This book is primarily intended for educational policymakers, administrators, and scholars (including graduate students) interested in educational reform and school change. The book also will be of interest to teachers, parents, and anyone else who is interested in learning more about the factors that influence the fate of school improvement efforts. And it will be especially interesting for those associated with more than 200 *MicroSociety* schools across the United States. The proposed book also could be used in a number of courses, particularly those in the area of educational administration.

OVERVIEW OF THE BOOK

The first part of the book introduces the *MicroSociety* program. Chapter 1 describes what it looks like, how it works, its underlying educational philosophy and rationale, and empirical research on its impact. Chapter 2 highlights the challenges encountered by schools in trying to implement the *MicroSociety* program. These challenges include lack of teacher buy-in, excessive time and work demands, and difficulty in making links between Micro and the core curriculum. Managing students who act out and staff conflict are two other challenges frequently involved in implementation. All of these challenges relate to a single, underlying problem: Many teachers do not understand the real essence of the program. Effective implementation of the program requires changing the mind-set of most teachers, and this is the greatest challenge of all.

The second part of the book presents a set of guidelines that pertain to the implementation process. Although these guidelines came primarily from my research on the *MicroSociety* program, they also came from the results of other research on the sustainability of school change. As such, they can help schools achieve success in implementing any whole-school reform model.

The first set of guidelines (Chapter 3) relates to the organizational context that exists before implementation of the program. The next set (Chapter 4) relates to the way in which the principal or others introduce the program to the school. A third set of guidelines (Chapter 5) pertains to the way in which the school manages the program once it is operational. The final set of guidelines (Chapter 6) involves the role of leadership in school change efforts. (I also have summarized these practice guidelines in Resource B.)

The third part of the book illustrates how the guidelines work in practice by presenting case studies of three different *MicroSociety* programs. These three case studies help show how important the implementation guidelines are for sustaining an effective *MicroSociety* program in a school. They also help to ground those guidelines in concrete experience. Chapter 7 describes one of the most successful *MicroSociety* programs, an elementary school that has become a showplace for the *MicroSociety* program concept. Chapter 8 describes another elementary school that attempted to implement the *MicroSociety* program, but in this case, the attempt ended in failure. Chapter 9 describes a middle school that achieved great success with the program and retained it for several years. Despite the initial success, however, the school struggled with some significant barriers that ultimately led to the program's demise. This chapter demonstrates why sustainability is a major challenge for the *MicroSociety* program and other reforms, and it points to the guidelines that can help schools to sustain school improvement efforts.

The book ends with a look at some implications for educational policy and practice. The last chapter begins with a set of guidelines related specifically to the challenge of sustaining change in schools (as opposed to just implementing it). Then the chapter highlights two central lessons that emerged from the research and their implications for educational policy. The chapter concludes with a discussion of the role of the external environment in school change efforts, especially in light of initiatives such as the federal No Child Left Behind legislation.

Despite a long history of efforts to reform public education in America, the results have been disappointing. Virtually every new approach to reform has struggled with the all-too-familiar problems of implementation and sustainability. Having a good model is not enough; reformers need effective strategies for implementing the model in a way that helps it to last. This book, based on an in-depth study of one such model, suggests how educators can begin to improve the quality of our schools through more effective school change efforts.

ACKNOWLEDGMENTS

It is particularly difficult to acknowledge all of the individuals who helped with a project such as this book. Literally hundreds of students, teachers, administrators, and parents in dozens of schools that implemented the *MicroSociety*® program have made important contributions. However, a number of individuals stand out and deserve special recognition. I hope I manage to name all of them here.

When it comes to educational matters, my greatest source of inspiration since graduate school days has been Seymour B. Sarason. It was Seymour who first made me interested in all of the topics covered in this work: teaching and learning, schools as social settings, the challenges of school change and educational reform, and the importance of organizational dynamics in the change process. Most important, Seymour helped me to see that organizational change could be an object of study and that only through studying the process can we hope to improve it.

For this particular project, the first important source of help was my friend and colleague Lew Gantwerk. Lew was the one who first made me aware of the *MicroSociety* program, and he has provided endless hours of help all along the way. His vast experience as an educator, a consultant to the *MicroSociety* program, and a psychologist have been invaluable. His compassion and friendship have been equally important.

George Richmond and Carolynn King also made an enormous contribution to this work. I am still amazed and grateful that they were willing to have a relatively unknown outsider come in and conduct an extensive study of their program's implementation. They not only allowed me complete access but also covered the costs of the research. And they were a constant source of insight and inspiration as the project developed.

Early on, I met Evans Clinchy, the consultant who was instrumental in the creation of the first schoolwide *MicroSociety* program. He filled in many gaps in the story of that first brave attempt, and he helped me to better understand the theory behind the *MicroSociety* program. For that, I am deeply grateful.

Another prominent educator whom I met as the result of this project was Roland Barth. Roland provided invaluable input on an early draft of the book, and he helped me to find the ideal publisher for it. I also appreciate his willingness to write the Foreword.

Then there were the many trainers, consultants, and staff members who have worked with MicroSociety, Inc., over the years. They all have contributed to my understanding of the model and its implementation, but those who have been especially generous of their time and knowledge include Pamela Coad, Dave Cronin, Sheryl Dunton, Philip Hawkins, Rachel Kharfen, Rob Kutzik, Tom Malone, Gilbert Moreno, Triana Olivas, Christyn Pope, Sylvia Sanchez, and Donna Wilson.

So many principals in *MicroSociety* schools also contributed their time and insight along the way, but those who deserve special mention are Cecelia Estrada, Sherry Malone, Tom Malone, Mike McTaggert, and Gary Moriello.

Finally, I'd like to acknowledge the help and support of my family. My wife, Deborah, has helped in so many ways, it is impossible to count them. Probably most important is the fact that she believes in me no matter what. My son, Joshua, has become a source of sage advice and insight about so many important ideas that relate to this book. I think it is fair to say that he now is one of my most valued colleagues, as well as my favorite son. Then there is my mother, Shirley, who was not only my first teacher but also the one who first made me interested in the world of ideas. The fact that she brought three children into this world, all of whom became teachers, makes me believe that she also must have had something to do with my interest in education and with this particular project.

Corwin Press gratefully acknowledges the contributions of the following individuals:

Sara Armstrong
Director
Sara Armstrong Consulting
Berkeley, CA

John Deasy
Superintendent of Schools
Santa Monica-Malibu Unified School District
Santa Monica, CA

Edgar Gill
Associate Professor
School of Education and Behavioral Studies
Azusa Pacific University
Azusa, CA

Frank Kawtoski
Adjunct Professor
DeSales University and Eastern University
Center Valley, PA

Seymour Sarason,
Professor Emeritus of Psychology and Education
Yale University
New Haven, CT

About the Author

Cary Cherniss currently is Professor of Applied Psychology and Director of the Organizational Psychology Program in the Graduate School of Applied and Professional Psychology at Rutgers University. He also has taught at the University of Michigan in Ann Arbor, the University of Illinois in Chicago, the Chicago Medical School, and the Illinois Institute of Technology. He received his PhD in psychology from Yale University in 1972.

Dr. Cherniss specializes in the areas of emotional intelligence, professional burnout, management training and development, and planned organizational change. He has published more than 50 scholarly articles and book chapters on these topics, as well as six books: *The Emotionally Intelligent Workplace* (with Daniel Goleman); *Promoting Emotional Intelligence in the Workplace: Guidelines for Practitioners* (with Mitchel Adler); *The Human Side of Corporate Competitiveness* (with Daniel Fishman); *Professional Burnout in Human Service Organizations; Staff Burnout;* and *Beyond Burnout: Helping Teachers, Nurses, Therapists, and Lawyers Recover From Stress and Disillusionment.*

In addition to his research and writing, Dr. Cherniss has consulted with many schools and school districts. He also has consulted with other kinds of organizations in both the public and private sectors, including American Express Financial Advisors, Johnson & Johnson, the U.S. Coast Guard, the U.S. Office of Personnel Management, Honeywell, and PSEG Power. He currently is the director and cochair (with Daniel Goleman) of the *Consortium for Research on Emotional Intelligence in Organizations.* He is a fellow of the American Psychological Association and past president of its Division 27 (Society for Community Research and Action), and he is a member of the Academy of Management.

CORWIN
PRESS

The Corwin Press logo—a raven striding across an open book—represents the union of courage and learning. Corwin Press is committed to improving education for all learners by publishing books and other professional development resources for those serving the field of PreK–12 education. By providing practical, hands-on materials, Corwin Press continues to carry out the promise of its motto: **"Helping Educators Do Their Work Better."**

I

Overview of the Program

1

The MicroSociety® Program

A DAY IN THE LIFE OF A
MICROSOCIETY® PROGRAM SCHOOL

Imagine that you are in a public elementary school somewhere in the United States and it is 7:45 a.m. School begins at 8:00, but already there are many teachers and students in the halls and classrooms, preparing for a new day. Everything seems normal as you walk around, until you pass a classroom and look in. There you see what looks like a television studio, with a dozen TV monitors spread around the room, several cameras, and many switches and dials. There are about 20 children of various ages scurrying around. Five of the children are sitting in front of some complicated-looking equipment, intently studying screens and adjusting controls. Suddenly, a 4-foot tall girl calls out, "Practice!" Then she counts down from 10, and a run-through for the morning show begins.

The title of the first segment is "Sittercize." Three kindergartners demonstrate various exercises while sitting in chairs as a recorded voice describes each routine. Then there is a pledge of allegiance, and you see an American flag waving in the breeze on all the monitors. Next, you see four kindergartners with sandwich boards do a weather report segment called "Pee Wee Weather." An announcer who is to give the daily lunch menu quickly follows them. Then there is a commercial, sponsored by the IRS (Internal Revenue Service), encouraging the students to pay their taxes and providing instructions on how to do it. The final segment presents another student announcer, who reads off "Important events on this date."

At 8:10 a.m., the actual show begins. A closed-circuit TV broadcasts it into all of the classrooms. The children watch intently as everything goes according to plan. There is just one problem. Something is wrong with the sound. It seems slightly distorted. The "soundman," a fourth grader, frantically tries to fix the problem, but nothing seems to help. When the show finally ends, you observe the soundman hitting his head repeatedly against his desk in exasperation. Two teachers, who up to now have done almost nothing, go over to him, put their arms around him, and offer gentle words of encouragement. Soon, the soundman recovers. Another day at a *MicroSociety*® program school has begun.

Life in the Classroom

The rest of the morning seems like any traditional public school. The children study reading, math, science, and social studies. However, as you visit various classrooms and listen carefully, you notice that occasionally there is something a little different. In one class, the children are studying simple math. However, instead of presenting problems on the board in the conventional way, the teacher refers to the *MicroSociety* program and asks, "What percentage do we pay in income tax in the *MicroSociety?*" "Twelve percent," responds one student. The teacher then begins to teach the children how to use what they have learned about percentages to compute their own income taxes in various ways.

In another class, the children are studying the Whiskey Rebellion as part of their social studies curriculum. The teacher asks, "How many of you think the farmers in western Massachusetts were right to resist paying a tax to the new government?" All the children raise their hands. Then the teacher says, "Well, what about in our *MicroSociety?* Do we pay taxes?" The children nod. "Why do we pay taxes? What is the money used for?" Several hands go up. One of the students says that some of their tax money goes to pay for the court, specifically the salaries for the judges, bailiffs, clerks, and other court personnel. The teacher then asks, "Is the court a good thing? What would happen if we didn't have a court?" More hands go up. The consensus is that the court is a very good thing and that the *MicroSociety* could not function very well without it. Now the teacher returns to the Whiskey Rebellion. "Ok, so what about the new government back in the late 1700s? Didn't they need money for courts also? And to get that money, didn't they need to collect taxes?" After some more discussion, the teacher asks the original question again. Now all students but one decide that the farmers were wrong to resist paying taxes.

Micro Begins

And so the day goes—normal except for the occasional reference to "MicroSociety." After lunch, however, something very different happens. It is 1:40, and there is still about an hour left of school. However, the teachers tell the children to put away their work and to "get ready for Micro." At 1:45, you hear a bell ring, and all of the teachers and children spring into action. However, they do not leave. You see some of them move desks and chairs around in several of the classrooms. In the lunchroom, dozens of students of all ages are scurrying around and putting up what looks like storefronts. Within 5 minutes, the lunchroom becomes a marketplace, and children in storefront booths begin to sell various items to other children who hurry into the lunchroom. The buyers have checkbooks and a local currency that looks like play money but which the buyers exchange for actual goods and services in the marketplace.

As you continue to walk around the marketplace, you find many kinds of stores. In one, the children are paying to have their faces painted. In another, children as young as kindergarten use their special currency (which they call the "Micro") to buy buttons with witty slogans. In another store, students pay to have their nails painted by other students.

You see only three teachers in the lunchroom, and they are just standing around observing. Occasionally, one of the students will go up to a teacher and ask a question, but most of the time the teachers just try to stay out of the way. The students, not the teachers, seem to be in charge here.

You leave the marketplace and begin to walk around the rest of the school. In one of the classrooms, you notice that a dozen children are busy working at computers. You see a sign that announces this is the office of the local newspaper. You go up to one of the children, a third grader who is typing away at one of the computers, and ask her what she is doing. "I just did an interview with the principal, and I'm typing it up for our next edition. Excuse me, but I can't talk anymore. I have a deadline." As you look around the room, you see some children run out with notebooks and pencils in their hands, and others come in and sit down at computers to type up more stories. Again, there is a teacher present, but she does not seem to be in charge. She seems to be more of a consultant.

In the room next door, you notice a sign above the door that says, "Manufacturing." You walk in and see children busy making some of the craft items you saw for sale in the marketplace. A teacher walks up to you and mentions that the students are particularly busy and excited today because they have just received a contract to make the costumes for the school choir's concert, which is coming up in just 2 weeks. In addition to the teacher, two parents help the children whenever they encounter a problem with an item.

Crime and Punishment

As you walk away from the manufacturing room, a student dressed in some kind of official-looking uniform comes up to you and asks to see your pass. You notice he has a badge that says "Crimestoppers." You have no pass; however, another similarly dressed student comes up and says it's okay, you are an authorized visitor and don't need a pass. A third student walks up and tells the other two students to resume their patrol. You discover that this is the chief of the crimestoppers. You ask him how he likes his job, and he admits that it is challenging. "I've been having some trouble because the other kids find me too bossy, but I think I'm getting better at it. Our facilitator has been talking with me about the problem and helping me to be less bossy." The chief then suggests that you visit the courtroom, where kids go if they receive a citation for breaking a law.

You enter another classroom that is set up very much like an adult courtroom. There is a raised platform at one end with a desk, and behind it sits a fifth-grade girl in a long, black robe with a gavel in her hand. Next to the desk is a seat where a somewhat younger student sits. He clearly is a witness sitting in the witness box. To the side, there are seats behind a rail. You realize that this is the jury box. In front of the judge's stand, there are two tables, with student lawyers sitting behind them facing the judge. One of the lawyers gets up and goes over to the witness box, where he begins to question the witness. You take a seat in the section reserved for spectators and listen to the proceedings. You discover that this particular case involves two students who were working together in class one day, and one wanted to see a paper that the other was working on. However, the other student did not want to show it to him. Therefore the first student took the paper away from the second student. The second student then hit the first student on the head with a clipboard. A crimestopper saw her and sent her to court. The trial ends as you sit and watch, and the jury walks out of the room to deliberate. They return in about 10 minutes. You listen intently as the foreman reads the verdict: guilty as charged. The student judge then hands down the punishment: The guilty party must pay a fine of 500 Micros, which you learn from a fourth grader sitting next to you is the equivalent of about 5 weeks' wages. You ask your new friend who makes the laws, and she directs you to the library, where the student legislature is in session.

As you enter the library, you notice that there are 24 students sitting at tables down at the far end of the room. The legislators have just assembled, and the president, a sixth grader, finishes writing the agenda on the board. The first item of business is what to do about the Micros left over from the previous semester. After some lively discussion, the representatives decide that they will consult with their classes and then come back to discuss the matter and make a decision. The next item on the agenda is to go over the calendar for Micro for the next 3 months. The legislators run out of time before they are able to deal with the last item on their agenda, which has to do with "the check-forging problem." The president announces that they will put off discussion of that issue until the next meeting.

It is 5 minutes before school is to end for the day, and the students and teachers dismantle their miniature society as quickly as they erected it. When the final bell rings, the school again looks very much like any other public school in America at the end of the school day. However, you realize that it is not like other schools. It is something different. It is a *MicroSociety* program school.

THE ORIGINS OF THE *MICROSOCIETY*® PROGRAM

In 1967, George Richmond had just graduated from Yale College and was in his first year of teaching. He was assigned to a fifth-grade classroom in Brooklyn, New York. Almost all of his students were from impoverished families who had only recently arrived in this country. Many of those families had become fractured and dysfunctional due to the strains of immigration and poverty.

Like many inexperienced teachers who find themselves in a less-than-ideal urban school, Richmond was struggling just to maintain some semblance of order in his classroom. The students had quickly sized him up and decided that here was the kind of teacher with whom they could have some fun. Within a few weeks, Richmond had just about abandoned any attempt to teach the students anything. His main concern was to try to regain enough control so that no one would get badly hurt, and he was failing more often than he was succeeding.

One night, as he wearily returned home from school on the subway, a radical idea came to him. He would turn the classroom into a kind of miniature society, at least for part of the day. It would be like "Monopoly," in which students would buy and sell sections of the classroom to each other. They would earn the money to do so by fulfilling basic attendance and achievement requirements. Richmond quickly printed up some money to use for the new activity, and he presented the plan to his class the next morning.

Although the students were suspicious at first, they soon became engaged in the activity, as almost any 10-year-old would. As the days passed and the activity unfolded, it evolved and became more complex. For instance, the students became embroiled in conflicts over their commercial transactions. Rather than become the arbiter, Richmond used the conflicts as "teachable moments." He explained to the students that such conflicts occurred in any society, and this is why citizens created laws, courts, and law enforcement agencies. If the students wanted to reduce the number of conflicts and deal with them fairly, they would need to create a constitution for their society. Then they would need to have a legislature, laws, and ways of enforcing the laws and adjudicating conflict. The students loved it. The process continued to unfold, becoming more engrossing—and educational—each day.

As the students became absorbed in their new activity, the classroom became more orderly. Many of the students actually seemed to look forward to coming to school. In addition, Richmond discovered that he could use the students' experiences in their miniature society to help them appreciate the value of what he had been trying to teach them. Suddenly, math and reading seemed to be useful and important. Social studies made more sense because it involved events and processes that were occurring right in the students' own society.

The miniature society not only provided examples that Richmond could use in teaching math, social studies, writing, and other subjects, it also began to change the culture of the classroom. The students became engaged in school and the learning process as never before, because now they had new ways to succeed. They also came to view learning as desirable for getting ahead, because those who possessed academic skills tended to be more successful.

For instance, there was Ramon, the student who became the society's banker. He got the job because he was the only student who could add, subtract, multiply, and divide. Prior to becoming the banker, Ramon was at the bottom of the status hierarchy within the student group. He was the one whom other students most often picked on and harassed. However, his role in their miniature society helped him to become one of the most respected students in the class.

One day, Ramon came to Mr. Richmond with a problem. He was having trouble collecting on loans that his bank had made to some students in the class. Richmond asked Ramon whether he wanted Richmond to collect for him. However, Ramon had a different idea. He wanted to employ Emilio, the class bully and the largest kid in the class, to help him collect from the other kids. Richmond found it an intriguing idea, especially because Emilio previously had been one of the chief tormenters of Ramon. Now they would be allies rather than adversaries. The plan worked. More important, such incidents taught the students vivid lessons about the values of cooperation, tolerance, and diversity; and they helped transform the atmosphere of the classroom. The miniature society in George Richmond's class transformed the classroom from an unruly, chaotic mob into a "context of productive learning" (Sarason, 2002).

Richmond eventually wrote a book about his experiment in that Brooklyn classroom (Richmond, 1973). After teaching a few more years, he returned to graduate school to secure a doctorate in education, and he went on to serve in a number of administrative positions at both the local and state levels. He did not write any more about the "MicroSociety," but interest in it was percolating.

THE *MICROSOCIETY*® IDEA SPREADS

In 1981, the city of Lowell, Massachusetts was under pressure from the courts to desegregate its schools. Like many other school districts facing such a mandate, Lowell decided to adopt a magnet school plan. There would be a variety of schools with different themes, and each school would be open to any student in the district. The hope was that each magnet school would attract a diverse group of students. One of the themes selected was "the city." The original notion was that the "City Magnet School" in Lowell would be a school without walls. The city itself would be the school, with students and teachers working and observing in various locales around the town. This plan, however, soon proved to be impractical. When the planners learned about Richmond's "Micro-Society" concept, they decided that they could accomplish their purpose by basing the entire school on it. In the fall of 1981, the City Magnet School in Lowell opened its doors, becoming the first schoolwide *MicroSociety* program.

During the next decade, the Lowell experiment began to attract national attention. Popular news shows featured it, such as Peter Jennings's nightly network newscast and the "MacNeil-Lehrer News Hour." *Time Magazine* and other print media highlighted it as well. Educators throughout the country became interested in establishing their own *MicroSociety* programs.

Richmond was spending much of his time responding to requests for information and assistance as other schools began to adopt the idea. Therefore in 1991, he and his wife, Carolynn King, established a small nonprofit organization to provide technical assistance and networking opportunities to schools that wanted to adopt the *MicroSociety* concept. (Carolynn King was an attorney who became interested in educational reform and went back to graduate school to earn a master's degree in education.) In the summer of 1993, they organized the first national training conference for educators and parents interested in learning more about the *MicroSociety* program idea. Attendance was good, and Micro-Society, Inc. (MSI), continues to hold a national conference for up to 400 educators each summer.

In 1998, the federal government approved *MicroSociety* program as a "comprehensive school reform model." This meant that qualifying schools could receive up to $150,000 over 3 years from the government if they adopted the *MicroSociety* program. This further spurred growth of the model. Within a few years, more than 200 schools in 40 states were employing the *MicroSociety* program.

Although the founder originally developed the model in an urban setting and many of the subsequent *MicroSociety* programs were in inner-city schools, there were many suburban and rural *MicroSociety* programs as well. Its appeal seemed to cut across class, regional, and ethnic lines. It also seemed to work well for a variety of ages. Students as young as kindergarten were involved, along with eighth-grade middle school students. About 60% of the programs are in elementary schools, and the rest are in middle schools.

As the model spread, it continued to receive recognition and support from different quarters of the educational community. For instance, the Northwest Regional Educational Laboratory approved the program for inclusion in its *Catalogue of School Reform Models*. In addition, MSI received support from numerous foundations and corporations, such as Morgan Stanley, IBM, ARCO Chemical, and the Annie E. Casey Foundation.

THE GUIDING PHILOSOPHY BEHIND THE *MICROSOCIETY*® PROGRAM

The *MicroSociety* program is based on two basic assumptions about learning. The first is that "real, sustained learning takes place when students are intrinsically engaged and motivated (usually in ways that are relevant to their lives) and experience successes in the process" (C. King, personal communication, January, 2005). The second is that children learn best by playing, working, doing, and reflecting.

In addition to these two assumptions, the *MicroSociety* program is based on a few guiding principles. The first is, "Empower the children. It is their society." What this means is that a good program is student run. The role of the teacher is not to solve problems, but to help students do so. As Richmond succinctly put it, "If you don't know what to do, ask the students" (Richmond & Richmond, 1996, n.p.).

A good example of this first principle was the program in which students who ran their own businesses initially went to a teacher if they encountered a problem. The teachers became increasingly overwhelmed and worn out from all the requests for help. Finally, they created the role of student manager for the mall, and student business owners who had a problem would go first to the mall manager for help. This change not only alleviated the strain on the teachers but also provided a more powerful learning experience for many students.

Second, problems that occur in the *MicroSociety* program are opportunities to learn. Rather than viewing such problems as potential calamities to be avoided, teachers and principals should view them as "teachable moments." The idea is not to create a smooth-functioning, problem-free society that dazzles the eye with its many fine ventures and agencies, but rather to create a realistic world in which students find themselves immersed in processes that provide rich opportunities for learning. As the *MicroSociety*® *Handbook* puts it, "The process is vastly more important than the product; indeed, the imperfections in the process lead students themselves to take charge and make it work effectively" (Richmond & Richmond, 1996, p. 3). The important thing in Micro is not the destination, but the journey.

In one school, the principle was put to the test when a student named Anton had a business that was failing. Some of the teachers wanted to intervene so that the business would not fail. However, they realized that allowing Anton's business to fail would be the best way of showing him what went wrong. So they allowed the business to fail, and when Anton started his second business, he refused to hire his buddies, who had a history of being troublemakers, and he changed his own behavior as well. The second business thrived, and Anton learned some important lessons about life.

The third principle is that learning in context is more effective than trying to learn facts in isolation. What this means in practice is that teachers should use Micro to make *all* learning activities more meaningful, including those that occur in the traditional classroom. There should be many connections between what the students are doing in Micro and what they are doing in their regular classes during the rest of the day. For instance, when students learn about percentages in their math class, the teacher might have them take out their Micro bank accounts and use percentages to compute how their interest payments would change with changes in the interest rates.

Fourth, educators cannot create a viable *MicroSociety* program without active community partnerships. As Richmond wrote, a Micro is like "stone soup. Everyone in the community brings his or her own ingredients to add to the soup. The more people contribute, the more delicious it will be" (Richmond & Richmond, 1996, p. 15). It is impossible for a group of teachers to know everything that one needs to know in order to help students create a viable society. Bankers, lawyers, police officers, and business people of various kinds must share their expertise. In addition, even though students do most of the work, it is difficult for teachers to carry the whole burden of organizing the program on their own. Parents and others in the community provide valuable hands-on help when it comes to establishing the different ventures or agencies and keeping them going.

MicroSociety program flexibly takes on a somewhat different shape at each school. In addition, once implemented, a *MicroSociety* program constantly evolves as students confront new problems and figure out their own solutions for dealing with them. Nevertheless, every *MicroSociety* program has certain common features.

BASIC ELEMENTS OF THE PROGRAM

During most of the day, a *MicroSociety* program school looks and functions like any other school. However, during the last hour of the day, the entire school becomes a society that is run by the students. Students in "Micro" do just about everything that people do in grown-up society: They have jobs, own and operate businesses, and make laws enforced by their own police force. They have courts, banks, and post offices. The "essential elements" are an internal currency, retail and labor markets, government agencies, nonprofits, businesses, and private and public property, along with parent and community involvement.

Like any society, the foundation of the *MicroSociety* program is its economic and political systems. Students earn money in a variety of ways. First, they receive a certain amount of money for attending school, turning in their work on time, and performing other duties associated with the student role. In one school, for instance, the students received five Micros for each period of class that they attended, and they received bonuses for special accomplishments such as an A on a test or helping another person in an unusual way. The teachers pay the students with a local currency that often has a colorful or meaningful name.

However, students also have jobs for which they are paid salaries; and as they become more skilled in their jobs, they stop getting paid for attendance, homework, and other student-related behavior. As in any society, there are literally hundreds of different kinds of jobs. Students may work as bank tellers, court bailiffs, or bakers. They may be journalists, manufacturers, or production assistants in the Micro Theater. Students also can start their own businesses, and when they do, they often employ other students. In their businesses, they make goods, sell them, and/or provide services. All students go to the marketplace at least once a week in order to buy the goods and services offered by their peers, using the money that they earned in their jobs or business ventures.

The Economic System

The heart of the economic system is the bank. Like the banks that grown-ups use, the *MicroSociety* program banks issue checking accounts and personal and business savings accounts to customers. The accounts pay monthly interest. The banks also issue loans, for which they charge interest.

As in the adult world, students in every *MicroSociety* program must pay taxes. There usually is an income tax, and the legislature must determine collectively what the rate will be. Then there is an "Internal Revenue Service" to collect the taxes. In some schools, the IRS must collect and keep track of income taxes, sales taxes, and business taxes. The IRS even uses W-4 and 1040 forms to manage the tax collection process in some schools.

The businesses in a *MicroSociety* program are numerous and varied. Many of the ventures involve manufactured items that students sell in the marketplace. These include posters, sports cards, origami, bird feeders, T-shirts, battery-charged race cars, and marionettes. Among the more creative ventures are a nursery where students grow and sell various kinds of plants and a venture in which a student made and sold an exercise video.

Often the most popular items for sale in a *MicroSociety* program marketplace involve food. In almost any *MicroSociety* program marketplace, one will find restaurants or food stands selling everything from pickles to potato chips. One school had a food court with 16 different concessions, including a root beer float stand, a pizza place, a popcorn stand, and a grilled cheese sandwich concession.

As in grown-up societies, many successful ventures in a *MicroSociety* program involve services and entertainment, rather than manufactured goods or food. There are puppet theaters, magic shows, art galleries, and travel agencies. There are companies that provide face painting, hair braiding, and manicures. In one school, there was a *MicroSociety* program chorus where students auditioned and then sang at various events throughout the year. In another school, there was a theater company where students wrote, produced, directed, and acted in skits and plays.

Health also has been a theme in many ventures. In one *MicroSociety* program, there was a "Wellness Company," which was a health center with a focus on exercise and nutrition. At another school, there was a health clinic where students worked as doctors, dentists, and nutritionists and performed health checkups on other students with real medical equipment.

The ventures often make connections with what students are learning in their academic classes. For instance, at one school, a multicultural education teacher helped a group of students to develop a "travel agency" venture for their *MicroSociety* program. Students paid to "visit" different countries whose cultures they were studying in their social studies classes. At another school, the science curriculum inspired a business called "Bug Hang Out," where students displayed and sold bug-related items. (The "Bug Greeting Card Series" was especially popular.) Other products included "Bug Books," which the students wrote themselves. Students visiting the Bug Hang Out also could examine a bug model under a magnifying glass.

Many *MicroSociety* programs also have private, nonprofit ventures that model the value of community service. In one school, there was an ice cream social to reward students who had participated in service learning projects. It was completely student run. In addition to the ice cream, there were tattoo booths and a DJ. Another school put on a *Micro-Society* program charity ball. To attend, students bought tickets with their Micro money, and the proceeds helped the *MicroSociety* community in various ways.

The Political System

As important as the economic system is the political system, which is based on a constitution that the students create themselves in a "constitutional convention." Each constitution is different, but it usually establishes some kind of elected legislative body and an executive. The constitution often is an elaborate document, and the students spend many weeks creating it and seeking the consensus necessary to adopt it.

The *MicroSociety* program's own legislature makes its laws. The student representatives meet regularly to debate many of the issues that confront any society. For instance, in one school, there was dissatisfaction with the salaries that some of the heads of the public agencies earned. Legislators were especially unhappy that the chief of police earned more money than they did. However, the chief's allies prevailed when they pointed out that the police force generated more income for the government through citations and fines than any other government agency.

Every *MicroSociety* program has a police force that enforces the laws established by the legislature. Often referred to as "the crimestoppers" or "peacekeepers," they enforce the school's laws by handing out citations to students who break the rules. Some of the rules relate specifically to Micro, such as being away from one's venture without a special pass. Other rules are more general, such as no fighting.

Students who receive a ticket for breaking a rule usually must go to court, where there is a trial with a judge, prosecuting and defense attorneys, and a jury. *MicroSociety* program courts also handle civil disputes, such as a conflict between a shopkeeper and a customer or between an employee and an employer. The court system relies on a cadre of judges, lawyers, clerks, bailiffs, court recorders, and juries. To prepare for their duties, the student judges and lawyers learn civil and criminal law as well as procedures for filing complaints and participating in hearings, pretrial conferences, and trials. The lawyers sometimes must pass a "bar exam" testing their knowledge of the laws and procedures before they are allowed to practice.

Training is important for many other jobs in a *MicroSociety* program. Blocks of time often are set aside at the beginning of the year and at other times throughout the year for the students to learn the special knowledge and skills needed to perform their jobs and function as effective citizens. Schools often refer to this training activity as "Micro Prep." In one school, the first 8 weeks of the fall term were devoted to training for Micro. During this time, all the students attended sessions covering topics such as "ethics" and "check writing." Students also learned how to present themselves in job interviews, open bank accounts, and calculate their taxes. In addition, the students who were going to manage business ventures attended a weeklong training session on "business planning," which was conducted by adults from the local Junior Achievement organization.

Students as young as prekindergarten have participated in Micro. The youngest students (kindergarten through first grade) often are "consumers." In one school, they learned about money—how to use it, why it is good to save it, and so on. They also learned about rules and the function of the crimestoppers. Like the older students, they were paid a certain number of Micros each month for attending school regularly and doing their work in the classroom. They used the Micros to pay for taxes, rent, and tuition. Then they went to the marketplace twice a month, where they used their money to purchase goods and services offered in ventures run by the older students.

Adult Roles

Teachers in a *MicroSociety* program are supposed to assume the roles of facilitators and consultants. Once they provide the students with training in how to operate their agencies or ventures, the teachers step back, but they do not completely withdraw. They continue to be available for consultation and guidance. For instance, in one *MicroSociety* program venture, two students spent most of their time "gossiping" instead of working. Rather than deal with the problem herself or ignore it, the teacher facilitator met with the president of the company and helped the president to think through various ways in which she might deal with the problem. By gently and skillfully asking questions and reinforcing good ideas that came from the president, the teacher helped the president come up with her own solution to the problem.

Some ventures do require more teacher supervision. For instance, in the IRS, the students have to labor constantly to keep up with the paperwork, so the teachers find that they often have to supervise more closely there. However, in the ideal *MicroSociety* program, the teachers spend most of their time observing, encouraging, and gently guiding. They also look for curriculum connections and instructional opportunities. Like management consultants in the adult world, they have special expertise and experience that they can offer the students to help them manage their society more humanely and effectively; but the responsibility ultimately is the students.' The students, not the teachers, run the *MicroSociety* program.

A *MicroSociety* program also provides many opportunities for parents to become involved. In some schools, the parents help by constructing the storefronts, courtrooms, and mailboxes that provide the *MicroSociety* program with a greater degree of realism. Parents also can help with training. For instance, in one school, a parent who was a self-employed computer consultant spent several hours each month training the teachers and students in how to run businesses. In another school, a group of parents worked in the companies and agencies along with the teacher facilitators and student employees. The parents even received wages paid in Micros and had their own checking accounts at the Micro bank. They used the money to purchase items for themselves and their children at the Micro marketplace.

Community partners also are a vital component of any *MicroSociety* program. They provide both expertise and financial support. Bankers come into the school and help the teachers and students to set up the *MicroSociety* program bank. Then the local bank may continue to provide support by printing the currency and checkbooks. Judges and lawyers often come into the school to train the teachers and students who work in the court. In addition, officers from the local police department frequently come into the school to train the crimestoppers. In some schools, the police department even donates equipment and supplies that the crimestoppers use in their work. Meanwhile, local merchants help by furnishing food for the food court ventures or supplies for the manufacturing businesses.

Despite the many permutations, the basic elements found in every authentic *MicroSociety* program are an economic system with its own currency and a variety of businesses, a legislature based on a written constitution and supported by taxes, laws enforced by a police agency, and the continuous involvement of parents and community partners. Using these elements and the guiding principles, teachers and students at each school create their own version of the *MicroSociety* program.

MICROSOCIETY® PROGRAM
OUTCOMES: WHAT THE RESEARCH SHOWS

To what extent are students in *MicroSociety* program schools more motivated to learn? Do they learn higher-order thinking skills? What about the *MicroSociety* program's impact on social and emotional competencies? How do students in *MicroSociety* program schools compare with other students when it comes to learning basic subjects such as math, reading, and writing?

Impact on Academic Skills

A number of evaluation studies have examined at least some of these questions. The *MicroSociety* program's impact on basic academic skills has received the most research attention: A number of different evaluation studies suggest that the *MicroSociety* program can help students to master the kinds of academic skills measured by standardized achievement tests. Data also strongly suggest that the program often improves school attendance and student conduct in school. There also is some indication that an effective *MicroSociety* program in a school can help increase teacher expectations for student performance and improve staff morale and cohesiveness.

Research on the first schoolwide *MicroSociety* program provided encouraging results. When Lowell's City Magnet School opened, it had full enrollment; and even 20 years later, there was a long waiting list of applicants. This was an important outcome in itself, because the district had implemented a citywide magnet program in which parents were free to send their children to any school. To be successful, a magnet school had to attract a diverse group of students. The *MicroSociety* program at Lowell clearly did so. But City Magnet did more than just compete favorably with other schools in attracting students. According to an unpublished report, a 1988 evaluation of City Magnet School found that eighth graders tested on average at the 9.3 grade level in reading and at the 10.4 grade level in math. Furthermore, these results reflected the best schoolwide performance in the city. The school's 96% student attendance rate also was the highest in the city.

Although these results are impressive, the Lowell experiment was unique in many ways. The first school to develop and implement a new educational practice often achieves impressive results, only to have subsequent efforts to replicate the original experiment fall short. The real test of a reform strategy is whether the positive impacts show up in schools that attempt to replicate the prototype. To what extent have other schools been able to match City Magnet's success with the *MicroSociety* program?

The research evidence suggests that a number of schools across the country have achieved similar results. An independent research organization reviewed the data from seven different evaluations of *MicroSociety* programs conducted between 1996 and 2002. They found that there had been an average improvement per year of 29% in reading and 42% in writing. Some schools did even better than that. For instance, at an elementary school in West Virginia, between 1997 and 2000, the test scores increased from 44% of the students reading at grade level to 60% (Arete, 2002).

The *MicroSociety* program schools also saw gains in math and science. The average improvement per year in math was 35%, and in science, it was 158%. At the school in West Virginia, the math scores went from 46% to 72% between 1997 and 2000, and in an elementary school in Detroit, the scores went from 9% to 56% in science during the same period.

In two schools, the researchers were able to conduct a more rigorous evaluation involving a comparison group. In one, a middle school, reading scores for the Micro group increased 12% in reading in 1 year compared with 0.3% for the comparison group. (The comparison group consisted of students in the same school who did not participate in Micro.) In the other, an elementary school, the difference was 4% improvement in writing for the Micro students compared with 0%. In this second study, other students in the district made up the comparison group (Arete, 2002).

The improvements in student performance associated with the *Micro-Society* program often occurred in schools with high percentages of disadvantaged children. For instance, an elementary school in Detroit had a student body that was 86% African American and 14% Bengali. Ninety percent of the students were from economically disadvantaged households. Nevertheless, after the school implemented the *MicroSociety* program, their students showed gains of 43% in math, 53% in reading, and 24% in science in just 1 year (Arete, 2002).

There also is the school in El Paso in which 97% of the student body were members of minority groups and 87% from economically disadvantaged homes. One year prior to implementing the *MicroSociety* program, only 29% of the students met state standards in reading, and only 33% met standards in math. After 5 years of the *MicroSociety* program, 92% of the students met state standards in reading, and 93% met the standards in math. (These data came from annual reports prepared by the school staff for local and state educational authorities.)

One problem with this kind of research is that there often are many other changes occurring in a school that implements a reform such as the *MicroSociety* program. Therefore it is difficult to attribute all of the positive gains to just one of those changes. A principal at one of those schools acknowledged this when she said that the improvement in student scores at her school really was due to the "whole community taking responsibility for all the children." However, she went on to add that the *MicroSociety* program had done much to contribute to those positive changes in the school's climate. For instance, she noted that with the *MicroSociety* program, "Teachers from different grades work together in ventures where they see kids from different classes and grades," and this helped create a caring community within the school.

The positive results relating to student performance are especially impressive because Micro does not directly target student test scores. Other reform models seek to teach directly the kind of information that is covered on the tests. Some even teach students test-taking skills. Micro does neither. Its impact is more indirect: It encourages students to come to school; it increases student interest in learning; and it provides students with additional opportunities to practice the basic skills that they learn in their classes and that the tests cover. The data indicate that these indirect effects of the program are powerful enough so that achievement test performance goes up when students participate in Micro, even though the program does not explicitly target such outcomes.

Nonacademic Outcomes

The data also suggest that the *MicroSociety* program can match other successful educational reforms in student test performance while producing a variety of other positive outcomes as well. Two of those other positive outcomes associated with the *MicroSociety* program involve student attendance and conduct. In one nationwide survey, every *MicroSociety* program principal reported improved attendance and reduced disciplinary infractions after program implementation. In another survey, 9 of 10 schools reported attendance increases (Arete, 2002). The results for a middle school in Iowa were typical. Following implementation of the *MicroSociety* program, average attendance increased from 74% to 98% in 1 year, and disciplinary infractions dropped from 6,234 to 1,802 over a 4-year period. The school previously had 17 active gangs; after 4 years of Micro, it had none.

In addition to the hoped-for improvements in student achievement, attendance, and discipline, the *MicroSociety* program also seems to have had a positive impact on teachers and parents. Here, the data are more anecdotal, but they are compelling.

A positive, unexpected outcome of the *MicroSociety* program involves teacher cohesiveness and collegiality. In several schools that implemented the program, the staff reported that teachers became more supportive of one another. For instance, after visiting a school in Iowa, a reporter wrote,

> Because all the teachers work cooperatively on *MicroSociety* program, whether they teach science or special education, they've gotten to know and appreciate one another more. In weekly meetings there is no longer a concern that one teacher may encroach on another's territory. (Poole, 1996, p. 1)

There also is evidence that the *MicroSociety* program can rejuvenate some teachers, helping them to become more enthusiastic and committed to teaching. For teachers who have become dissatisfied with teaching in the traditional classroom, *MicroSociety* program can provide an alternative source of fulfillment and an antidote to burnout. As one teacher put it, "Teaching should be exciting." He then went on to say that what he was most excited about was his venture in Micro. Another teacher admitted that Micro was "a lot of work," but then said, "It's worth it because of what it does for the kids."

One other way the *MicroSociety* program seems to affect teachers is through its impact on teacher expectations. Research on learning has consistently suggested that teacher expectations are critical for student learning. When teachers expect more from students, student performance improves (Weinstein, 2002). A number of teachers with whom I spoke said that they had raised their expectations for their students because of what they had seen them do in Micro. In some cases, the teachers' behavior in the regular classroom reflected this change in their view of the students.

The Micro program also has had a positive impact on parents. First, it provides a vehicle for positive parent involvement. In a school serving a largely disadvantaged population, the parent coordinator said that many parents cannot read and this discourages them from becoming involved with the school. Nevertheless, they do come to the school in order to help with Micro, because they know they do not need to be able to read in order to be helpful there. In one case, a parent began to work in the program as a volunteer, then became a coteacher, and eventually became an assistant to the program coordinator. She also went back to school to secure a teaching credential, in large part because of the positive experiences she had had through helping with Micro.

The program also can help parents develop some of the same academic and practical skills that their children are learning. For instance, one school served an impoverished community made up largely of immigrants from Mexico. In this community, most parents did not have checking accounts. Some did not even know what a checking account was. However, because of the *MicroSociety* program, children learned about checking accounts, went home, and taught their parents.

THE PROBLEM OF IMPLEMENTATION

Many schools have seen positive results when they have successfully implemented the *MicroSociety* program, but not all schools have been able to do so. One evaluation study found "wide variety among schools in the fidelity of their implementation of the *MicroSociety* model" (Arete, 2002, p. 1). In addition, the research indicates that the program's impact on student learning has varied. For instance, one review of the studies found that while 11 schools showed gains in reading tests, 4 did not. And even when schools have implemented the program with high fidelity and the documented impact on learning and behavior have been impressive, it has not always been sustainable over a long period of time.

There are many reasons why some schools are able to implement and sustain the program with high fidelity and positive results while others do not. In the next chapter, I discuss the major challenges that schools have encountered in trying to implement and sustain the *MicroSociety* program. Then, in the next section of the book, I present three case studies that depict the experiences of individual schools when they set out to implement the *MicroSociety* program. In one case, the effort was successful, and the school sustained the program over a long period. However, in another case, the attempt ended in failure; and in the third case, the school terminated a program despite its success. Together, these case studies highlight the obstacles and challenges involved in trying to implement change in public school environments. The case studies also reveal the factors that help schools to succeed.

CONCLUSION

The *MicroSociety* program transforms the school into a miniature society run by the students themselves. It has all the components that one would find in any adult society, including an economic system with its own currency, banks, and businesses and a political system with a constitution, laws, legislature, and courts. Students earn money through work and use their money to buy goods and services provided by other students. As students assume more responsibility, teachers become facilitators and consultants. There also are roles for parents and community partners.

The *MicroSociety* program concept began in the late 1960s in a fifth-grade classroom in Brooklyn, New York. Since then, it has spread to more than 200 schools in 40 states, and the federal government has approved the program as a "comprehensive school reform model."

A number of studies indicate that when schools are able to implement it effectively, the *MicroSociety* program can have a positive impact on both academic and nonacademic outcomes. However, not all schools have seen equally impressive results. Ultimately, the impact of the program depends on how well schools are able to implement it. Thus for the *MicroSociety* program, as well as many other educational reforms, it is important to understand the typical challenges that schools encounter in trying to implement the program.

2

Challenges Encountered in Implementing the Program

Those who visit a successful *MicroSociety*® program or view one of the documentary videos on it see children and adults engaged in a fascinating series of activities. The scene is lively, but it is orderly as well. Everyone seems happily absorbed in the life of a miniature society. It is a very appealing picture. What the viewers or visitors do not see are the challenges that the staff and students had to overcome in order to achieve such a result. This is unfortunate, because when teachers and administrators decide to implement the program in their own school, often all they have seen is the happy outcome of sustained struggle. The struggle itself remains hidden. As a result, when a new group of implementers encounter these challenges, they usually are unprepared. Caught off guard, they flounder and sometimes fail.

There is a danger, of course, in describing the challenges that educators typically encounter in trying to implement the *MicroSociety* program or other innovative educational strategies: They may become so discouraged that they will decide not to implement the program. However, if merely becoming aware of the challenges is enough to dissuade them from trying, perhaps it is better if they do not attempt it. For those who do decide to implement whole-school reform, knowing about the predictable problems may help them to handle them more effectively and with less stress.

LACK OF TEACHER BUY-IN

Of all the challenges that schools encounter in implementing the *MicroSociety* program, the most significant in terms of its impact probably is lack of teacher commitment or "buy-in." At the 2002 summer conference, I asked a group of about 40 teachers and administrators from *MicroSociety* programs around the country to identify the biggest challenges that they had encountered in their programs. The one that was mentioned most often was "getting teachers to genuinely buy into the program." This response did not surprise me, because I had found teachers who had reservations about the program in virtually every school I had studied, including those with the strongest programs and the most enthusiastic teacher participation. There even were teachers who made it clear that they would not be doing the *MicroSociety* program if they felt they had a genuine choice. Also, an extensive, unpublished evaluation study, involving 14 *MicroSociety* program schools and more than 2,000 student survey responses, found that while students generally were very positive about the *MicroSociety* program, "Teachers are not as universally positive as students about the value of the *MicroSociety* program. Significant numbers of teachers are not convinced as yet that participation in *MicroSociety* contributes to students' academic or personal growth" (Kutzik, 2003, p. 34).

This lack of commitment among some teachers proved to be a challenge for program coordinators, and it adversely affected the more committed teachers as well. This lack of uniform support among the teachers also could affect the students and the program's impact on them.

Lack of teacher buy-in has been a perplexing problem for other reform models as well. Berends, Bodilly, and Kirby (2002) found that this was one of the problems that the New American Schools (NAS) reform models encountered when implemented in schools. Haynes, Emmons, Gebreyesus, and Ben-Avie (1996) also noted that lack of desire for change on the part of school staff hindered implementation of Comer's Social Development Program model.

Some of the resistant teachers were responding largely to the discomfort that often accompanies change. As one principal noted, "Teachers are used to knowing their stuff well. They're reluctant to take on something new that they don't know as well." Once these teachers had done the program for a while and felt more efficacious with it, their resistance faded.

Some even became strong supporters of the program. However, other teachers remained critical.

Also, new teachers who came to the school after the school had established the program might not be as enthusiastic as the pioneers were. Principals usually attempted to screen out new teachers who might not be supportive of the *MicroSociety* program when they hired them, but inevitably, some less committed teachers slipped through the process.

Some of the opposition to the *MicroSociety* program related to philosophy. For example, there were teachers who believed that "slow learners" miss time they need for extra help because of the *MicroSociety* program. For other teachers, their resistance to the program had more to do with their own interests and what they most enjoyed doing. One critical teacher said that reading was "her love" and that she wanted to spend more time teaching reading, not doing the *MicroSociety* program.

Whatever the cause, a lack of teacher commitment has proved to be a major impediment to effective implementation of the program. Without strong teacher interest and support, the ventures are not likely to be as engaging and meaningful for the students. As one principal put it, "The program doesn't work as well when a teacher in charge of an area lacks zippidy-do-dah." As principal, she could require that her teachers participate in the program, but she could not mandate the level of interest and enthusiasm that are necessary for effective implementation.

Lack of teacher commitment also contributed to interpersonal conflicts among the staff. In the traditional school structure, teachers have considerable autonomy once they go into their classrooms and close the door behind them. This allows them to adopt a "live-and-let-live" attitude toward teachers who embrace different philosophies and methods, which defuses conflict. However, a schoolwide program requires that all the teachers participate, and when some do so with less enthusiasm, conflicts are likely to become contentious and troublesome. Morale can plummet among the less committed teachers who feel pressured to participate in a teaching method they do not like, and the teachers who are strong supporters of the program may become demoralized by the resistance of those who are less committed. Coordinators and administrators who are in the middle increasingly feel as though they are under siege.

EXCESSIVE TIME AND WORK DEMANDS

Next to lack of teacher buy-in, the challenge that workshop participants most often mentioned was the amount of extra time and effort that implementing the program requires. Some teachers felt that implementing the

MicroSociety program was "like adding a second curriculum." One teacher said that she spent an extra hour each day just preparing for Micro. Other teachers reported that they spent as much time preparing for the *MicroSociety* program as they did for the rest of the day. One teacher complained that she spent even *more* time preparing for her *MicroSociety* program venture (the bank) than for her classes.

Excessive teacher effort has been the undoing of many other reform efforts. It was a major reason that schools dropped out of the NAS program (Berends et al., 2002). Muncey and McQuillan (1996) also found that implementing Sizer's Essential Schools approach required substantial amounts of additional time and effort for teachers and that "the increase in workload . . . led some teachers to return to previous teaching practices or otherwise disengage from reform work" (p. 267).

Much of the extra time and effort required for the *MicroSociety* program went into planning. One of the coordinators said that teachers who were "really into it" would spend a whole summer planning for it. Some teachers also complained about the amount of paperwork involved in doing Micro. A first-grade teacher became exasperated with the payroll forms, tax forms, and attendance forms that she had to complete on a regular basis for the program.

Teachers who took on special roles spent even more time on the program. For instance, the teachers who serve on the management team for the program often will meet after school for 1 or 2 hours each week to deal with problems that come up and to make decisions. If the program encounters a great deal of difficulty, the management team may end up meeting even more often. In a school that struggled with implementation, the management team met two or three times per week just to try to keep up with all the problems.

Time also was a challenge at the coordinator level. Every *MicroSociety* program school is supposed to designate one teacher (or other professional staff member) as the coordinator. This individual provides administrative support as well as training and consultation to other teachers and students. Ideally, there is money in the school's budget so that the coordinators can be released from other responsibilities. But in the schools I studied, the coordinator's *MicroSociety* program commitment often was simply added to their other commitments. A teacher at one school said that the coordinator was so overcommitted that she often was not able to give teachers the guidance and support they needed. The coordinator agreed that she was "swamped" with all the tasks associated with the role, such as organizing students' jobs (she placed all the students in their ventures), writing memos, completing forms, and showing visitors around the school. (At this point, I apologized for taking up so much of her time. She responded with a sheepish grin and a shrug.)

Even when teachers felt that they could manage the extra planning time, they sometimes were concerned about the hour or so that the *MicroSociety* program took from "regular class work" each day. The problem as they saw it was that they still had to cover a prescribed curriculum, and the *MicroSociety* program meant that they had an hour less each day to do it. Some teachers felt that other areas of the curriculum suffered because of "all the time they had to give to Micro." This added to the pressure and stress that they felt.

Because the teachers felt so burdened, they often did not have the time or energy to do the things necessary to make the program better. All of the extra work prevented many teachers from learning what they needed to know in order to implement the program effectively. The added work also made it harder for teachers to find the time to meet with community partners. In addition, the staff neglected evaluation because of the heavy time demands.

Fortunately, the work demands associated with the *MicroSociety* program seemed to become less onerous over time in the more successful schools. Although the first year of implementation always involved many hours of additional work for the staff, by the third year, many teachers felt that the workload had diminished. In addition, many of the teachers willingly did the extra work associated with the *MicroSociety* program because it was so rewarding. For instance, at one school, the teachers indicated that the *MicroSociety* program still involved extra work after 10 years of existence, but they willingly did it because they saw the positive impact it had on the students. Nevertheless, the additional time and effort the *MicroSociety* program required of teachers could become problematic.

Many factors contributed to the work and time pressure that the *MicroSociety* program imposed on the staff. A major one was that most teachers in most schools lacked adequate time for planning during the regular school day. Ideally, additional funding would accompany the introduction of a new program such as the *MicroSociety* program, and the school would use this funding to pay for additional planning time. However, there usually was not enough funding to support the kind of additional planning that teachers needed to manage all of the demands on their time. As a result, implementing the *MicroSociety* program became an added burden.

Lack of funding has been a chronic problem in the history of school reform efforts. Schorr (1997) observed that "inadequate funding" and "an unwillingness to invest the necessary resources" (p. 20) have been major impediments to scaling up successful reforms. Inadequate funding was the single most important reason for schools sponsored by the NAS project to drop a design. The primary reason that lack of funding was so detrimental was because it led to overloads on teachers (Berends et al., 2002).

Another reason that the *MicroSociety* program seemed to impose such a burden was that the administration often expected the teachers to implement other mandates at the same time. In one district, an official in the central office said that in addition to the *MicroSociety* program and the regular curriculum, the teachers had to start a new science program and develop a social skills program.

The most intrusive mandates involved the growing emphasis on testing and standards in the public schools. At one school, the board of education announced that all schools in the district had to develop two performance-based assessment tests for each educational goal set by the state. The school eventually terminated the *MicroSociety* program in order for the teachers to have more time to prepare the students to take the achievement tests. In another school, the principal said he was disappointed with the school's performance on the statewide tests during the previous year, and consequently the teachers had to focus more on test-taking skills. This new focus on testing added to the burden of implementing the *MicroSociety* program.

Research on whole-school reform efforts associated with the NAS project also found that implementation was hindered by "high-stakes testing." Such testing led to competing mandates from the state and district levels (Berends et al., 2002).

Whatever the source of the competing mandates, they took their toll on the teachers in *MicroSociety* programs. One teacher summed up the effect of all these different mandates when she said, "I would like to do one thing well, and I can't when there are so many different programs to implement."

The most common way in which the schools dealt with the additional time demands on the teachers was to scale back the program. In one middle school, the *MicroSociety* program began as a two-period activity; but in the face of competing demands, the principal reduced it to one period a day. In an elementary school, the program initially ran for 90 minutes each day. Eventually, in response to pressure from the teachers, the principal agreed to scale it back to 50 minutes a day. In yet another school, the principal dealt with time demands by reducing the number of weeks during the year that Micro ran. She also would cancel Micro whenever there were additional demands, such as testing or parent conferences.

Another common strategy was to scale back other requirements. For instance, in one school, the principal allowed the teachers to abandon another program that they were trying to implement at the same time. Unfortunately, schools cannot completely avoid mandates by definition, and so this strategy often proved to be of limited value. The school was more likely to scale back the *MicroSociety* program, which was not a mandate, than to scale back other demands on the staff's time.

However, some of the schools found ways to make the workload manageable without scaling back the program. At one school, for instance, the principal and teachers tried to alleviate the burdens by creatively combining different parts of the standard curriculum. For instance, because Micro cut into the time normally set aside for teaching social studies, the faculty tried to combine social studies with language arts by having students read material relating to the social studies curriculum during their language arts period.

The most effective way of reducing the added workload demands on the teachers utilized the program itself. When teachers were able to give the students more responsibility for managing ventures, the workload on the teachers greatly diminished. For example, in one school's marketplace, both buyers and sellers would bombard the two teachers in charge with questions and problems every day. By the time Micro was over for the day, the teachers were exhausted. Then someone had a brilliant idea. They created a new position for the students called "mall manager." The job of the mall manager was to assist shoppers and shopkeepers in the marketplace whenever they had a problem. Students with problems would go to a mall manager rather than one of the teachers. If the mall manager could not solve the problem, then he or she would go to a teacher for help. The teachers selected three students who had been successful shopkeepers during the previous year to fill the position. The result: Almost immediately, the burden on the teachers diminished. In fact, after only 1 week, they found that they had gone from being overwhelmed during Micro time to having little to do.

Unfortunately, many teachers found it difficult to give up the control that was customary for their role. They had learned over many years of socialization that teachers should be in charge. Although they could not articulate it, at some level, they believed that if they were not in charge, chaos and pandemonium would ensue. This anxiety prevented teachers from allowing the students to take over in *MicroSociety* programs, and this, as much as anything else, created a situation in which the teachers felt burdened with additional work.

This aspect of the problem became especially clear at an elementary school where one of the ventures was a fully equipped television studio. The local university had provided the school with a grant of several hundred thousand dollars to purchase the equipment. The school began each day with a news show put on by the students, complete with weather reports, news headlines, and so on. Given how expensive and fragile the equipment was, the three teachers assigned to the TV station were especially nervous about letting the students do too much without direct supervision by the teachers.

Then came a week when all of the teachers assigned to the TV station were going to be away for 3 days. What should they do about the TV station? Many of the staff thought they should shut down the TV station for those 3 days. However, the principal pointed out that the students had been putting on the morning show every day for several months and they now seemed capable of doing it on their own. With great trepidation, the teachers allowed the students to run the show on their own during those 3 days. The students did so without any mishaps.

When the teachers returned and found that the students had been able to manage on their own, they realized that their close supervision was no longer necessary and that the students were capable of far more responsibility and independence than the teachers had thought. Unfortunately, many teachers never had the opportunity to learn this lesson, and the result was that the *MicroSociety* program imposed a heavy burden on them.

MAKING LINKS BETWEEN THE *MICROSOCIETY*® PROGRAM AND THE CORE CURRICULUM

In theory, the *MicroSociety* program is supposed to demonstrate, reinforce, and provide practice for what students are learning in the classroom. Addition and subtraction become more meaningful when students have their own checking accounts at the *MicroSociety* program bank and they must reconcile their checkbooks and bank statements each month. The political conflicts over taxation, which have shaped American politics since the founding of the republic, become more comprehensible when students must pay taxes themselves and decide what public services they should provide as part of the *MicroSociety* program. Students have an opportunity to develop writing skills when they apply for jobs and write business plans.

In practice, however, many teachers came to see the *MicroSociety* program as another "add-on." Rather than enhancing the core curriculum, the new program seemed to be competing with it by taking time away from covering it. The *MicroSociety* program coordinator at one school said that even though many teachers thought that students learned "a lot of social studies" through the program, they then complained that Micro "cut into the time set aside to teach social studies." If the teachers had been more able to link the program to the curriculum, they would have seen it as part of the curriculum and part of the day, rather than another add-on.

Other school reform efforts also have encountered the "linkage" problem. For instance, teachers in Coalition for Effective Schools (CES) schools found it difficult to implement the "less-is-more" principle because of their concern about departing from the traditional curriculum. They were afraid that they would not be able to cover all the subjects that they were supposed to cover, and they worried about "how the new standards would be integrated with existing district- and state-level requirements" (Muncey & McQuillan, 1996, p. 265).

Increasing pressures to raise student scores on achievement tests tended to exacerbate this problem in schools that implemented the *Micro-Society* program. For instance, one teacher complained that she needed to spend more time focusing on raising her students' test scores and that the *MicroSociety* program took "time away" from this work.

The difficulty in making links to the core curriculum varied with the students' jobs. For instance, students who were members of the legislature received a strong dose of social studies, and students involved in publishing received much practice in reading and writing. Those who worked in the bank were able to practice math skills. Managers of agencies and ventures also had many opportunities to engage in high-level literacy and math tasks. However, students who did piecework in manufacturing ventures had little opportunity to use math or reading skills.

The extent of the problem also varied with the teacher. Although many teachers complained that it was difficult to make the links between the *MicroSociety* program and the standard curriculum, some teachers found it easy to do so. For instance, in a school where several teachers struggled with making links between Micro and the unit on Latin American history, one teacher was able to use the students' experience in Micro to explain more clearly why peasants in several Latin American countries became interested in socialism and revolted.

These examples suggest that the challenge of making links with the curriculum relates to the way in which teachers think about and approach teaching. As one insightful program coordinator noted, "Teachers tend to think, 'Here's the math segment, here's the Micro segment.' They don't see connections unless they're told to look for them and shown how to make them. They are used to top-down management. They wait to be told how to do it."

To make the links between Micro and the rest of the curriculum, the teachers need to *see* the links as they emerge either in the classroom or in the *MicroSociety* program and then figure out ways to make those links come alive for the students. As one teacher noted, "You need to constantly look for ways to make a link between Micro and the required curriculum. You can't necessarily plan for it all the time. For instance, when teaching writing in the classroom, you could do book brochures for the publishing strand rather than just use traditional book reports."

The *way* in which teachers teach also can make it easier to make links between Micro and the rest of the curriculum. A teacher in one of the more successful schools thought that students could make the links themselves, "if you teach the regular curriculum using the discovery method." However, if the teacher just gives students information, the students will not make the links.

Unfortunately, many teachers seemed to be at a loss for how to make the links, and they looked to others to provide the answers. They thought that there should be more guidance provided at the summer conferences or, better yet, a "curriculum" that would make the links for them.

However, it is too simplistic to blame the teachers. They work in a setting where there is a heavy emphasis on curriculum standards and on covering a certain amount of material in a certain amount of time. It also is a setting where textbooks tend to drive the teaching process. Teachers tend to teach "by the book" because early in their careers they have been punished (or seen others punished) for not doing so. The culture of schooling makes it difficult for the typical teacher to make the connections between Micro and the core curriculum (Sarason, 1996).

One of the original *MicroSociety* program teachers in Lowell made an observation that illustrated this point particularly well. He noted that the best year in the school's history was when they were in a temporary location, waiting for their permanent building to be renovated. "At that point, we had no books, so we had to work on the theme more." Because the teachers had no schoolbooks, they made up their own lessons, and those lessons made many links between Micro and standard subjects. Another one of the original teachers added, "Lessons can't be traditional lessons that are schoolbook oriented. The teachers need to make up lessons that are linked to Micro activities." Although the teachers were glad to get regular textbooks the next year, in retrospect, they realized that those books made it harder to link Micro with the rest of the curriculum.

The way in which schools of education train teachers also contributes to the problem. As one report on the *MicroSociety* program noted, "In general, teacher certification programs don't provide preparation for the extensive use of experiential learning" (Kutzik, 2003, p. 34). Without this foundation, many teachers find it difficult to utilize *MicroSociety* program activities in the service of academic learning.

The growing emphasis on standards and accountability during the last decade has made the linkage problem worse. More than ever, there is pressure on teachers to make sure that their students cover prescribed material in a prescribed amount of time. School districts increasingly evaluate administrators on how well their students perform on standard tests. The pressure to cover what is in the curriculum, what is in the book, and what is on the test has never been greater. One effect of this growing emphasis on standards and accountability has been that teachers have become more concerned about the links between Micro and the rest of the curriculum, and they have found it more difficult to make those links.

The problem of integrating the *MicroSociety* program with the rest of the curriculum also relates to the principal's leadership and the school's commitment to the program. The weaker the school's commitment to the program, the weaker the teachers' willingness and ability to make the links. For example, at one school, the teachers found it relatively easy to make links between Micro and the rest of the curriculum during the first few years. Then there was a change in principals. The new principal, who had not been at the school when the program began, knew little about it and was much less committed to it than his predecessor had been. One teacher in this school observed that since the new principal took over, there had been "deterioration in the connection between what goes on in the traditional classroom and Micro activities." The teacher believed this was because "the first principal stressed it, and you need to keep it on people's minds for the connections to occur."

Lack of time for reflection and planning contributes to the linkage challenge. Although the connections between Micro and the core curriculum sometimes are obvious and easy for a teacher to make, often they are subtle. It would be helpful if teachers had time specifically set aside time to think of how to make those connections. Unfortunately, there usually is not much time left over once they finish doing all the other prep work they need to do.

For instance, a Micro coordinator at one school suggested that one solution would be for teachers to "write questions that make the link between Micro experiences and what is being covered in class." However, this kind of work takes time, and the Micro program already overwhelms many teachers with additional time demands. On the other hand, if the teachers could make the links more effectively, the time demands would decrease.

The schools tried to deal with the challenge of making connections in a number of ways, none of which was ideal. The original school at Lowell created a special role called "Micro specialist." The Micro specialist was a teacher who had a certain amount of release time each week to devote to helping implement the program. Several teachers served in this role. One of the regular duties of the Micro specialists was to help achieve some linkage between the regular classroom experience and Micro by teaching Micro-related lessons in every classroom every week.

In another school, the coordinator helped students develop test-taking skills by writing practice test questions that used Micro activities and concepts. Another school tried to link Micro to the state's core curriculum objectives by incorporating some of the objectives into the terminology of each strand. (The *MicroSociety* program initially was organized around six major components or "strands." These were Economy, Academy, Citizenship and Government, Technology, Humanities and the Arts, and Heart.) They also used the state's objectives as the basis for a posttest for each strand.

One way to make the links between Micro and the traditional curriculum is to bring examples from the Micro program into the regular classroom. However, in one school, the teachers used the opposite strategy: They brought what they needed to cover in the regular curriculum into the Micro program. One of the teachers explained that he did this by thinking about his regular curriculum objectives when he created his venture. Rather than just developing a venture that seemed fun or interesting, he designed his venture so that it contributed directly to the curriculum goals.

Unfortunately, none of these solutions was ideal. The Micro specialist role is useful, but most schools lack the resources necessary for creating and sustaining such a role. Having the coordinators take on responsibility for making the connections adds to their already heavy burden. Moreover, creating ventures with the curriculum in mind does not always work out. In one school, a teacher created a venture called "Live Poets Society," which linked well to the writing curriculum, but few students wanted to work there, and few students were interested in buying their products. Thus making links between Micro and the core curriculum has continued to be a vexing challenge, one that further weakens many teachers' commitment to the program.

WHAT TO DO WITH "PROBLEM" STUDENTS?

One of the greatest benefits of the *MicroSociety* program is that it provides a chance to shine for students who do not succeed in the regular classroom. Students who are "behavior problems" the rest of the day, because of boredom or short attention spans, usually become engaged in the *MicroSociety* program and present no problem at all. In fact, most schools have found that the number of disciplinary problems drops significantly during the application phase of the *MicroSociety* program. However, a few students always seemed to have trouble fitting in during Micro time, and they often became disruptive. What to do with these students posed a dilemma.

The behavior problems associated with Micro usually were minor. A few students might "goof off" when they were supposed to be working, or they might act as though they did not care and refuse to participate. Nevertheless, a lack of engagement and productive activity on the part of some students was a source of frustration for many teachers and administrators. It fueled the feeling that Micro was taking time away from regular class activity, because the educators assumed that those students would have been more productive if they had been in a regular class. Too much down time for students also could be a precursor to more serious behavior problems.

When behavior problems did occur, some teachers blamed the students. For instance, they might conclude that some students just were not "mature enough" for Micro. Other teachers believed that students misbehaved or became restless because of the kinds of homes and communities from which they came. Although there might be some validity to these beliefs, the problem with them is that many *MicroSociety* program schools located in large urban districts, with many students who come from disorganized homes, experience few behavior problems. In fact, George Richmond's first classroom was located in such a setting.

Student behavior problems during Micro time seem to be more a function of the way in which the program is implemented and the school's organizational dynamics than of the students or their backgrounds. For instance, at one of the schools I studied, the teachers said that only "one or two kids" posed problems, while at another, student behavior problems were endemic. Both schools were located in urban communities, and most of their students came from disadvantaged families. However, effective leadership and positive relations among the staff characterized the first school, and teachers were strongly committed to the *MicroSociety* program there. At the second school, the principal provided weak and inconsistent leadership, and teacher commitment to the program varied.

The quality of the venture in a *MicroSociety* program also influences the students' behavior. When the students like their job and have choices, their behavior usually is no problem at all. Even at the school that had the most behavior problems, there were specific ventures in which student behavior was exemplary. One teacher, for instance, complained that student discipline was "a big problem" in his venture. However, he conceded that student behavior had not been a problem during the first 2 years when he was working with another teacher who "was very good." When I asked him what made his colleague so "good," he replied that she made the venture interesting and successful for the students.

Student behavior problems also can be a reaction to the distribution of power and responsibility in a *MicroSociety* program. The students in a *MicroSociety* program are supposed to be in control. When teachers or administrators step in and impose limits on the students, the students are more likely to lose interest in the program and act out.

For instance, in many schools, teachers struggled with the question of what to do about "wealthy entrepreneurs," students who are especially adept at starting successful ventures and who amass far more money than their peers. It is not clear that students worry about this problem, but some teachers do. The most frequent response is for the adults to make up rules limiting how much money students can earn, even from their own businesses. However, when adults intervene in this way, students tend to lose interest in the program, and then student behavior deteriorates.

A better way for the teachers to deal with such a challenge is to view it as a "teachable moment" and begin by exploring with the students why the uneven distribution of wealth may be a problem. Teachers might ask the students to think about how it makes them feel when a few of their peers amass large amounts of money. Teachers also might help the students explore the consequences that a concentration of wealth in a few hands has for the *MicroSociety* program's economy. For instance, the teachers might ask, "Does the concentration of wealth tend to encourage or discourage productive, entrepreneurial activity by students who do not have as much capital to invest?" Then if students feel that there are problems with unbridled entrepreneurial activity, there are ways of dealing with the problem that do not involve limiting directly how much a student can earn. These methods include graduated income taxes, business taxes, and policies that encourage more competition. In using these mechanisms to deal with the problem rather than relying on adult authority or arbitrary rules, the potential for learning is much greater.

When student behavior becomes a problem, the same principle applies. Teachers can, and should, use the program to help students deal with those challenges themselves. Too often, however, the teachers jump in and deal with the problems by making rules and enforcing them. An example was a bank robbery that occurred at one school. Two or three students discovered how to break into the bank, and they stole all of the money that was stored there. The teachers were very upset by what had happened and suggested various draconian measures for dealing with the problem. Fortunately, the principal did not give in to their desire to step in and punish the students in a traditional way. Instead, he came up with a way to use Micro to punish the students and make a point at the same time. He proposed that the *MicroSociety* program have an auction the next week and let the bank robbers outbid the other students. The auction took place, and the bank robbers did outbid the other students on virtually every item.

Up to that point, many of the students thought the bank robbers were "pretty cool." However, when the other students discovered that the bank robbers' behavior had deprived the rest of them of all the items put on auction, their sense of fairness was aroused. They turned on the bank robbers and ostracized them. Overnight, the robbers went from being heroes to pariahs. After 3 days, the robbers confessed their crime and gave back all of the items that they had purchased at the auction.

The best approach to dealing with student behavior problems associated with the *MicroSociety* program, however, involves prevention. For instance, effective teachers prevented student boredom and misbehavior from occurring by helping students choose work wanted, either by starting their own ventures or by ensuring that they secured one of their top job choices. As one teacher put it, "Kids want to see results right away." She said she learned this lesson the first year she did the program. The students got restless easily, and she soon discovered that she did not have enough jobs for them to do. The next year, through brainstorming with a colleague, she was able to come up with more jobs for the students, and student behavior improved.

THE PROBLEM OF STAFF CONFLICT

Interpersonal conflicts are inevitable in any complex organization, and schools are no exception. In addition, any attempt to introduce change is likely to increase tensions and conflicts among the staff. However, a school-wide *MicroSociety* program can make such conflicts even more apparent and disruptive because teachers need to work together more closely. There is greater interdependence among teachers in a *MicroSociety* program, and thus more opportunity for open conflict to disrupt the work process.

Sometimes conflict resulted from "personality differences among the teachers." This was especially true for teachers who shared responsibility for a venture. Differences in values also can be a source of conflict in Micro programs. One teacher said that she was disturbed that another teacher had opened a "pub" as a venture. (The pub sold hot chocolate, coffee, and sodas.) She also objected to the modeling agency venture. "We need to remember this is a school," she said indignantly. "You need structure and discipline!"

One of the most common conflicts resulted from uneven adherence to rules. Invariably, some teachers would become upset because some of their colleagues were deviating from certain rules or allowing their students to do so. On the other hand, there were the teachers who resented attempts by their colleagues to impose "too much structure."

The most serious conflicts related to differences in commitment to the program. Even when all of the teachers initially agreed to participate in the program, some were less enthusiastic about it than others were. These differences in degree of commitment often became sources of bitter conflicts. In one school, a particularly committed teacher complained, "A group of teachers here don't do anything!" On the other hand, some of the teachers who were "less gung ho" about the program resented the way in which those who were more committed looked down on them. Less involved teachers also resented the extra "perks" that the more committed teachers sometimes managed to acquire.

Philosophical differences often contributed to conflicts over degree of commitment. In one school, the principal was a proponent of progressive and humanistic educational methods, and she regarded the teachers in Grades 4 through 6 as "very rigid and traditional." The principal saw Micro as a vehicle for getting the teachers to loosen up. Not surprisingly, the teachers resisted the principal's efforts, and they waged their war over educational philosophy through battles over Micro. This conflict between the principal and the teachers eventually led to the termination of the program.

Often the conflicts related to power and authority issues. In one school, for instance, several teachers complained that the coordinator "tells the teachers what to do and then goes over our heads when we don't do it." The coordinator, on the other hand, complained that many of the teachers resisted every effort to implement the program. She said, "Even now, after doing the program for over a year, every issue seems to require discussion and debate."

Other whole-school reform efforts also have found that such change invariably generates conflict among staff and others in a school. These conflicts between teachers who vary in their commitment to the reform effort have adversely affected other school change initiatives. For example, the RAND study of whole-school reform efforts associated with the NAS initiative also found that uneven commitment among the teachers in a school was a major problem (Berends et al., 2002). Similarly, faculties in schools that adopted the CES model often became polarized around it, with one faction supporting the new approach and the other opposing it. As Muncey and McQuillan (1996) put it, "Tensions, uncertainty, and divisiveness commonly accompanied these efforts at change" (p. 265). As with the *MicroSociety* program, the major sources of conflict associated with implementing the CES model involved teaching philosophy, power, status, autonomy, and resources. Muncey and McQuillan also found that "teaming with other teachers proved problematic" (p. 268) in the CES schools they studied.

Whatever the cause, these conflicts were disturbing for many of those involved. A teacher at one of the oldest programs still remembered the bitter arguments that occurred among the staff during the first year of implementation. He said that the conflicts were so upsetting that he sometimes "threw up on the way to work." Not only were such conflicts disturbing for the teachers, but they also impeded implementation of the program. In three of the schools that eventually terminated the program, unresolved conflict was a significant factor in each program's demise.

The conflicts were especially disruptive because teachers did not expect them. In addition, when conflict did develop, teachers who were used to working on their own often did not have the tools for dealing effectively with it. Most of them had learned how to manage conflict between students, but they were less sure about how to respond to conflict between themselves and their colleagues.

The most common way in which teachers dealt with conflict was to avoid open discussion of differences and disagreements. For instance, at several of the schools I studied, I found that teachers who were unhappy with the program would express their unhappiness to me, an outsider. However, they would not come forward to try to work out their differences with those involved. One of these teachers said she did not do so because "it takes too much time." She also felt that it would "not do any good." This avoidance strategy sometimes worked, but often the pressure would build up and the conflict would erupt into shouting matches that accomplished nothing and left the participants feeling shaken and depressed. Alternatively, teachers might act out the conflict in passive-aggressive behavior. Thus the problem ultimately is not conflict, which probably is inevitable in any educational setting, but rather the way in which the staff thought about and dealt with it.

THE "FOG OF CHANGE"

Another challenge that every new program encountered was the confusion that seemed to engulf teachers and students during the first few weeks or months of implementation. Even when the staff had the luxury of months of planning, invariably they would get off to a "rocky start." As a third-grade teacher put it, "I didn't understand anything about it that first year. . . . Even after reading about it and seeing the Micro video at a faculty meeting, I still didn't get it!" (Grote, 2002, p. 87). Moreover, this teacher worked at a school that had spent a year planning for the program before it became operational. Even with all of that planning and training, many staff members still were overwhelmed.

Teachers repeatedly commented on how there was "just so much going on at one time." In addition, there always were challenges that the teachers had not anticipated in advance. These were often simple things, such as how to handle the students' transition from class to Micro or how to handle demand in the warehouse when students from four different businesses came in at once with orders. The teachers and students usually figured out how to deal with such challenges, but it often took considerable time and experience to work out all the kinks. Moreover, it took time to adjust to the very different tempo that occurs in a *MicroSociety* program compared with a traditional classroom.

Unexpected events beyond the school walls often added to the uncertainty and disruption associated with change. For instance, one new *MicroSociety* program school encountered stiff opposition from parents because it was associated with a forced desegregation plan. Many parents who might have otherwise supported the program opposed it because it was part of an unpopular policy. Then to make matters worse, a grand jury indicted the superintendent who initially supported the program, for embezzlement. This unfortunate event occurred at the end of the first year of operation. The superintendent's successor was not nearly as supportive of the *MicroSociety* program as he had been. Not long after this, the district laid off 100 teachers because of budget cuts. All of these external events diluted support for the new program.

Inflexible rules often posed another unexpected challenge as staff began to translate an abstract reform model into a concrete educational program. For instance, when the teachers and parents at one Micro school tried to design their own report card, bureaucrats in the central office intervened and forced them to keep the district's standard report card.

THREATS TO SUSTAINABILITY

Even when a *MicroSociety* program school managed to overcome the initial barriers and burdens associated with change, new challenges often emerged over time. One such challenge involved a gradual decline in support from the district and wider community. In one case, the Micro program started as part of a districtwide school choice initiative based on the magnet school concept. Because the *MicroSociety* program school was one of the first magnets, it received much attention and support from the central office. However, as new magnet schools were created with different themes over the next few years, interest and support for the Micro school within the district waned. Then as time passed, other initiatives came to the fore, such as the implementation of a new middle school concept. The teachers and parents who had been associated with the school for many years felt that these changes in priorities made it difficult for them to sustain the program.

Previous research on whole-school reform also has documented the importance of support from the district level (Berends et al., 2002; Haynes et al., 1996). Portin, Beck, Knapp, and Murphy (2003) found that such support not only was necessary during the early stages of implementation but also continued to be important. A gradual loss of such support over time put the reform effort in jeopardy.

Another threat that became more significant over time involved the growing concern about standards and accountability in American public education. The *MicroSociety* program concept is not necessarily antithetical to such a concern, but how schools performed on standardized tests became more important to local school board members and central office personnel than promoting a specific innovation such as the *MicroSociety* program.

Yet another challenge associated with the passage of time was turnover among administrators, teachers, and students. In one Micro school, the administration announced layoffs at the end of the first year of implementation. The school eventually lost half of the staff as a result of the layoffs and the "bumping" that occurred along with them. At the same time, the district implemented a new "controlled choice plan," which allowed many parents to send their children to different schools in the district. These changes meant that there were many new teachers and students in the school at the start of the second year. These newcomers knew little about the program, and they were not necessarily as supportive of it as the original group had been.

Of all the threats that can occur, a change in leadership often poses the greatest challenge for a *MicroSociety* program. A new principal often brings a different set of values and concerns and thus creates an unsupportive environment. As a result, even successful programs sometimes decline and fail following a change in principals. (See Chapter 9 for an example.)

The *MicroSociety* program is not unique in this respect. Hargreaves and Fink (2003) noted that "Changes in leadership always pose a threat to sustainable improvement" (p. 697). One of the most renowned examples of whole-school reform, which took place in Memphis during the 1990s, abruptly ended when the progressive superintendent who supported the effort left in 2001 and her predecessor quickly dismantled it (Finnan & Meza, 2003).

One other challenge to sustainability involved the diminution of enthusiasm and growing routine over time. Although the *MicroSociety* program concept has the capacity to reinvent itself constantly, many older programs struggle with the problem of how to maintain interest and enthusiasm. In one such program, newer teachers and outsiders observed that many of the teachers who had been there for a long time "lack enthusiasm. . . . They are going through the motions." One teacher believed that some faculty members were doing "the same thing they were doing from the beginning." A parent complained that after a few years, "The faculty became comfortable with it," and at that point, they became "more traditional." The older faculty tended to confirm this view. One said, "The curriculum hasn't grown in the last few years." Another one of the original teachers, who eventually left the school, said he felt he had reached a point where he needed a change: "Personally, I had just run out of ideas."

However, the decline in faculty enthusiasm was not universal, even in the oldest programs. For instance, a teacher who had been continuously involved with Micro for over a decade had recently created a new venture (a peer mediation program) that rejuvenated her. She said she was never bored and that "time goes fast here—for the teachers as well as the kids."

Another teacher with many years of experience in the program also said that maintaining enthusiasm had not been a challenge for him because he had been able to change what he was doing within the program.

These individual experiences suggest one way that teachers can forestall the increasing sameness and loss of excitement that can occur over time. Part of the solution involves making a change in what one is doing, but it is a particular kind of change, one that involves creating a new venture—or, in some cases, re-creating a venture. The peer mediation program provides a good example. By developing a new intellectual and professional interest, pursuing it through professional development activities, and then making it the basis for her work in Micro, a teacher rediscovered the excitement and stimulation that existed during the first few years.

Allowing the students to take more control over what happens in their ventures probably is the best way to prevent the stagnation that sometimes sets in after many years of doing Micro. One teacher said that she never found Micro to be monotonous because she begins each year by asking the kids in her venture (publishing) what they want to do with it. Each new group of students inevitably goes off in a different direction, which keeps the experience fresh and interesting for the teacher.

CONCLUSION

Educators who attempt to implement the *MicroSociety* program encounter a number of challenges. (See Table 2.1 for a summary of the most common challenges.) These challenges have many different sources, but one common theme involves the principle of student empowerment. The essence of the *MicroSociety* program is that students are empowered to create and manage their own society. Implementing the program in a way that is consistent with this principle requires a significant change in the role of the teacher. Teachers must become facilitators, and they must have faith that their students can handle the responsibility that is involved in managing a society. Many teachers find it difficult to make this transition. This difficulty to give up control and empower the students causes, triggers, or exacerbates many of the problems associated with implementation.

For instance, teachers become overwhelmed with additional demands on their time because they are reluctant to allow students to do much of the work involved in running a society. Moreover, because the teachers become overwhelmed, they do not have the opportunity for the periods of calm reflection that would help them make links between Micro and the rest of the curriculum. In addition, because students do not play a significant role in running their own society, they are more likely to become bored and

Table 2.1   Most Common Challenges Encountered in Implementing the
MicroSociety® Program

- Lack of teacher buy-in
- Excessive time and work demands
- Making links between Micro and the core curriculum
- "Problem" students
- Conflict among the staff
- Confusion and uncertainty during the first few months of implementation
- Threats to sustainability over time
  - Decline in support from district and wider community
  - Growing concern about "standards" and accountability
  - Turnover among administrators, staff, or students
  - Decline in enthusiasm and increasing sense of routine

apathetic, and student behavior may become more problematic. Ultimately, all of these problems undermine teacher commitment to the program and contribute to the greatest challenge: lack of teacher buy-in.

The teachers' need to maintain control and its negative impact on reform are not unique to the *MicroSociety* program model. For instance, Muncey and McQuillan (1996) found that many teachers who tried to implement the CES philosophy "had reservations about giving up their role of authority in the classroom" (p. 264). Their ambivalence about key aspects of the program was "rooted more in a concern about giving up control of their classrooms, no matter how temporarily, to students" (p. 264).

Rigid control of student behavior is part of the culture of schools. A report on a school improvement project sponsored by the Ford Foundation in the 1970s stated, "As students of any age are given more freedom to talk, to move, and to decide where, when, how, and what to study, parents, community, and even teachers become apprehensive" (quoted in Muncey & McQuillan, 1996, p. 287).

Although all of the schools encountered these challenges to a greater or lesser degree, some fared much better than others did. What were the factors that made a difference? Why did some schools manage to implement the program effectively despite these challenges, while others faltered and, in some cases, even failed? Finally, what guidelines emerge from the assessment that can help those in the future who wish to implement sustainable whole-school reform models? The next part of this book provides answers to these questions.

II

Guidelines for Successful Implementation

3

Creating a Favorable Context

Implementing a reform is like planting a flower: Much depends on the environment. In the case of the flower, the relevant factors include soil, light, and temperature. No matter how well the gardener plants the flower and tends to it, its chances of survival are slight if the soil is poor, the light is inadequate, and the ambient temperature is too hot or too cold. Similarly, no matter how skillful and dedicated a group of educators are, they will find it difficult to establish viable school change unless the organizational context is favorable.

Unfortunately, those who wish to replicate successful educational reforms rarely focus much attention on the context of the initial, successful prototype effort. They assume that it is what the teachers and students did that is important, and not where they did it. It is as though, after successfully growing a new kind of cactus in the California desert, one assumed that one could grow the same plant, in the same way, in a New Jersey marsh. Agricultural innovation has progressed much further than educational innovation in part because context is seen as important.

Those who wish to implement sustainable change in their school first need to consider the contextual factors that are critical for success. Although it is impossible to come up with a definitive list, a comparison of the *MicroSociety* program schools that succeeded with those that failed can suggest some of the more important ones. It also is worthwhile to consider the distinctive context out of which the first, successful schoolwide prototype in Lowell, Massachusetts, emerged.

When I looked at the organizational contexts out of which the different *MicroSociety*® programs that I studied emerged, there were four factors that seemed to be especially important in influencing their subsequent outcomes. One factor was the quality of relationships in the school, especially the relationships between the principal and teachers and among the teachers. A second factor that seemed fateful was the "goodness of fit" between Micro and the school's priorities and needs. Third, the extent to which there was a history of community partnerships and parent involvement in the school also made a difference. Finally, the extent to which the principal supported the program influenced both the process and outcome of implementation efforts. These four factors suggest an initial set of implementation guidelines. (All the guidelines in this and the following chapters are summarized in Resource B.)

GUIDELINE 1: RELATIONSHIPS AMONG TEACHERS AND PRINCIPAL

Relationships among teachers and the principal in the school should be positive. If they are characterized by mistrust and conflict, then efforts should be directed toward improving those relationships before attempting to implement change.

The social climate of a school is particularly important for the implementation of a reform model like the *MicroSociety* program. As we saw in the previous chapter, the implementation process is fraught with unexpected problems and challenges. These challenges can be disruptive for even the most seasoned teachers. Positive relationships between the principal and the staff and among the staff provide a store of good will and trust that can be drawn upon when conflict and frustration become particularly taxing. Positive relationships provide the social lubricant that facilitates the group planning and problem solving necessary for an effective program.

Also, if the principal is a strong advocate of the program, positive relationships between the principal and the staff make the staff more willing to go along with the program. When the teachers respect and trust the principal, it is easier for the principal to secure teacher support for the program. For instance, at one school I studied, many teachers had doubts about the program. However, they committed themselves to it because the principal was a strong supporter of the program, and the teachers liked and respected him.

Relationships among the staff are especially important in *MicroSociety* program schools because the teachers are more interdependent than they are in a traditional school. They often work together within agencies and ventures, and they also must cooperate with teachers in other ventures. As one teacher put it, "In Micro, teachers need to be able to trust their colleagues. They need to feel, 'When I send my kids to you, they'll learn.' That's the sort of trust that's necessary." She went on to say that this level of trust among teachers "often doesn't happen."

Positive relationships among the teachers and between the teachers and the principal were one of the factors that characterized the creation of the original schoolwide *MicroSociety* program at the Clement G. McDonough City Magnet School in Lowell, Massachusetts. At first sight, it might appear that there were no relationships before the program was implemented, because the school did not exist before the *MicroSociety* program was adopted. The school was created to be a *MicroSociety* program school, and the program began the day the school opened. However, the staff and principal already had become a highly cohesive group when the school opened. The close bonds were forged through self-selection, team-building exercises, and shared staff development experiences. Several months before the school was to open, word went out to all the teachers in the district calling for volunteers. About 20 teachers initially answered the call. They began to meet together regularly after school to develop the concept of a school that would have "the city" as its theme. The principal, who also was a volunteer, was part of these early team-building experiences. The group then together attended a 4-week summer workshop at a local university to plan more intensively. The final group of 11 teachers who began the school was selected based on these early experiences. By the time the school opened and the program became operational, the staff and principal had become a close-knit group.

The principal at City Magnet School played a particularly significant role in this team-building process. He had been a psychologist before becoming a principal, and some informants believed that this background helped him to appreciate the importance of forging positive relationships among the staff from the beginning. Some people also believed that this background and training gave him some of the competencies necessary to forge those relationships. In any case, the staff clearly admired the first principal and enjoyed working with him. All the original teachers spoke glowingly of him.

Most of the other successful *MicroSociety* program schools that I studied also had enjoyed strong, positive relationships among the staff and the administration for some time prior to adopting the program. A particularly successful program was established in a school that had had a reputation for being a "friendly" place for many years. Several teachers said that they had wanted to work at the school just for that reason. Several staff members also commented that there was a real "family atmosphere" among the staff. One teacher said that there was "a real bond among the teachers here." This teacher went on to say, "You couldn't have the Micro program here without the positive atmosphere, because of the need to be flexible." Positive relations among the teachers made them more willing to help each other out and to make the accommodations needed for successful implementation. This positive atmosphere provided the social glue that helped the Micro program to thrive.

On the other hand, in the schools that ultimately failed to implement a successful program, lack of trust and respect among the teaching staff and between the staff and the principal were common features. For instance, in one school where the program was discontinued after 3 years, there was a deep rift between the principal and a powerful group of teachers. The source of the conflict was philosophical: The principal, who had been at the school for 6 years, was a strong advocate of progressive education. The teachers who opposed her were, in the principal's words, "very rigid and traditional." The teaching staff also was divided based on these philosophical differences, with some teachers supporting the progressive views of the principal and others lining up against them.

The *MicroSociety* program became enmeshed in this conflict from the beginning. The principal was the one who brought the program to the school, seeing it as a way to make the "rigid" teachers more flexible and student oriented. Not surprisingly, those teachers opposed the program. The principal gave the resistant teachers the opportunity to transfer out of the school, but they refused to leave. Their attitude seemed to be that it was their school, and if anyone transferred out, it should be the principal. In this climate, it would have been difficult to implement any educational reform.

In some cases, the relationships within the school were adversely affected by union-management conflict that permeated the entire local school system. In one school, the program suffered because teachers rarely came together to discuss the program and plan together. The primary reason was that there had been a history of bitter conflict between the teachers' union and the school board; and in the most recent contract, the teachers' union won a clause that said teachers were not required to attend any faculty meetings unless they were paid extra. Although some of the teachers in the *MicroSociety* program school would have been willing to attend planning meetings on a voluntary basis, their colleagues saw such an action as undermining the union's position. And when the teachers did have meetings in this district, the animosity that existed between the teachers and administration made those meetings unproductive. As one teacher put it, "People just use the time to bitch."

As union-management relations deteriorated, the staff became polarized. Many administrators and some teachers complained about the "blue-collar mentality" of the pro-union teachers. An older teacher complained that many of his fellow teachers "won't do anything unless they're paid for it." On the other side, many teachers blamed the administration rather than the union for the teachers' lack of commitment. One teacher characterized the school board as "anti-union." He also described the managerial climate within the system as "top-down from the central office."

In this hostile climate, it was difficult for teachers in the school to generate much enthusiasm for the *MicroSociety* program, and any creative initiative was discouraged. For instance, one of the teachers had put together, on his own time, a curriculum to integrate Micro with basic skills teaching. This initiative was ignored, and the teacher became disaffected and "demotivated" as a result. Without a context of positive relationships among the teachers and between the teachers and administration, it was difficult to establish an effective *MicroSociety* program.

Other research on educational reform has reached similar conclusions about the importance of good relationships among the staff prior to implementation. For instance, in their research on the New American Schools initiative, Berends, Bodilly, and Kirby (2002) found that implementation was more successful at schools that were "relatively free of strife and had stable leadership" (p. 89). And Firestone and Corbett (1988), in their review of research on planned organizational change in schools, observed that the extent to which faculty are divided into factions and the level of interpersonal tension are two contextual factors that will determine success.

Thus the first guideline: If those who wish to implement a *MicroSociety* program, or any other reform, in a school find that relationships among teachers and administration are poor, then it is better to work on improving those relationships before one proceeds with implementation of the change. Otherwise, much time and effort probably will be wasted, and support for any innovation in the future will be weakened as the staff becomes demoralized and cynical about the prospects for change.

GUIDELINE 2: GOODNESS OF FIT

The second guideline states that there should be a good fit between the proposed change and the school's priorities and values. In the most successful schools, the *MicroSociety* program seemed to meet a pressing need, or it fit well with some of the school's most important priorities and values. For instance, another reason that the first schoolwide *MicroSociety* program at City Magnet School was successful is that Micro fit a particular need of the district and the school so well. The wheels were set in motion years before the school was created when the courts ruled that the school district in Lowell was illegally segregated. The courts then ordered that the district develop and implement a desegregation plan. Because Lowell is so close to Boston and the memory of riots over forced busing there was so fresh, the idea of using a magnet school model as a way of voluntarily desegregating the schools was an appealing one.

The plan was to eventually make every school in the district a magnet or "school of choice." Each school was to have a distinctive theme. A parent council, which was established to help develop the plan, surveyed parents in the community concerning their preferences for various themes that had been considered. Of the five choices that were given to the parents, a "city" school and an "arts" school received the most votes. A "back to basics" theme came in third, and these became the bases for the first three magnet schools in the system.

The original plan for the city school was to make the whole city the school. The students would spend the entire day studying and working in different settings around the community. However, as the teachers and parents began to plan for this concept, they ran into many logistical problems. This created what Evans Clinchy, one of the original consultants, referred to as a "planning crisis." At this point, the consultant remembered meeting George Richmond a couple of years earlier and reading his book on the *MicroSociety* program, and it occurred to the consultant that a schoolwide *MicroSociety* program could solve the problem by "making the school into a city." The idea appealed to the teachers, parents, and principal, and they began to develop a schoolwide *MicroSociety* program.

There was a good fit between the school's needs and the *MicroSociety* program in the case of other successful *MicroSociety* program schools that I studied. One of those schools also had been designated a magnet school as part of a plan to promote racial integration in the district. Also like City Magnet, this other school adopted a theme, "business and government," that was highly compatible with the *MicroSociety* program. In this case, however, the teachers had been struggling for more than 4 years to develop the business and government theme, with little success, before they ever heard about the *MicroSociety* program concept. The teachers had tried to develop units dealing with the stock market, government agencies, and money, but they could not figure out how to teach economic concepts to elementary level students in a way that made the material interesting. A few of the teachers even had created programs similar to the *MicroSociety* program in their own classrooms, but these were isolated efforts that had little impact on the school as a whole. Meanwhile, the central office had been putting pressure on the school to make the magnet program stronger and to better develop the business and government theme.

Such a school provided particularly fertile ground for planting the *MicroSociety* program. There was a natural fit between the *MicroSociety* program concept and the school's theme. Also, because the teachers had been struggling without much success to implement the theme, they were especially receptive to the program when they became aware of it.

One other school that I studied adopted the *MicroSociety* program as part of becoming a magnet school or "school of choice." In this case, the principal was under pressure from the superintendent to come up with a distinctive theme for his school as part of the district's new school-of-choice plan. As the principal and his staff considered various possibilities, they discovered the *MicroSociety* program. The program appealed to the teachers and principal for a number of reasons. Particularly important was the fact that there had been a strong emphasis in the district on "career education." Micro seemed to fit that priority well.

In all of the more successful schools, there proved to be some kind of natural affinity between the school and the *MicroSociety* program prior to adoption of the program; and in the schools that ultimately failed, there was much less of a fit. For instance, one such school adopted the *MicroSociety* program precisely because it was so radically different from what they had been doing in the past. The principal of this school was under pressure to raise test scores quickly, and he thought that the *MicroSociety* program might "do the trick." Although there were many other factors that contributed to the eventual demise of the program in this school, the lack of fit between Micro and the school's character did not help.

Educational researchers have long recognized the importance of "goodness of fit" in facilitating change. For instance, Berman and McLaughlin (1976) wrote, "The better the fit between a change project's objectives and school and/or district priorities, the greater the likelihood that change will result" (p. 334).

Thus the second guideline suggests that those who wish to implement a reform in a school should look for some connection between the reform and what the school already is trying to do. If the reform does not seem to fit one of the school's priorities or core values in an obvious way, then the implementers may need to work on changing the school's priorities or values in some way before proceeding with implementation of the innovation.

GUIDELINE 3: PARENT AND COMMUNITY INVOLVEMENT

The third guideline states that there should be a history of parent involvement and community partnerships at the school. To be successful, *MicroSociety* programs need to tap community resources. The most successful programs have police officers come in and train their crimestoppers, and local attorneys come in to train their student attorneys. The local bank sends employees to help train the teachers and students assigned to the *MicroSociety* program bank, and then the bank may help further by donating checks and checkbooks for the students to use. Parents also can be a valuable resource within a *MicroSociety* program. And as with any educational innovation, active parental involvement and support are invaluable for helping to sustain the program in the face of political opposition (Dow, 1991; Fullan, 2001).

Parents played a prominent role in the creation of the City Magnet School in Lowell, and they became strong supporters and advocates for the program. When the school was created, district parents had several choices. They could send their children to any of the first three magnet schools, or they could keep them in their neighborhood schools. Thus many of the parents who chose to send their children to City Magnet began with a strong affinity for the school and the *MicroSociety* program. In addition, several of the parents who chose to send their children to the new *MicroSociety* program school had been members of the parent council that studied the desegregation problem and made recommendations for how to desegregate the schools. This experience helped them become a strong and cohesive group.

The first principal at City Magnet saw this strong parental contingent as an asset rather than a threat. He valued parent participation, and he went out of his way to make the parents feel welcome. For instance, the principal allowed the parents access to all parts of the building, including the teachers' lounge. He even let parents bring in playpens so that they could leave their infants and toddlers in a secure place when they came in to work in the school. Parents also continued to be involved in helping to set policy at the school. They met virtually every week and considered a variety of issues. The first principal at City Magnet also helped minimize the barriers between parents and teachers. One important way in which this happened was in a series of workshops that the teachers and parents attended together even before the school opened. I talked with several of those original parents, and they agreed that the first principal "had a lot of respect for the parents and their power. He didn't try to stop them when they wanted to do something."

Parental involvement and support at City Magnet was further strengthened by a sense that they had something to prove to the rest of the community. When the school was first established, there still was opposition to it and to desegregation more generally. This brought the parents and staff together. As one parent put it, "It was like a family in the beginning.

We all became friends outside of school, including the teachers. There was a 'we-they' feeling among us because we felt like we were fighting a common enemy." Led by a core of 10 to 15, the parents met at each other's homes, where they would have "wine or beer together, and make it a social thing." Although the most involved parents made up a relatively small core group, they "could get a lot more parents involved when necessary," according to one of them.

The parents decided early on that they "wanted to do more than just bake cookies." They raised money to buy supplies. They helped fix the dilapidated building that was given to the school after the first year. Parents even took over responsibility for filling the school secretary position: During the first 3 years, the school did not have a secretary, so the parents organized themselves and took over different shifts so that this important function was filled.

Parent support was especially helpful when it came to the political battles waged during the early years. There was considerable opposition within the community to the new magnet school arrangement and to desegregation in general. When a new school board tried to discontinue the magnet program 1 year after it began, the parents at City Magnet mobilized themselves and fought vigorously to save the school. They wrote letters to the local newspaper and testified at board meetings. As a result of this strong pressure by the parents (as well as pressure from the state), the board backed down and allowed the program to continue. A year or two later, the parents again fought for the school when the city of Lowell tried to deny them the building that they had been promised. And again, the parents were successful. It seems likely that the school at Lowell would not have survived without the involvement of an active group of parents.

Other successful *MicroSociety* program schools similarly built on a foundation of strong parental involvement. In one school, there had been an active Parent–Teacher Organization (PTO) for many years, and the principal worked closely with them when he and the teachers began to develop the *MicroSociety* program. The principal encouraged the PTO to set up a "Micro Executive Board," composed of PTO members who were especially excited about the new program. The board quickly became a strong and loyal group of parents who helped with the implementation of the program in various ways, including fundraising.

This same school also had a mentoring program before the *Micro-Society* program came along, and the district had a "partners in learning" program that brought community members into the schools to help in various ways. The principal used these existing programs to facilitate the kind of community support and involvement that are crucial for a *MicroSociety* program.

At Lowell, the parents proved to be valuable political allies when resistance to the program developed in the local community, and parents played a similar role at some of the other successful schools. In one school, the innovative superintendent who helped the program get started and provided strong support during its first 3 years was fired by an obstreperous school board. The new superintendent and board viewed the *MicroSociety* program much less positively. Fortunately, this school had a tradition of strong parent support and an active group of community partners, and this constituency rallied to Micro's defense in a way that helped the program survive a less hospitable political climate.

A history of community partnerships and parent involvement characterized most of the successful *MicroSociety* program schools, and the schools that struggled most with implementing the program tended to have little prior history with such involvement. Lacking such a history, the administration and staff found it difficult to mount the kind of concerted effort in this area that is necessary for a viable *MicroSociety* program. Thus another important guideline is that implementers of a school reform need to examine how actively the target school has involved parents and nurtured community partners in the past. If there is not a strong tradition of parent involvement and community partnerships, the implementers should begin to develop such a tradition before moving ahead with their plans. Otherwise, the new program will not have all the resources and support necessary for long-term viability.

GUIDELINE 4: PRINCIPAL SUPPORT

The last guideline relating to the context is probably an obvious one: Success is more likely if the school's principal supports the school change effort. The importance of this factor became especially apparent in those *MicroSociety* program schools that began with a supportive principal but then saw a change in the principal after the program had been in existence for some time. It became hard to sustain even a successful *MicroSociety* program if the principal was not particularly interested in it.

The support of the principal was guaranteed in the first schoolwide *MicroSociety* program in Lowell. The first principal of the school, like all the teachers and parents, was a volunteer. He had been working in the district for many years, and when he heard about the opportunity to participate in creating a new school based on the city as a theme, he jumped at the chance. Along with the rest of the staff, he saw the *MicroSociety* program as an ideal way to bring their theme to life when he first heard about it. When the school finally opened and the program became operational, there was a knowledgeable and committed principal in charge.

Other research on school change has confirmed the importance of principal endorsement. For example, research on the implementation of a national school renewal initiative called "KEYS to Excellence in Your Schools" concluded that there needed to be a supportive principal (Portin, Beck, Knapp, & Murphy, 2003). In fact, opposition from the principal was always fatal.

However, even though ensuring the principal's support seems to be both an obvious and basic guideline, it does not necessarily lead to success. At least two schools I studied failed to establish a successful *MicroSociety* program even though the principals were strong supporters and advocates of the program. Their advocacy and support were not enough in part because the implementers failed to follow the other guidelines I have presented. There was little trust and much conflict between the staff and the principal in these schools; relationships among the staff tended to be weak or conflicted; and there was not a particularly strong fit between the school's prior orientation or needs and the *MicroSociety* program. These schools also had relatively little in the way of parent involvement or community partnerships.

Thus it probably is fair to say that the support of the principal is necessary but not sufficient for the establishment of a successful *MicroSociety* program. It is hard to imagine a group of teachers establishing a viable schoolwide *MicroSociety* program without the principal's blessings, but having such support is only the first of many pieces that must be in place in order for the program to thrive.

A supportive principal, positive relationships among the staff, a history of parent involvement and community partnerships, and a good fit between the proposed change and the school's current needs or priorities are the contextual factors that provide a rich and fertile environment for implementation. If these factors are in place before the school adopts the program, the chances of success are greatly enhanced. However, a favorable context by itself is not enough. The way in which the program is introduced to the school also is fateful. We turn to this aspect of implementation in the next chapter.

4

Introducing the
Program to the School

Seymour Sarason (1972, 1998) has suggested that the way in which a new setting is created will strongly influence its subsequent development and long-term viability. The *MicroSociety*® program schools that I studied seemed to support Sarason's thesis. The way in which the program was introduced to the school, starting with the adoption process and continuing through the initial planning, differed in successful and unsuccessful schools. By the time the program became operational, certain decisions and processes had occurred that seemed to shape the program's subsequent development and outcome. These findings suggest a set of guidelines relating to the way in which a reform is introduced to the school. One of the most important has to do with the extent to which the teachers participate in the decision to adopt the program.

GUIDELINE 5: GIVING TEACHERS
A MEANINGFUL VOICE

One of the best-known principles of planned change involves the value of "participation." We are told repeatedly that in order to reduce resistance to change, those who will be affected by the change, and particularly those who will be implementing the change, should have a voice in the planning process (Berman & McLaughlin, 1976; Evans, 1996). For this reason, many educational innovations require that teachers have a say about whether or not to adopt them. In Levin's "Accelerated School" model, 90% of faculty, staff, and parents must vote in favor of the project (Levin, 1987; Schwebel, 2003). The "Success for All" model requires that at least 80% of the faculty in a school vote by secret ballot for its adoption before they agree to work with the school (Schorr, 1997).

Unfortunately, schools do not always follow the "participation principle" in practice when they adopt a new practice. For instance, Muncey and McQuillan (1996), who conducted extensive field research in several schools that adopted Sizer's "Coalition of Essential Schools" model, found that most schools "did not establish a working consensus about the need for change before implementing a Coalition program" (p. 283).

Perhaps because the participation principle has become so widely accepted, I found that in virtually every *MicroSociety* program school that I studied, the teachers had a voice in the adoption process. Usually this took the form of an actual vote. Thus in both the successful and unsuccessful schools, teachers usually had an opportunity to vote on whether to participate in the program.

However, when I looked more closely at how the teachers actually participated in the change process that followed, I found that they had a more meaningful voice in the successful schools. Thus the study did not simply provide more support for the "participation principle"; it helped to elucidate the difference between *meaningful* participation and "just going through the motions." What is crucial for securing teacher buy-in and effective implementation is not just their participation in the process, but rather their *empowerment*. Participation can lead to empowerment, but not necessarily. Empowerment depends on *how* teachers participate.

True empowerment of the teachers began with the way in which the initial decision to participate in the program was made. A close look at the first schoolwide *MicroSociety* program in Lowell is instructive. All of the original teachers in the Lowell program were volunteers. Furthermore, before they made the final commitment to join the experiment, they were able to attend many weekly planning sessions after school with the principal and other teachers. The group also attended a 4-week summer workshop. Out of the 20 teachers who initially expressed interest, only 11 ended up joining the faculty of the new school in the fall.

The teachers at Lowell's City Magnet School also had a meaningful voice in shaping the new program. The superintendent believed strongly that in order to maximize teacher buy-in, teachers had to play a significant role in the development of the curriculum, and this began in the planning workshops prior to the school's opening. Evidence for the teachers' clout comes from the fact that both the external consultant and project director would have liked the school to do Micro all day, rather than just one period at the end of the day. According to the consultant, however, the teachers "couldn't buy that." In this instance, as in many others, the teachers' voice prevailed. By the time the school opened, the teachers truly felt that it was *their* program.

In none of the other schools that I studied did teachers have as much voice as they had in the beginning at Lowell. In this sense, they were not true replicates of the original program. However, the more successful schools did give the teachers a more meaningful voice than did the schools that failed to establish the program.

For instance, at one of the most successful schools, the principal carefully orchestrated the adoption and planning processes so that the teachers came to feel a strong sense of ownership for the program. It began when the principal took three carefully selected teachers to the national *Micro-Society* program conference. She selected one teacher from the third, fourth, and fifth grades, and she picked teachers she knew would like the program, were respected by the other teachers, and had varied teaching styles. When the teachers returned in the fall, they began to discuss what they had learned informally with the other teachers. They also passed around articles on the *MicroSociety* program for people to read and think about. Then the principal arranged for a group of six teachers to visit an actual *MicroSociety* program school in an adjoining state. To make it a "fun trip," the principal "rented a van and arranged it so that the staff could stay over Saturday night." The plan worked. On the way back in the van, the exuberant teachers took the initiative and began planning the program on their own. The principal gave the teachers the rest of the fall to plan, and then they started the program in January. Initially, they ran the program only for the fourth and fifth grades, because the third-grade teachers were "not quite ready to jump in at that point." The next year, they decided that they wanted to do it on their own as a separate program, and they were allowed to do so. The K–2 teachers were even more hesitant, but eventually they all chose to implement the program in their own classrooms. The process took 3 years, and each subgroup of teachers had considerable latitude in when and how they implemented the program. But eventually, the whole school was doing it.

In another school, the teachers also played a significant role in the program's initial development, but as the process unfolded, many teachers assumed a more passive role, which eventually weakened the program and led to its demise. The process began when the magnet resource person in the district's central office told the principal about a federal grant opportunity and encouraged her to develop a proposal. The principal convened a group of teachers to work on the proposal, and she gave them the freedom to develop whatever ideas appealed to them, as long as they were consistent with the school's business and government theme. There were 15 teachers in the original core group that worked on the proposal, with at least one from each grade.

The idea of establishing a *MicroSociety* program originally came from one of the teachers in the proposal-writing group. She had just seen an article about a *MicroSociety* program school in Yonkers, New York, and it looked like a particularly good way to develop the school's business and government theme. She brought the article in to show to the other group members, and they quickly became sold on the idea. The principal was supportive at this point, but she initially thought that they should start the program on a more modest scale. It was the teachers, led by a few particularly enthusiastic individuals, who wanted to go ahead with it on a larger scale.

Three of the most enthusiastic teachers became the informal leaders of the change effort. They attended the next national *MicroSociety* program conference, and when they returned in the fall, they helped to sell the program to many of the other teachers. They provided particularly effective leadership because they were highly respected by the other faculty at the school.

However, even though some teachers played a major role in the development of the program at this school and all of the teachers seemed to support the decision to adopt the program, not all the teachers were equally enthusiastic about doing so. One teacher, a strong advocate of the program, admitted that "there were a lot of frustrated teachers forced into the program." She believed that many teachers really were not sold on the idea when they adopted it, even though the program seemed to be teacher initiated and teacher driven.

This ambivalence among some of the teachers seemed related to the subtle dynamics that occurred during the adoption process. Once the core group had decided on basing the proposal on the *MicroSociety* program, they went out to get other teachers involved. In reflecting on the process, one of the early leaders said that it was a "hard sell" because many of the teachers felt "overwhelmed." Despite these misgivings, the school moved ahead and implemented the program in the upper grades.

Once the school adopted the program, teacher choice became more limited. All upper-grade teachers were told that they had to participate. The principal did assure the teachers that they could move to a lower grade or transfer to another school if they did not want to be involved in the program, and some teachers did transfer out. However, others decided to stay because the only schools in the district that had openings were schools where the work climate was less favorable. And one teacher complained that she tried to transfer to another school but was not able to do so because she "did not have enough seniority." (I heard similar stories at other schools where the teachers had the option to transfer to another school after the decision was made to adopt the program. It suggests that even when teachers are allowed to opt out through transferring to another school, the choice may not be a meaningful one for the individual teacher.)

Teachers had even less choice about participating in the program as it worked its way down to the lower grades. One year after the program started in the upper grades, the lower-grade teachers were told that they would have to implement it. A few of these teachers had been part of the original proposal-writing group and were eager to begin. However, most of the K–2 teachers were in the position of implementing a program that had been developed by others. Even though these "others" were their colleagues in the upper grades, the two groups of teachers had little contact with each other and viewed themselves as having different concerns, values, and tasks. Thus there was little sense of ownership among the lower-grade teachers. Not surprisingly, the greatest opposition to the program came from the lower grades.

This school provides a particularly rich and revealing glimpse at how complicated the participation principle can be in practice. In this case, teachers initially played a central role in developing the program. The principal was supportive, but the idea originally came from the teachers, and it was teachers who provided the leadership. Also, all of the teachers initially had a vote about whether or not to participate. However, a closer look at the actual process suggests that there was considerable social pressure and passive acquiescence as those who were passionately in favor of the program tried to "sell it" to those who were more reluctant. The school eventually developed one of the best *MicroSociety* programs in the country, but it did not last. Continuing pockets of resistance within the faculty, combined with a change in principals, led to its demise.

This particular case thus suggests that it is desirable for teachers to take the lead and that the program comes to be seen not as the "principal's program," but as the teachers'. However, there still will be resistance unless all of the teachers participating in the program freely choose to do so *based on a process of reflection and inquiry rather than "selling."* And this resistance ultimately may prove fatal.

This case and others also suggest that simply giving teachers the opportunity to vote on whether to adopt the program does not constitute meaningful participation. In several of the schools that conducted such a vote, I heard teachers say afterward that although they voted in favor of adoption, it was not a meaningful choice. For instance, at one of these schools, the teachers voted by secret ballot on whether to adopt the *MicroSociety* program, and all but one teacher voted to go along with the program. However, the vote occurred right after the staff participated in a workshop with the theme of "resistance to change." The implicit message was that "change is good" and that it is "wrong" to resist it. Several of the teachers who voted in favor of adoption later said that they did so because they felt that the program "was coming anyway," and they wanted to "appear supportive." Some of the teachers had misgivings about the program, and many felt that they did not have enough information about the program to make an informed decision. But the social dynamics of the situation led them to vote in favor of it despite these concerns.

Schwebel (2003), has noted that the top-down authority structure in school systems leads to "rubber stamping of decisions" (p. 217) when participatory mechanisms are developed. The role of teachers in the adoption process in many of the schools that I studied tended to involve such "rubber stamping." The result was a lack of the teacher buy-in that is so crucial for effective implementation of a school change model.

One final example suggests that the *MicroSociety* program *can* be introduced into an existing school in a way that provides *all* the teachers with a meaningful voice in the adoption process. The *MicroSociety* program at this large urban elementary school began on a small scale. Two teachers initiated it as part of the school's summer program. (The summer program was voluntary for both students and teachers.) The *MicroSociety* program continued as a summer activity for 6 years, becoming more elaborate, refined, and engaging each year. Then one of the two teachers who started the program became the principal of the school. One of her goals was to bring the *MicroSociety* program into the regular school curriculum. However, rather than mandating it or asking the teachers as a group to vote on it based on limited information, she merely made it possible for more teachers to work with the existing *MicroSociety* program during the summer. (Several teachers already had worked in the program during previous summers.) Teachers who did not want to work in the summer program were encouraged to come in and just observe it.

Most of the teachers who had worked with the program during the summer were enthusiastic about adopting it, and the principal allowed them to do so in their own classrooms. Some teachers just wanted to implement certain aspects of the program. For instance, a few teachers chose to use the court for dealing with discipline in their classes. Others started to use brainstorming techniques to involve their students in making various kinds of decisions about how to organize the day. The principal made it clear that it was okay for the teachers to adopt just certain aspects of the program.

After many teachers had had an opportunity to observe and experiment with various aspects of the program, they were ready to adopt a schoolwide version during the regular academic year. Again, however, the approach was a gradualist one. The first year, they began with just the government strand, and the next year, they introduced the court system.

One problem with such an approach is that it is much slower. However, faster methods of securing teacher buy-in, such as having the teachers read some material on the *MicroSociety* program, spend a meeting or two discussing it, and then vote on whether to adopt it, usually lead to mixed support. It may well be that there are faster, more efficient ways of giving teachers a meaningful voice in the adoption process. However, long-term success will be in doubt unless a reform is implemented by a group of teachers who begin with the kind of enthusiasm and active participation that the first group at Lowell City Magnet had for the *Micro-Society* program.

Experience with implementation of other new educational practices has tended to confirm the importance of ensuring that there is more than perfunctory teacher participation in the adoption process. Berends, Bodilly, and Kirby (2002) found that there were higher levels of implementation in NAS schools when teachers felt they were "well-informed about the design they selected and allowed free choice of design" (p. 89). Both choice and being well-informed were important. Similarly, Muncey and McQuillan (1996) discovered that effective implementation of the Essential Schools philosophy depended on striking the right balance between principal leadership and faculty leadership.

Thus in order to secure teacher buy-in, it is critical that teachers have a meaningful voice in adopting and implementing the program. However, it is not enough just to give them a vote based on limited knowledge of the program. The choice needs to be informed, and this usually means an extended period of time during which the teachers have an opportunity to observe the program in other schools and think about how it might work with their own students and teaching styles. Implementers also need to be skilled in sensing whether teacher compliance represents a meaningful choice to participate or simply a desire not to make waves. And when the teachers are not ready to commit, implementers need to be able to spend more time with those teachers in order to help them move toward a commitment to participate that is based on an adequate understanding and a true choice.

GUIDELINE 6: PLANNING BEFORE THE PROGRAM BEGINS

Before the program begins, there should be a planning period that includes effective staff development and a "pilot run." Moving too fast can adversely affect more than just the process by which teachers come to accept the program. It also can result in an inadequate planning process and insufficient staff development.

In the prototype schoolwide program at Lowell, many months were devoted to selecting the teachers, preparing the teachers and parents, and developing the initial plan for the school. Fortunately, the original state and federal desegregation funding provided money specifically for planning. According to a consultant who worked with the school, there was enough money for "hour-long curriculum and staff development workshops every day, with the teachers being paid extra for the meetings." The teachers had weekly after-school workshops all during the spring semester before the school opened. There also was the 4-week summer workshop at the local university. The teachers used this time to meet frequently with the educational consultant who introduced the program to the school. He arranged for them to meet with George Richmond, the founder of *MicroSociety* program, during this period as well. Thus the planning phase included a rich mix of staff development activities as well as "nuts-and-bolts planning." And considerable time was allocated for these activities.

Another important aspect of the initial *MicroSociety* program at Lowell, which is often overlooked by those who have tried to replicate it, is that it began on a rather small scale. Initially, there were only 11 teachers and 224 students in the school, and it remained about this size for the first 6 years of its existence.

Unfortunately, some schools that attempted to replicate the original model allotted much less time for planning and began on a larger scale. A rather extreme example was the school that devoted just *one day* for planning before launching the program. Not surprisingly, the teachers were overwhelmed when they began the program with so little preparation, and they eventually abandoned it.

Another school devoted adequate amounts of time for planning and staff development with one group of teachers but not with another. This school began the program with the upper grades and then added the K–2 grades a year later. Before the upper-grade teachers began the program, they spent 2 hours every other week in planning and staff development activities. In contrast, the K–2 teachers were given only one day to plan prior to starting the program—and they received this day only *after* they complained that they had not been given enough time. The coordinator later said that she and the principal believed the K–2 teachers "did not need as much time to plan" because their program was "less intense," by which she meant that it ran only 2 days a week. The coordinator and principal also may have believed that the lower-grade teachers needed less time because the upper-grade teachers already had developed and implemented the program at the school. Unfortunately, this mind-set led to a split in the faculty. The upper-grade teachers generally liked the program and were committed to it, but the lower-grade teachers, with a few exceptions, were resistant. Although the program flourished (at least in the upper grades) for a few years, it eventually was eliminated.

However, it is not just the amount of planning time that is important. Also vital is how the school uses the time. For instance, in one school, the teachers were able to devote 2 hours every week, for more than 6 months, to planning for the program before launching it. Nevertheless, they felt overwhelmed and unprepared when they finally began the program. After 6 weeks, they had to stop and spend the summer revamping the program. The problem in this case lay in how the teachers used the planning time. No teachers attended a national *MicroSociety* program conference or visited another *MicroSociety* program school. No trainers or consultants came in to work with the teachers. In fact, there was little if any in the way of staff development. The teachers spent almost all of the time writing "curriculum guides" for the program.

Most schools did allocate time for staff development prior to starting the program, but their experience suggests that some staff development activities are more helpful than others. Observing one or more *MicroSociety* programs in action, for instance, seemed to be more helpful than merely reading about the *MicroSociety* program or having a few teachers attend the national conference. One teacher said that the first time she "really understood" the program was when she and some others went up to Lowell to observe it there.

However, some teachers and principals found that even spending a few hours observing in another school was not enough. In one case, a few teachers had managed to spend one day observing in an existing *Micro-Society* program school prior to starting their own program, but this proved inadequate. In retrospect, they believed that more extensive observation, such as observing Micro for a whole week, would have prepared them much better. Another teacher said that having a trainer available to guide them during the observation also would have made the observation more helpful. Observing in more than one other school also can be helpful; a few teachers who had the opportunity to do so found that it was both informative and "liberating" to see that different schools could do Micro in different ways.

There also is value in having a trainer or consultant on-site. At one of the more successful schools, the principal and coordinator initially visited the program at Lowell, but they found this experience to be relatively "unhelpful." Three teachers also went to the national conference; this too was not very helpful. (This was the first national conference that MicroSociety, Inc., organized, and it may have been less effective than subsequent conferences.) The most significant help, according to the principal and coordinator, came from one of the teachers at Lowell, who came out to the school to consult with the staff for 3 days. This same teacher then returned to the school a few months later and spent a whole year there as a regular teacher. This kind of intensive, ongoing consultation from an experienced *MicroSociety* program teacher proved to be by far the most helpful source of guidance in implementing the program.

Other research on educational change has come up with similar conclusions about what kind of staff development is necessary for success. Schorr (1997), who studied the implementation process in a number of different types of educational and social programs, concluded that an "intensive approach to professional development is the key to changing the school culture" (p. 253). This means long-term efforts that include "feedback, trial and error, and problem solving over time" (p. 255). Similarly, Elmore (1996) has argued that educational practice is unlikely to change "without some exposure to someone who could help the teachers to understand the difference between what they were doing and what they aspired to do." (p. 24) He believes that teachers also need to be able to consult regularly with others when problems arise and that they should have "direct experience with the kind of practice they are expected to engage in" (p. 24).

Other reformers have recognized the importance of good staff development for effective implementation. For instance, the founder of "Success for All" wrote that effective implementation requires "a great deal of professional development over an extended period of time" (Slavin & Madden, 2001, p. 201). Staff development for this school reform model relies heavily on observation, shadowing, and mentoring rather than the written or spoken word (Schorr, 1997).

Ultimately, however, there may not be one approach to staff development that works for all teachers. Teachers, like students, differ in their learning styles and preferences. Some teachers, for instance, blossom when they are able to take the basic concept and then use their own imagination to develop the program. This appeared to be the case at one successful school, where observers described the initial group of teachers as "strong, experienced, cohesive, and receptive to the new program." The principal at this school thought it was good that they did not spend too much time planning, but instead just "jumped in." It also helped that once the teachers started the program, they were able to spend up to 2 hours each week for planning and group problem solving.

A teacher's previous training and experience also will determine what kind of staff development will be most useful. For instance, I found at one school that a particularly committed and effective teacher there had been trained to teach via the "discovery learning" method in one of her education courses. This teaching approach fits the *MicroSociety* program concept particularly well. Also, she originally had been a business major in college.

Thus for this teacher, the *MicroSociety* program seemed easy and natural, and relatively little in the way of formal staff development was necessary.

On the other hand, there are teachers who, because of their background and learning style, need a great deal of structure and guidance in order to implement the program effectively. Ultimately, most teachers probably need some guidance and structure before they are ready to "take the plunge." This kind of staff development, however, requires more time than is often allocated for the purpose.

The content of staff development activities is as important as the process. The schools that implemented the *MicroSociety* program found that they needed to address three different areas in their staff development efforts. First, in addition to just teaching the teachers about the program in general, they found that many teachers needed help with basic economic principles and business practices. One coordinator, for instance, said that the teachers at her school should have had some training in how to use ledgers and set up cash boxes. "The money management system was very loose. They didn't realize that to the kids, it's real money."

Second, in addition to learning basic economic principles and business practices, the teachers needed to learn how to help students run the ventures. One of the community partners at one school, the manager of a local bank branch, said that there was insufficient time for many teachers assigned to the bank to learn what they needed for their particular venture. And the bank was not unique. Whether it was a restaurant, a publishing venture, or a TV station, the teachers often needed to learn how to run the activity in order to help the students do so. (In fact, ventures often worked best when the teachers in charge already were familiar with the activity due to previous personal experience. For instance, a teacher who had worked in publishing before changing careers was particularly effective as the facilitator of the publishing strand at her school.)

The third staff development area that needs to be addressed in implementing many school changes involves *team building*. The original teachers and principal at Lowell spent time not only on planning for the program but also on activities designed to help them develop into a cohesive and effective work group. Because the *MicroSociety* program requires such a high degree of interdependence among the teachers, providing time for effective team-building activities before the program becomes operational can make a big difference.

In the end, no matter how good the preparation has been for starting the program, there appears to be nothing as valuable as actually "doing it." Teachers repeatedly said that no matter how long one plans, and no matter how much one reads about the program or attends summer conferences or even observes other programs, it is impossible to anticipate all of the problems that one will encounter until one actually tries to do the program. But then there needs to be a period when the teachers can stop, sit down together, discuss their initial experiences, and make corrections in what they are doing. As a teacher at one school reported, a short (3-week) initial tryout session in the spring of the first year was helpful because it showed them that "a lot had to be revamped." During the summer and early fall, they made the changes necessary for the program to work better.

The trial run, however, was not helpful at one school that had particular difficulty implementing the program. The problem there seemed to be that the trial run occurred during the summer program. While this initial experience was helpful in some ways, it also was limited in value because the conditions in the summer program were so different from those that existed during the regular academic year. There were fewer teachers and children, and the staff had much greater flexibility. To be really helpful, the initial trial run needs to be realistic.

Research on other educational reform models has confirmed that adequate time for planning and training is especially important for the successful implementation of school reform models such as the *MicroSociety* program. As Fullan (1993) has argued, liking a reform idea or attending a 1-day workshop simply is not enough for a teacher to feel that sense of competence or mastery that is so important for effective change. Even with adequate preparation, materials, and technical assistance, a certain amount of confusion and trial-and-error learning is inevitable during the initial stage of implementation. As Firestone and Corbett (1988) noted, "Implementation is in large part a learning process. Even with innovations that seem clear, people experience substantial ambiguity—along with feelings of confusion, anger, and exhaustion—when they begin using new practices" (p. 330). Without a certain amount of appropriate staff development before implementation, these feelings will most likely overwhelm the teachers' efforts and leave them feeling incompetent. And teachers will tend to resist any change that requires them to take on tasks that make them feel incompetent (Cherniss, 1995; Levine & Levine, 1973). Perhaps Schwebel (2003) put it best when he wrote,

> Teachers, like other professionals who have been trained to function in a particular fashion, cannot by fiat suddenly transform themselves, and it is psychologically threatening to them to demand that. With understanding, support, and assistance they can and do change. (p. 158)

Thus in introducing a change like *MicroSociety* program to a school, there should be adequate time for planning and staff development. Some development activities, such as observing several MicroSocieties in action and having ongoing consultation, are more effective than others are. Also, the content of staff development is important: For successful implementation of the *MicroSociety* program, teachers need to learn how to run their ventures and agencies, and they also need to learn about basic economic principles and practices. Ultimately, however, there needs to be a realistic but time-limited trial run followed by an opportunity to sit back, reflect on what was learned from the experience, and revise the program based on the process of reflection.

GUIDELINE 7: SECURING ADDITIONAL FUNDING

The time and effort necessary to implement the previous two guidelines suggest that implementing a reform requires additional funding. For example, in their research on the implementation of the New American Schools reform models, Berends, Bodilly, and Kirby (2003) found that lack of funding for professional development was the single most important reason for schools to drop a design.

It is almost a truism that meaningful organizational change requires additional resources (Firestone & Corbett, 1988). In the case of educational reform, there have been too many attempts to introduce change that have not been adequately funded. When the efforts failed, the fault often was assigned to the nature of the innovation rather than the lack of resources necessary to implement it.

The *MicroSociety* programs I studied varied in the amount of additional funding implementers had to start the program. Although a large amount of additional funding did not guarantee success, all of the successful programs began with a considerable amount of additional funding dedicated to the program, and the most notable failures were resource starved.

The first schoolwide *MicroSociety* program at City Magnet in Lowell was relatively well funded throughout the first decade of its existence. Federal and state desegregation money was available, even before the school opened, to pay for planning. Once the school became operational, this grant money continued. For the first 7 or 8 years, City Magnet had planning money that allowed the staff to meet once a week after school hours. This funding also paid for a facilitator, part-time paraprofessionals, and materials. There also was money for extra workshops and staff development related to the program. This additional federal money was essential for the program's operation. By 1991, the program at City Magnet cost $50,000 more than was allotted by the city and state.

Some of the funding supported the "Micro specialist" position, which was an especially useful resource at Lowell. The specialists, who were regular teachers, taught Micro-related skills to the students in their classroom groups every week. They also pulled students out of class to work on Micro-related tasks. The specialists were resources for the teachers as well.

There was a specialist for each strand (government, publishing, etc.), and each specialist oversaw a venture. One of the original teachers said that getting the Micro specialists was a "peak" in the history of the program.

In addition to the Micro specialists, the program at City Magnet had a facilitator. In this respect, the program was not unique; in many other *MicroSociety* program schools, one of the teachers served as a facilitator or coordinator for the program. But not every school is able to come up with funds to release the program facilitator from regular teaching duties. Sometimes the position is voluntary, and the facilitator continues to carry a full teaching load. At Lowell, the federal desegregation money made it possible for the program facilitator to devote full-time to that role. The facilitator was especially valuable because he was able to go out and find additional resources. As one teacher put it, "Without a facilitator, there is no one to get money to keep stocks up."

Like City Magnet, the most successful *MicroSociety* program schools benefited from additional outside funding. One school, as a magnet in a large urban district undergoing court-ordered desegregation, had access to about $400,000 in additional funding each year during the first few years of its existence. Initially, the staff used these funds to provide each teacher with several hundred dollars for supplies, along with 4 or 5 days of release time for planning. This outside money also helped fund the program coordinator position.

It is impossible to say how much additional funding is necessary for a school to establish a successful *MicroSociety* program or any other new program. The amount probably varies depending on each school's unique situation. Also, some successful schools have done much with relatively little. For instance, in one school, the principal served as the program coordinator, which meant that there was no need for additional funding for this position. In another school, two teachers worked together to coordinate the program and did so voluntarily, taking on the additional burdens without any reduction in teaching duties or additional compensation. But these were highly unusual situations. In the first case, the principal was extremely dedicated to her work in general and to the *MicroSociety* program in particular. An older woman with few family responsibilities (her children were adults and living on their own, and her husband was retired), she reportedly started work by 5 a.m. every day and usually did not leave the school building until 8 p.m. or later. It is not likely that too many principals would have the ability or desire necessary to take on the coordinator's responsibilities as this woman did. Similarly, while many enthusiastic teachers might be willing to serve as program coordinator without any reduction in teaching responsibilities or additional pay, very few can continue to do so for any length of time without suffering some degree of psychological strain (Levine & Levine, 1973).

Thus an important guideline for introducing an educational innovation to a school is that there must be adequate additional funding to cover the costs associated with implementation. In the case of the *MicroSociety* program, MicroSociety, Inc., now believes that the costs of implementation at the minimum should include money for training, a full-time coordinator, supplies, and teacher stipends. Without this additional funding, the chances for successful implementation are greatly diminished.

GUIDELINE 8: MATCHING TEACHERS WITH VENTURES

One other factor that strongly influences how teachers will respond to the *MicroSociety* program is the way in which they are matched initially with the *MicroSociety* program's ventures. The more interesting and meaningful the venture is for the teacher, the more likely the teacher will feel enthusiastic about the program. Also, when teachers enjoy their ventures, they are more likely to invest the time and thought necessary for the ventures to work well. The most successful schools recognized from the beginning that if the program were to succeed, the fit between the teachers and their ventures would need to be a good one.

One aspect of the matching process that made a difference was the degree to which teachers had a choice about their ventures. In a school that encountered considerable teacher resistance and eventually discontinued the program, teachers initially had no choice. They were assigned to ventures by the administration. After the first year, some teachers were allowed limited choice, but many still were assigned to their ventures. Teachers who were arbitrarily assigned to a venture were much more likely to be dissatisfied with the program and to become vocal critics of it.

However, even when the teachers were given a choice, they could end up in unrewarding ventures. For instance, in one school, a teacher developed a venture that seemed promising at first. It involved having students write poetry and then sell their poetry to other students or give poetry readings during Micro time. Unfortunately, the venture proved frustrating because most of the students did not speak English well and the teacher did not speak their language (Spanish) at all.

Another example shows how teachers usually need certain competencies in order to succeed with their ventures. Back in the mid-1990s, a teacher who was in her early 60s and close to retirement initially took on a publishing venture. It seemed like a good venture for her because she liked reading and books. Unfortunately, she discovered that much of the work involved using computers; she had no expertise in computers, nor did she have any interest in developing this expertise at that point in her life.

Another teacher had a more positive experience because she developed a venture that built on interests and competencies she already possessed. This teacher, who was the multicultural resource teacher for the school, came up with the idea of a travel agency. This venture allowed her to expose students to multicultural learning in creative ways. The students loved the venture, and it was very successful.

This teacher, like many, came up with a rewarding venture on her own. However, many other teachers needed help to come up with ventures that would tap into their enthusiasm and competencies and also appeal to the students. An example was the program coordinator who sat down with a teacher and encouraged her to think about activities that she did outside of school and that she particularly enjoyed. The teacher's initial response was "reading." However, this was the teacher who had just tried and failed with a publishing venture. So the coordinator encouraged her to think more, and eventually the teacher remembered that she also enjoyed sewing. The coordinator suggested that this might be the basis for a rewarding venture. A month later, the teacher had established a very successful venture in which the students sewed articles for other students. The teacher, who initially opposed the *MicroSociety* program, became one of its strongest supporters in the school.

Giving teachers a choice is better than assigning teachers to ventures, but several teachers initially made poor choices. When they did so, they could become vocal opponents of the program. Thus in addition to giving teachers a choice, it often is useful for a skilled coordinator to sit down with the teachers and help them to develop a venture that will be successful and rewarding, such as the sewing venture. Alternatively, a well-designed staff development activity could provide teachers with some guidelines for choosing their ventures or agencies. Whatever the approach, it is important that implementers help teachers to become associated with agencies or ventures that fit well with the teachers' interests and abilities.

GUIDELINE 9: REALISTIC GOALS AND TIME PERSPECTIVES

Even when teachers have a meaningful voice in adopting the program and there is adequate time for planning and staff development, if expectations are unrealistic, their commitment can be undermined once the program becomes operational. Schools that saw the *MicroSociety* program as a panacea or hoped it would lead to dramatic improvements in test scores within a short period of time found it difficult to recover from the disappointment of failed expectations.

The City Magnet School at Lowell was not created initially to raise student test scores. The primary purpose was to help desegregate the school district, develop the "city" theme, and foster choice. These relatively modest goals could be realized soon. The school also was expected to perform well based on student performance on standard measures, but the teachers and principal had several years before they needed to achieve this more ambitious goal. During the first few years, when the program still was in its formative stage, expectations were few and modest.

The most successful schools, like City Magnet, all began with relatively modest goals and expectations. Two of them were magnet schools that adopted the *MicroSociety* program primarily to attract students from diverse backgrounds and different parts of the district. In one case, they also saw Micro as a way of developing the school's "business and government" theme. And even for these relatively modest goals, the district's time perspective was realistic. The magnet resource coordinator in the central office said that the district was willing to "give the school time to accomplish these goals because the school's location and overcrowding would make it difficult initially to attract many middle-class children from other parts of the district." Improving achievement scores also was a goal, but initially, it was of secondary importance. Reducing the racial imbalance was the primary concern. It was assumed that achievement scores eventually would rise if integration occurred.

The principal at this school had an additional goal, which also was appropriate for the *MicroSociety* program. She wanted "to make kids from disadvantaged backgrounds familiar with other career options." She herself had grown up in a barrio, and until she was a senior in high school, she had planned to go to beauty school following graduation. Then she became aware of only two other career options: teaching and nursing. She said that she wanted the students in her school to be aware of other options.

These goals were more appropriate and realistic than the goal at another school, which was to substantially raise student test scores within 2 or 3 years. Students at this school scored on average at the sixth percentile on the standard tests, which put it near the bottom among all schools in the district. The school's students performed so poorly that the school was one of a handful that had been placed on probation by the superintendent. Without a dramatic improvement in a relatively short period of time, the school would be closed. This situation led to unrealistic expectations for the *MicroSociety* program, and the school abandoned the program after 3 years when scores showed only a modest improvement.

Unrealistic expectations can be a problem on the level of the individual teacher as well. Some teachers became frustrated with the program because they initially expected too much of it and of themselves. For instance, one teacher came to dislike the program in part because of her "perfectionism." She had many ambitious ideas for her venture (a snack shop), and she also felt that she needed to write a curriculum for it. After taking on so much, she became frustrated and impatient. And she blamed the program for her burden rather than her own unrealistic expectations.

One principal tried to discourage this kind of perfectionism in her teachers by sending them to observe a relatively modest *MicroSociety* program in another school. She said that she would not let her teachers go to a *MicroSociety* program school with "lots of bells and whistles." Instead, she looked for a poor school with a program that was less flashy but "conceptually sound." This principal also repeatedly advised her teachers to adopt the "KISS" ("Keep it simple, stupid!") philosophy. A teacher at another school said that she wished she had known about that philosophy in the beginning.

Program coordinators also can be guilty of expecting too much from themselves and others. In several of the schools, the coordinators expected much greater teacher support and commitment than initially occurred. When some teachers failed to respond with as much enthusiasm as the coordinators thought was appropriate, the coordinators became frustrated and angry. This reaction can adversely affect relations between coordinator and teachers, which then will impede development of the program.

The principal's expectations concerning the quality of implementation also are important. One MicroSociety, Inc., consultant observed that in many schools, the principals and coordinators want "a Micro school without the sloppiness that Micro should be." She thought that many teachers become "overwhelmed" because too much is expected of them initially. She said it would be better if principals and coordinators "listened to the staff more" and were more accepting of a "piecemeal approach" to implementation. "The critical thing," according to this consultant, "is to prevent frustrations from going too high."

Implementing a complex school change like the *MicroSociety* program can put added stress on everyone. Murphy's Law ("Whatever can go wrong will go wrong") is validated repeatedly. When the initial expectations and time perspective are unrealistic, the stress is magnified. Each false step, each unforeseen problem, increases the pressure on the teachers and principal. It is difficult to create any kind of meaningful change in such an environment. For this reason, many school reform models try to build in a longer-term time perspective for change. Levin, the founder of the Accelerated Schools model, has said that it takes about 6 years for the complete transformation of a school to occur (Schwebel, 2003). Success for All's founder has written, "We must be prepared to engage with schools for many years, perhaps forever" (Slavin & Madden, 2001, p. 201). These beliefs about the need for a long-term time perspective are supported by research on school reform. Berends et al. (2002) found that financial and political pressures led the New American Schools corporation to try to scale up too soon, which resulted in uneven implementation and much frustration.

CONCLUSION

Those responsible for implementing a *MicroSociety* program usually understood that how they introduced the program to the school was crucial. For this reason, they gave the teachers an opportunity to vote on adopting the program. However, a comparison of the successful and unsuccessful schools suggested that more was necessary in order to maximize chances of success. By following a few basic guidelines for introducing the program to the school, implementers can make it more likely that their schools will be successful as well. (See Resource B for a complete list of the guidelines.)

5

Keeping It Running

Once the *MicroSociety*® program is up and running, there are a number of factors that become important for its viability and success. The first has to do again with resources. The most successful schools were particularly effective in seeking out, finding, and creatively utilizing both material and human resources for the program. The second factor has to do with what management theorists refer to as "organizational learning," that is, how well the principal, teachers, students, and parents are able to reflect on their experiences and, in doing so, anticipate and solve problems. The third factor concerns power, authority, and decision making. In the most successful schools, the teachers and students participate meaningfully in running the *MicroSociety* program. These findings suggest another set of guidelines for those who might implement a *MicroSociety* program.

GUIDELINE 10: EXPAND STUDENT RESPONSIBILITY

Once the program is up and running, the most important guideline concerns the role of the students. Every decision, every policy, every action should be evaluated in terms of this guideline: To what extent does it enhance student autonomy and responsibility? Teachers especially need to avoid doing anything that reduces student control over the *MicroSociety* program, and everyone in the school needs to think about ways that they can enhance student control.

Enhancing student responsibility—or what might be called the "student empowerment principle"—is important for the students and what they ultimately get out of the experience. But it also helps make the experience better for the teachers. Implementing the *MicroSociety* program, as we have seen, can require a significant amount of additional time and effort for the teachers. Whether this additional energy expenditure continues and how draining it feels depend on how much the teacher is willing to turn over control to the students. One of the teachers who did not feel particularly burdened by the *MicroSociety* program said that the key for her was that she "made the kids responsible for solving problems when they arose" rather than trying to solve all the problems herself. Another teacher who initially felt overwhelmed said that the program became much easier for her when she realized that she could have students do much of the administrative work, such as filling out forms, rather than do it herself.

Involving students more formally in decision making for the *MicroSociety* program also enhances program efficacy. At the most successful schools, there were effective structures for ensuring that the students had a meaningful role in making decisions concerning the *MicroSociety* program. For instance, at one school, in addition to the usual governmental bodies, the presidents of all the ventures and agencies met with the program coordinator each week to discuss operational problems and to make decisions about how to address them. This presidents' group helped to empower the students as a group within the program, and it strengthened the leadership of the presidents within their own agencies and ventures.

In the less successful *MicroSociety* programs, students never got to exercise much power, even in their own ventures and agencies. Teachers would take charge and make all the operational decisions. The teachers, in effect, were the bosses, and the students were their employees. Even in the legislature, the teachers in charge would dictate to the students and maintain firm limits on what they could and could not consider. Whenever there was a disconcerting event, such as a bank robbery, the teachers as a group would take over and decide on how to handle it rather than allowing the students to deal with it as responsible members of their own society. In this kind of teacher-directed authority structure, the students soon lost interest in the *MicroSociety* program, the teachers became increasingly overwhelmed with the burden of keeping everything going, and the program eventually was terminated.

Unfortunately, many teachers found it difficult to share control with the students. As one *MicroSociety* program coordinator said, "Some teachers forget the purpose of the program, which is to give kids more responsibility."

One teacher conceded that it took her several months to "back off and just let the kids do it." Another teacher, who eventually became one of the best *MicroSociety* program teachers in the country, said that giving up some of her authority was "the hardest change of all" for her to make when her school adopted the *MicroSociety* program.

Allowing the students to take responsibility for the *MicroSociety* program requires a radical change in the teacher's role. It also involves a major change in power relations between teachers and students. And, as an educational consultant who worked with the *MicroSociety* program noted, "It is hard to convince school people to trust kids, even when presented with evidence." He went on to describe how he had tried in vain at one school to get the teachers to share more power with the students. He believed that part of the problem was that educators, as well as the general public, have an image of what is a "real school." The kind of involvement envisioned for students in the *MicroSociety* program—and the less central role relegated to the teacher—just does not seem like "real school."

One of the parents at a *MicroSociety* school believed that it was fear that prevented teachers from allowing the students to run their *MicroSociety*. He said, "This school has always been afraid of the Micro concept, of turning kids loose." Perfectionism on the part of the teachers also can be a factor. One teacher who oversaw the yearbook had trouble letting her students take more responsibility for doing it because she had such high standards.

There is no doubt that allowing the students to take over and really run the *MicroSociety* program makes for a "messier" situation, at least in the beginning. However, there is some evidence that in the long term, a student-run program works just as well. The principal in one school did a study in the second year of the program in which half the students were assigned to a teacher-directed version of the program and half to a student-directed version. Although the teacher version "took off more quickly," the student-directed version eventually caught up.

Although many teachers found it difficult to allow the students to assume meaningful roles in the *MicroSociety* program, some teachers were able to do so. A notable example was the teacher who oversaw the publishing strand at her school. She described how she began each year by asking the students what *they* would like to do, rather than simply assigning them to predetermined roles and activities. The teacher said her goal was "to get kids to the point where they wouldn't need me." Evidence that she had succeeded came when the students in her venture became so confident and independent that they decided to send her on vacation!

Another positive example was the teachers who oversaw the marketplace, whom I described in Chapter 1. They came up with a new role for students, "mall manager," which transferred responsibility for solving problems from the teachers to a group of students. This change greatly relieved the burdens on the teachers.

Fortunately, as teachers gain experience with the *MicroSociety* program, many do see students take on more responsibility, and as a result, some teachers begin to change their views of what students are able to do for themselves. In Chapter 1, I described how the teachers in charge of the television station at one school allowed the students to assume more responsibility after all the teachers had to be away several days for a conference, and the students ran the morning show themselves without any major problems.

Once the students are allowed more responsibility, it becomes easier for the teachers to let go. As one teacher put it, "It's easier to share responsibility now because everything is student directed. The teachers are just facilitators." A teacher in an elementary-level program conceded that she even had learned "useful things" from the more experienced students in her venture!

GUIDELINE 11: SEEK OUT ADDITIONAL RESOURCES

In the last chapter, I indicated that successful programs began with a certain amount of funding, which usually was provided by the district and other external sources. Once the programs are up and running, they continue to require additional resources. Thus to be successful, *MicroSociety* programs continually need to seek out, identify, and utilize various kinds of resources within the school and in the larger community. The most effective schools stood out in how extensively they utilized existing resources and in how much effort they put into seeking out new ones.

MicroSociety programs require several different kinds of resources to operate. In addition to a certain amount of funding, programs require space, adults to oversee the program and provide support to the students, and community partners with their special expertise. They also need a steady supply of materials for the manufacturing ventures. And many of the ventures need special equipment, such as sound systems or popcorn makers.

In the most successful schools, resource development was a high priority that received constant attention and support from the program's leadership. It began with funding: The most successful schools augmented their initial grants by seeking out new funding on their own. For instance, one school began the program with several hundred thousand dollars per year that came from district funds. They then used part of this money to support grant-writing efforts, which eventually led to a 3-year federal grant that provided $100,000 per year for the program. Another school began with a grant of almost $200,000, which was followed by another grant of $450,000 a few years later.

In the more successful schools, the principals were resourceful not only in obtaining new funding for the program but also in leveraging existing funds. Several principals, for instance, utilized some of their Title 1 money for developing the program. At one school, the principal used district staff development funds to pay a group of staff to write a manual for the *MicroSociety* program during the summer.

Although a certain amount of additional funding is vital, other kinds of resources are equally important for long-term viability. The first school-wide *MicroSociety* program at Lowell was blessed with more than just an unusually large amount of initial funding for the program. The staff also was able to rely on an active and talented group of parent volunteers. These parents became an invaluable resource for the program, spending hundreds of hours during the early years helping to establish it.

The most successful schools utilized parents in ways that are more meaningful. For instance, in one school, a group of parent volunteers constructed a number of physical structures within the school that provided a high degree of realism for the *MicroSociety*. These included storefronts in the marketplace and a mock courtroom with a judge's bench and witness stand. Several parents with relevant expertise also provided technical assistance to various agencies and ventures. Eventually, more than 80 parent volunteers worked in the *MicroSociety* program on a regular basis in this school.

In another school, at least 20 parents were involved as volunteers—some every day, others more occasionally, with about 10 to 15 involved on any given day. The parents helped supervise students during Micro time and sometimes helped teach the students Micro-related skills. One parent described how in one venture, she had helped students to translate from English to Spanish. In another venture, a recycling center, she helped get material to recycle.

Not all schools were effective in developing parents as a resource for the *MicroSociety* program, and those programs tended to fare worse. At one large urban elementary school, only about eight parent volunteers helped out in the *MicroSociety* program. As a result, the teachers were overwhelmed with the amount of work involved in running the *MicroSociety* program. They often found themselves alone running huge agencies and ventures, sometimes with 40 students. After 3 stressful years, the school gave up and discontinued the program.

Unfortunately, often it is not easy to recruit parent volunteers. In an impoverished community made up largely of new immigrants, many of the parents cannot read or write in their own language, much less English. They are intimidated by the school and do not believe that they can help.

And they work all day, every day. Even in a more affluent community, the parents often are so busy juggling demanding jobs and extracurricular activities for their families that they feel they have little time or energy left over to donate to a *MicroSociety* program.

One virtue of the *MicroSociety* program is that it provides a way for parents to become more involved in schools. It can be an effective "hook" by which schools involve parents in a positive and meaningful way. Simply having a *MicroSociety* program, however, is not enough for attracting parents to the school. The most successful schools displayed an unusual degree of commitment, skill, and sensitivity in using the program to involve parents.

It often begins with making the parents feel truly welcomed. At Lowell, the first principal went out of his way to make the parents feel that they were welcomed and to treat them with respect. The other successful *MicroSociety* programs used the same approach. One of the schools even developed a separate "parent program" and hired a director for it. Their primary goal, according to the director of the program, was to "make the parents feel their time is valuable to the school. . . . We try to make them feel important." She went on to say that the "parents are treated as one of the teachers in the way they're referred to in front of the children." The school also stayed open late every day and offered many different kinds of programs for parents and their children.

In addition to making the parents feel welcomed and nurtured at this school, the staff used specific strategies to involve the parents in the *MicroSociety* program. The simplest one involved having parent meetings at which parents were invited to brainstorm ideas for the *MicroSociety* program. A more elaborate strategy was implemented at a meeting of the parent advisory committee: They began by having two students speak about their experiences in the *MicroSociety* program. Then they asked for volunteers to help "evaluate" the program. They gave the volunteers some training and then had them observe the program while it was going on. After the parent volunteers did the observations, the staff invited them to volunteer in the program on an ongoing basis.

The first schoolwide *MicroSociety* program provides an interesting example of how important parent involvement is for school reform. The first principal, as we have seen, was a strong supporter of parent involvement and found many ways to include parents in the implementation of the *MicroSociety* program there. However, when he left after several years, the next two principals were much less supportive of parent involvement. This change in the principal's attitudes toward parents at Lowell "did a lot of damage," according to one informant. It led to escalating conflicts between the principal and the parents and a drop in parent involvement, which deprived the program of valuable resources. The *MicroSociety* program suffered as a result.

Parents can play a crucial role in the implementation of any significant school change. For instance, the lack of parent involvement hinders implementation of Comer's School Development Program, one of the most popular whole-school reform models (Haynes, Emmons, Gebreyesus, & Ben-Avie, 1996). Fullan (2001) also has noted that lack of parent support hinders implementation efforts.

In addition to parents, community partners are an important resource for *MicroSociety* programs, and the most successful programs were especially effective in seeking out and utilizing community partners. Given that business and economics provide a foundation for any society, including the *MicroSociety*, partnerships with the local business community were particularly valuable in implementing the program. The most successful schools tended to invest more time and energy into building on the ties they already had with this part of their community. They also were creative in using other kinds of community partners. One successful school worked extensively with a local university in developing their program. For instance, the teachers who oversaw the *MicroSociety* television station were able to take a 1-week course at the university on how to operate the equipment, and then they had access to professors and graduate students in the university's communications department. Another school developed formal partnerships with five different departments at a nearby university and used these links to develop a "Micro Science Museum."

Community partnerships are an explicit part of the *MicroSociety* program, and so virtually all of the schools tried to develop them. The most successful schools, however, showed great initiative and ingenuity in establishing more effective and enduring partnerships. For instance, almost every school I studied had sought out the help of the local police department when they set up their "crimestoppers." But in the most effective programs, the police continued to be involved with the crimestoppers on a regular basis. In one school, for instance, a police officer assigned to the school for security purposes became the coordinator for crimestoppers. She not only supervised the student officers and detectives each day during Micro time but also provided them with considerable training. And she used her connections with the police department to secure various kinds of materials and supplies for the crimestoppers.

Similarly, most of the schools sought help from a local bank when they established the *MicroSociety* bank, but in some cases, the local bank became a relatively inactive partner once the teachers and original group of students learned how to run their bank. In one successful school, however, the adult community bank played a more significant, ongoing role. In addition to providing supplies, such as printed money and checkbooks for the students, the bank manager assigned two employees to work with the school 1 hour each week.

The most successful schools made the development of community partnerships a priority. For instance, in one school, the principal established as a goal having at least one community partner for each agency and venture. Although the school had not fully achieved that goal when I studied it, they had developed an extensive network of community partners and had involved them in meaningful ways.

A particularly useful and innovative community partnership involved the local credit union. Their staff developed a six-unit curriculum for classroom use, and one of their counselors came into each classroom to teach it to the students. This partnership was invaluable because many teachers had felt overwhelmed with all the other things they had to do, and they did not know how to teach money management to the students. As a result, the *MicroSociety* program bank was swamped with many "bounced checks." Once students began to learn more about money management from the credit union volunteers, the bounced-check problem became more manageable.

Another valuable resource for *MicroSociety* programs lay especially close at hand: noncertified staff, such as paraprofessionals or nonteaching professionals. Aides or teaching assistants, clerical staff, custodians, school nurses, media specialists—virtually any paid employee in the school building could be used to help implement the *MicroSociety* program. Use of these staff members reduced the burden on teachers. Involving noncertified staff in meaningful ways also could increase the sense of community within the school.

The most successful schools also used noncertified staff in more varied, creative, and effective ways. At one school, the media specialist helped to set up and run the TV station. At another school, the school nurse supervised the students who operated the "health clinic." And a teacher's aide was enlisted to teach a unit on *MicroSociety* to all the kindergarten classes. This experience helped prepare the children to enter the program in the first grade.

Whether it was developing community partnerships or seeing new ways to utilize nonprofessional staff for the program, the most successful *MicroSociety* programs seemed to have at least one person in the school who constantly scanned the environment for possible resources. At one school where the principal served this function, she said, "Whenever I see someone, I ask for something!" This principal also nurtured partnerships by going out and getting herself placed on the boards of different community organizations. Through this involvement, she was able to make contact with many different potential partners, and she had an opportunity to develop these contacts in a congenial setting.

This example suggests that "resource development" is both a skill and a role that needs constant attention (Sarason & Lorentz, 1989). Schools that had a skilled person who took on that role tended to be more successful in implementing the *MicroSociety* program. While it sometimes is hard to find someone to fill this role and to be effective in this role, it is necessary for a strong, effective program. Filling this role should take priority over other roles in any major school reform effort.

Other school reform models do not require the special kinds of resources that the *MicroSociety* program requires. However, given the resource constraints and enormous demands faced by public education today, any school change effort will be more likely to succeed if there is a staff person whose role involves seeking out and utilizing additional resources, such as parent volunteers and community partners.

GUIDELINE 12: CREATE A CULTURE OF EXPERIMENTATION

The schools I studied never began with all the answers. No matter how well they prepared for launching the *MicroSociety* program, unanticipated problems emerged once the program became operational. The most successful schools succeeded because of the way they responded to problems. When they made mistakes, they were able to learn from them. These are the attributes of a "learning organization" (Fullan, 1993; Senge, 1990).

In many ways, the first schoolwide *MicroSociety* program functioned as an effective learning organization, and this was another characteristic that helped make the original school at Lowell so successful in the early years. The staff at City Magnet spent many months together planning for a new school based on the *MicroSociety* program. But as one of the original teachers said, "We read George's book, then planned, and then threw out the plan on the first day." He went on to refer to their program, even after 15 years, as "still a work in progress."

What made it possible for the staff at Lowell to "throw out the original plan on the first day" and then create an exciting, vibrant program was their ability to sit down together and learn from the problems they were encountering. This, in turn, required relationships characterized by respect and trust. The collegial relationships that developed among the staff prior to the City Magnet School's opening continued for some time after it became operational. Meetings were "very informal." They often took place at people's homes and went on for hours. And there was a feeling among the teachers, parents, and principal that they "were involved in something revolutionary and that you could shape it."

The physical setting also enhanced the collaboration and mutual assistance at City Magnet in the early days. Because they started the first year in one big open space, there was much opportunity for shared learning and collaborative problem solving.

Although each school's experience is unique, the most successful *MicroSociety* programs, like Lowell's, excelled in organizational learning. Schools, like individuals, differ in how they approach problems and value learning, and these differences in the organizational culture had a significant effect on teacher commitment and implementation of the *MicroSociety* program. In one school, the staff seemed to deal openly with problems and conflicts as they arose, and they resolved those problems in a collaborative way. The *MicroSociety* program thrived at that school. At another school, the climate was very different: The staff was divided and spent more time arguing. Teachers accused each other of "refusing to listen" to each other or to the program coordinator. Disagreements would be discussed without any resolution. One teacher said, "We'd debate an issue and then drop it." Not surprisingly, the *MicroSociety* program ended in failure after 3 years at this second school.

In every school, there seemed to be a distinctive problem-solving climate that influenced how the staff thought about and reacted to problems, and this problem-solving climate greatly affected the implementation process. In implementing a school change like the *MicroSociety* program, mistakes are inevitable. (As the manual developed by one *MicroSociety* program noted, "A lot of our original ideas didn't work.") The difference between success and failure often comes down to how administrators, teachers, and students react to those mistakes. A teacher put it well when she said, "The most important lesson I've learned from this experience is that you have to be a risk taker." A program coordinator expressed the same idea when she commented, "You have to be comfortable with chaos. Things change from day to day." To help teachers and students maintain the resilience and flexibility necessary for effective implementation, there needs to be a positive problem-solving climate that supports experimentation.

The problem-solving climate at a school often was apparent in the tone set at staff meetings. In one of the more successful *MicroSociety* programs, I observed a planning meeting in which the leadership was shared among the teachers. I saw them help each other brainstorm ideas for their ventures. They made decisions with much give-and-take. At another meeting involving a larger group of teachers, the teachers felt free to raise problems and then brainstorm together to find solutions. As the meeting progressed, teachers continued to identify problems. Sometimes the program coordinator had the answer or solution to a problem; sometimes the faculty would come up with a solution after brainstorming; and sometimes there was no solution, but the coordinator wrote down the problem to explore it further. None of the meetings I observed was like the all-too-common faculty meeting, where an administrator stands in front of a group of teachers and makes announcements, while the teachers are silent except for an occasional complaint or request for information.

The group process at planning meetings was not always smooth and problem free at the successful schools. At one school, group members sometimes became "very dogmatic," in the words of one staff member. Feelings could be hurt when something had to be cut. Not everyone was active all the time; there could be a certain amount of passivity, disorganization, side comments, and unresolved tension. However, meetings at the most successful schools, despite these inevitable lapses, also involved active, collaborative give-and-take, and this positive problem-solving climate seemed to be crucial for successful implementation.

Unfortunately, the school climate does not always support experimentation and problem solving. Instead, teachers and administrators focus on avoiding mistakes and problems. The ultimate goal seems to be smoothness of functioning. And this goal affects the way in which the *MicroSociety* program is implemented. The teachers and principals become preoccupied with getting the *MicroSociety* program to run smoothly. Rather than seeing the "messiness" as providing opportunities for students to learn and grow, they see it as a calamity that needs to be stamped out—the sooner, the better. Smoothness of functioning becomes an end in itself.

This value placed on smoothness of functioning is especially apparent in the way *MicroSociety* programs deal with their constitutions. Once the constitution gets written, the teachers and students do not go back to do it again. They do not seem to realize that the greatest learning comes from the process of writing a constitution and it is the *learning* that is more important than getting a constitution written, so that the *MicroSociety* can function the way it "should" and look like a "real" *MicroSociety* program. As a result, only the first group of students and teachers participate in one of the most engaging and valuable activities associated with a *MicroSociety* program.

At the most fundamental level, it is fear that prevents some teachers and administrators from implementing the program effectively. It is a fear that something terrible will happen if things do not go according to plan or the teacher loses control. However, the problem is not just fear. To some extent, a certain amount of anxiety about how things are going is inevitable and even desirable. When problems and mistakes occur, some concern about the consequences is not a bad thing. What matters is the way in which the administrators and teachers respond to that concern: the way in which they *manage their fears* and the fears of their students. When educators are not able to effectively manage the anxiety associated with "messiness," then a poor problem-solving climate develops and implementation suffers.

The most successful schools developed processes that helped the staff to manage the anxiety associated with implementing a *MicroSociety* program. At one school, the staff periodically would take time at the beginning of a meeting to share success stories and complement each other on what went well. The program coordinator believed that this technique had contributed to a better process at meetings. It may have done so in part by helping staff to avoid becoming overwhelmed with anxiety about the program's functioning.

The principal, *MicroSociety* program coordinator, and other key leaders within the school also help create a good problem-solving climate by being positive models. In all of the successful schools, the principal continually modeled a positive problem-solving attitude.

Other school reform experiences have demonstrated the same principle: The implementation process requires the school to function as a flexible learning organization. For instance, there is the example of Central Park East (CPE), one of the better-known examples of an urban public school that became a successful educational alternative. An outside researcher who studied the history of CPE found that part of what contributed to the school's success was "the organization's ability to learn and grow" and its ability to overcome "past major mistakes," to improve on "inadequate theories and practices," and to develop "new capacities unimagined at the time of the school's establishment" (Bensman, 2000, p. 7). Also important was the school's ability to "define problems, seek help and expertise from others, and continuously improve its practices and performance. CPE was an organization that learned how to learn" (Bensman, 2000, p. 123). Similarly, in her study of how successful educational alternatives "scaled up," Schorr (1997) found that success required a process that allowed for some degree of flexibility in order to respond to the unique conditions of each case.

Thus another key to successful implementation of school change involves the way in which schools approach problems. There needs to be a positive problem-solving climate as well as a culture that values experimentation and learning more than smoothness of functioning. The staff and students need to reflect on their own experience in implementing the program, and to learn from it. The school, in short, must become an effective "learning organization."

GUIDELINE 13: CONTINUE TO SET ASIDE TIME FOR PLANNING

Another important part of the Lowell story is that the staff had the time they needed for organizational learning and productive group problem solving during the early years—in fact, they had lots of it. The original state and federal desegregation funding continued to provide money for ongoing planning after the school opened. Thus once the school became established, the staff continued to have Monday afternoons available for meetings as a large group and in the different strands. These planning meetings were invaluable. As one of the teachers noted, "I don't know how you'd start a new *MicroSociety* program without that." And another one of the original teachers proclaimed, "The most important thing for a Micro is communication. And if teachers and students don't have enough *time* to communicate about what is happening, it won't work."

In addition to weekly meetings, the faculty at Lowell was able to spend time together planning before the beginning of school each fall. One teacher remembered that when she first came to the school 5 years after it had opened, there was a weeklong workshop on the *MicroSociety* program for all the teachers during the week before school started. The workshop provided not only training but also opportunities for curriculum development, problem solving, planning, and team building among the staff.

Like Lowell, the most successful *MicroSociety* programs set aside the time necessary for ongoing planning, problem solving, and staff development. In one of these schools, the teachers spent 1 to 2 hours per week in group brainstorming and problem solving during the first year of the program's operation. Then in August prior to the start of the second year, the teachers went off to the mountains to take stock and plan for the coming year. When they returned to school in the fall, they put off the start of the program until November so that they could continue to plan. Finally, they decided to run the program only 4 days a week and use the fifth day for more group problem solving and planning.

Another highly successful school had retreats each summer for the staff to reflect on and improve the program. They also had a weekend retreat in the fall during the first 2 years of operation. And they used these retreats for team building as well as planning. According to the principal, "The retreats have helped a lot in making things run smoother. We can get a lot done and really focus on what we're doing." In addition to the retreats, the staff at this school consulted with staff at other *MicroSociety* programs more often than was the norm. Especially helpful was networking with teachers in other schools who worked with the same strands.

Schools that used different kinds of meetings for planning and professional development found that larger blocks of time often were more productive. For instance, at one school, I observed two kinds of planning meetings. One was a large meeting that involved all the teachers from Grades K–2 or 3–5. These meetings occurred twice a month and lasted 60 to 90 minutes. The other kind of meeting was much smaller, consisting of five or so teachers in the same grade. This meeting went on all day. It was arranged so that the teachers could do the bulk of the planning necessary for the *MicroSociety* program during the upcoming term. The second type of meeting was much more productive, partly because of the smaller group size but also because the teachers had a much larger block of time with which to work. The *MicroSociety* program coordinator agreed that there was not enough time at the larger meetings to deal with issues in an adequate manner.

To be consistent with the *MicroSociety* program philosophy, the *students* as well as the teachers should have opportunities to engage in planning and problem solving. The most successful *MicroSociety* programs did have mechanisms for involving the students in this way. For instance, in one school, the students used their *MicroSociety* period 1 day each week for training and group problem solving. During this time, they met in their occupational areas, and these meetings were not like a traditional class. They were more like a staff meeting or a training workshop that might be conducted in a business setting.

Training for the teachers also seemed to make a difference. In fact, it appeared that staff development became even more useful once the program was up and running than it had been before the program became operational. Many teachers said that whether it was visiting other schools, attending the summer conference, or even reading George Richmond's original book, such activity proved to be more valuable once they had some experience trying to implement the program. For instance, one teacher said that she reread Richmond's book *after* she had been doing the program for a while and realized that she was "doing too much for the kids." She began to give them more responsibility, and many of her problems diminished.

The national training conferences held each summer were especially valuable experiences for teachers and administrators once they had some experience trying to implement the program in their own schools. They found it comforting to be surrounded by other teachers who were working with the same program model and encountering the same difficulties. Equally helpful were the many workshops taught by veteran teachers and administrators in which practical techniques and solutions to problems were exchanged. The teachers almost always left these conferences with a renewed sense of commitment, as well as a better understanding of how to resolve the implementation issues they had confronted. As one principal put it, "The summer conference is a very supportive place. It's different from most other professional conferences. People there are excited and committed. They want to share what they have." A teacher from another school said, "Things began to improve as more teachers went to the summer conference. They got ideas and became inspired. Even skeptics would come back inspired. They became converted. They would start working together. . . ."

Teachers and principals from other *MicroSociety* programs also could offer much in the way of guidance, especially once a program became operational. A school that eventually became one of the best *MicroSociety* programs in the country called a *MicroSociety* program in an adjacent state "a lot" during their first year of operation in order to get advice on how to deal with the problems that were emerging.

Valuable technical assistance could come from non-*MicroSociety* sources as well. Lack of knowledge about business principles was a particular problem at all the schools because the economic system is the foundation of the *MicroSociety* program and most teachers have not had any courses in economics. (The most successful *MicroSociety* teachers, interestingly, often did have some background in business and economics.) Thus consultation from local business people could be especially valuable. At one school, in fact, one of the most helpful "interventions" occurred at the end of the second year, when they had some business people come in and teach them how to price goods and services.

A teacher who had benefited from most of these sources of information said that while all were helpful, there was no substitute for actually observing a *MicroSociety* program at another school. Her belief was confirmed by a teacher in another school, who said that the first time she "really understood" the program was when she and some others went to observe the program in operation at another school.

Setting aside time and providing opportunities for planning and ongoing training are helpful, but the teachers' *attitudes and values toward their own learning* are important as well. Teachers need to be willing, if not eager, to put in extra time for reflection, brainstorming, and personal learning. This was the case at the most successful schools. For instance, at one successful school, many of the teachers sought out help on their own. The teacher in charge of the Internal Revenue Service was typical: She pulled out her old college economics books to learn what she needed and also studied a video on taxes geared for kids. At the schools where implementation was problematic, many of the teachers were reluctant to spend additional time for learning and problem solving. They would use excuses such as union contracts to avoid investing extra time and effort into professional development or brainstorming sessions. A newer teacher at one such school stated that "a lot of the faculty have been here a long time. They are in the habit of repeating past practices. They are not reflecting on what they are doing. They aren't growing."

Thus the staff and students in schools that are implementing school change need time to identify problems and collectively come up with solutions. There also needs to be time set aside for them to continue to learn and grow through participation at conferences, observations at other schools, and reading. And continual learning, on both an individual and an organizational level, must be valued.

GUIDELINE 14: CREATE AN OPEN AND FLEXIBLE DECISION-MAKING STRUCTURE

Another factor that influenced organizational learning at the schools was the way in which power and authority were exercised once the program had become operational. Ideally, it is the students who run the *MicroSociety*. But teachers also need to play a significant role. Successful schools followed this pattern. Power was shared among all the important stakeholders, including the teachers. In the less effective programs, teachers had little power.

In the original program at Lowell, the teachers, along with several parents, played a significant role in the development of the program before the school opened. This pattern continued once the program became operational. During the first year of its existence, there were only 11 teachers and the principal. The entire school was crammed into one large room. In this setting, everyone had a say about what went on. Important decisions were made collectively. There was no strong distinction between the leaders and the led as far as the *MicroSociety* program was concerned.

In the *MicroSociety* programs that came after Lowell, teachers rarely were as empowered as they had been at Lowell in the early years. Authority for making important decisions concerning the program usually was concentrated in the hands of the principal, the program coordinator, and/or a management team. This more hierarchical decision-making structure diluted the power that teachers exercised. As a result, some teachers became less committed to the program over time, and their ventures or agencies usually reflected this fact.

In one of the schools where the program ultimately failed, the decision-making structure was an elaborate, hierarchical one, in which no one felt that they had much power to influence the direction of the program. In addition to a program coordinator, there was a teacher put in charge of each of the four strands implemented in that school. These strand leaders formed a "board of directors," which met regularly with the program coordinator to plan. When teachers had a problem or suggestion, they would have to take it first to their strand leader, who then would take it to the board of directors. The principal reviewed all of the board's decisions, but he did not attend their meetings. So once the board made a decision, the program coordinator would have to take it up to the principal for his review.

Thus there were four levels of authority from teachers to principal. Many teachers at this school complained that the board of directors made all the important decisions. The board of directors, on the other hand, felt that they had little power because the principal vetoed many of their decisions and the teachers often ignored the rest.

One of the successful schools created a more open and flexible authority structure by having the program coordinator position rotate among several teachers. Each year, a different teacher filled the position. This practice meant that leadership ultimately was vested in the teachers as a group rather than in a single program coordinator. As a result, it was less likely that the program would come to be seen as "belonging to" a single person. By rotating the position among the teachers, the program came to be seen as something for which everyone was responsible.

In addition to the authority structure, the way in which people in leadership positions exercised their authority had a significant impact on the *MicroSociety* program. In the more successful schools, the leaders led in ways that increased the teachers' participation in decision making. For instance, the principal (who also served as the program coordinator) at one of the successful schools was a strong believer in sharing power with her teachers, and she tried to involve the teachers in making many decisions concerning the program. There were certain "nonnegotiables" for the principal (such as whether to have a *MicroSociety* program). But there were few issues that could not be discussed and influenced by her teachers. The principal also understood that the best way to involve teachers was not necessarily to discuss an issue in a large faculty meeting and then ask the teachers to vote. Her typical approach was to begin with a small committee or task force of teachers to work out the details. Then the committee's report and proposal would go to the full faculty for discussion and a decision.

At another school, the principal increased the teachers' voice in a particularly dramatic way. Many of the teachers were unhappy with the program after the first year of operation because it seemed so onerous. So the principal scheduled a meeting to discuss the future of the program. She began the meeting by telling the teachers that the *MicroSociety* program was very important to her but it could not continue without their support. If they wanted to terminate the program after a thorough discussion, they could. She then presented her arguments for continuing the program. And then the principal stopped and turned it over to the teachers. During the rest of the meeting, which was highly emotional and went on for 3 hours, the principal said little. She listened with sympathy to the teachers' concerns. At the end of the meeting, the teachers decided to keep the *MicroSociety* program but to scrap another initiative that they had been trying to implement at the same time.

The principal at another successful school had the same philosophy about empowering teachers. She encouraged initiative on the part of the teachers, and she was flexible about many aspects of the *MicroSociety* program. For instance, she acceded to teacher requests to suspend the program on days when the teachers needed to prepare for special events such as parent conferences. Like the other principals at successful schools, she seemed to feel that teachers should play a role in running the school and that their concerns should be taken seriously.

In some ways, the sharing of authority was more difficult for coordinators and management teams. As teachers, they were not used to exercising power over other teachers, and they had no formal authority on which to rely for compliance. As a result, they often would swing back and forth between being too laissez-faire and too authoritarian in the way they supervised the program.

For instance, at one school, the coordinator initially tended to "push" the other teachers because she was so enthusiastic about the program and wanted her fellow teachers to implement it "properly." Many of the other teachers reacted against her rather heavy-handed approach by becoming more resistant and less cooperative.

Over time, the coordinator tried to back off and become less "pushy." However, a daylong planning meeting I observed suggested that in her effort not to be "too pushy," the coordinator often failed to provide the teachers with guidance that they needed and wanted. The coordinator left the teachers on their own to figure out what to do, but at one point, one of the teachers called the coordinator over as she walked by and asked her a question about how much money to pay students. The coordinator answered, "It's up to you. You can do it any way you like." The teacher clearly was disappointed that she had not received more help.

Part of the art of leadership is finding the right balance between autonomy and support. In their research on the Coalition of Essential Schools model, Muncey and McQuillan (1996) found that the most successful principals were strong advocates for the program but they also knew when to,

> Back off and allow faculty to direct change efforts. . . . At schools that sustained their Coalition reform efforts, the principal's role involved a balancing act, one that required knowing when to be directive and assertive and when to back off and allow faculty to direct change efforts. (p. 270)

As Firestone and Corbett (1988) put it, participation by teachers often increases commitment to change, but too little control by administrators can lead to "confusion, frustration, and bad technical planning, all of which undermine the implementation effort" (p. 332).

CONCLUSION

MicroSociety programs, like any other human community, evolve. They do not remain fixed in time. Thus no matter how favorable the context initially is, and no matter how well the founders of the program introduce it into the school and school system, there will be unforeseen challenges as time passes. Some of the challenges will come from within, while others will come from the outside. To withstand those challenges, *MicroSociety* programs need to have the capacity to identify and develop all kinds of resources. They also need to have processes and norms that encourage students, teachers, and administrators to experiment and to learn from mistakes, to solve problems collaboratively, and to resolve conflicts constructively. (See Resource B for a complete summary of the guidelines covered in this chapter.)

The guidelines in this chapter, as well as many in the previous chapters, point to the importance of one other aspect of the change process that is particularly important: leadership. In the next chapter, I present the last set of guidelines based on the various ways in which leadership can either help or hinder effective implementation of school change efforts.

6

Leadership: The Critical Ingredient

Although all of the guidelines presented thus far are important for successful implementation, my research, as well as that of many others, suggests that the most critical ingredient in school change is leadership. One reason that leadership is so critical is that many of the success factors and guidelines (presented in the previous chapters) depend on it. In a variety of ways, principals and other leaders, such as program coordinators and teacher advocates, provide both the fuel and the grease that are necessary for success.

Research and theory on school change have long recognized the importance of leadership (Fullan, 2001). For instance, Louis, Toole, and Hargreaves (1999) noted that "the classic RAND study of Educational Change found that teachers rarely muster the will and motivation for significant changes without support from the school administrators or district officials, a finding that has been widely replicated" (p. 267). Schorr (1997) identified "skillful leadership" as one of the factors crucial for scaling up innovative educational programs and suggested that leaders in effective programs have certain qualities, such as,

> The willingness to experiment and take risk . . . to tolerate ambiguity; to win trust simultaneously of line workers, politicians, and the public; . . . to be collaborative in working with staff; and to allow staff discretion at the front lines. (p. 9)

And Retallic and Fink (2002) asserted, "The importance of leadership in an organization is one of the few ideas in the change literature about which there is fairly consistent agreement" (p. 91).

Recent research on whole-school reform has tended to confirm previous findings on the critical role of leadership. For instance, James Comer and his colleagues have found that the principal is the key to overcoming all of the challenges to implementation of their model (Haynes, Emmons, Gebreyesus, & Ben-Avie, 1996). As a result, a central part of the School Development Program implementation process involves training principals how to develop and use a more collaborative, less judgmental leadership style. Research on the New American Schools initiative, which included several of the better-known whole-school reform models, found that the teacher's perception of the principal's leadership was "the most important indicator of implementation level achieved" (Berends, Bodilly, & Kirby, 2003, p. xxxiii).

While leadership is crucial for successful school change, the research has shown that it can come from sources other than the principal. For instance, implementation of the KEYS program in Memphis was greatly helped by the active support of a local union official. She served as a kind of facilitator for all 12 of the schools, and when she left after 2 years, implementation suffered (Portin, Beck, Knapp, & Murphy, 2003).

Although there are many ways in which leadership influences the implementation process, the principal's role as an active advocate for the program proved to be one of the most fateful for the implementation of the *MicroSociety*® program. This finding leads to the next guideline. (All of the guidelines are listed in Resource B.)

GUIDELINE 15: THE PRINCIPAL AS ADVOCATE

In Chapter 3, I suggested that a positive attitude toward *MicroSociety* on the part of the principal helped create a favorable context for implementation of the program. Once the program became operational, the principal's support continued to be important. However, at the most successful schools, the principals not only had a favorable attitude toward the program but also provided more tangible support.

Principals did not need to become actively involved in the program in order to provide the necessary support. What was critical was that the principal support the program *politically* (rather than oppose it or neglect it in favor of other initiatives) and provide *tangible assistance* when needed.

In the successful schools, the principals were advocates for the program within the school. For instance, a staff member at one school described the principal as "very positive about the program. She shows it off to everyone who comes into the building." The principal's support for the program also was reflected in the physical environment of the school. There was much evidence of the *MicroSociety* program in the halls, library, and other public spaces: student art with the *MicroSociety* as the theme, names of the *MicroSociety's* student officers and senators posted in the library, and other signs and posters related to the program throughout the school. This principal also demonstrated political support within the school when some teachers objected to the amount of time that the program required. While the principal was willing to make some accommodations in order to lessen the time demands, she made it clear that the program itself was not "negotiable." She was willing to give on many issues, but not on the *MicroSociety* program. As one teacher said, "The principal has been very consistent in her support for the program, and that has been important."

Principals at the successful schools also were strong advocates for the *MicroSociety* program beyond the walls of the school. They actively lobbied for the program with the central administration and the larger community. For instance, when student test scores declined after the first year the program was implemented in one school, the principal went to the superintendent and pointed out that scores "usually go down at first whenever there is a change." She argued that the program should have at least 3 years to prove itself. The superintendent agreed, and by the end of the third year, test scores had not only rebounded but were also significantly higher than they had been before the program had been introduced to the school.

In addition to political support, principals with the most effective programs often played a crucial role by helping teachers to overcome problems and providing encouragement. For instance, at one school, the principal tried to alleviate pressure on the teachers who were involved in the program by relieving them from other duties whenever possible and by providing them with some additional resources, such as extra paraprofessional help. He also tried to give the teachers "lots of strokes" for what they were doing in the program. In another school where teachers took the lead in implementing and running the program, the principal provided symbolic support by consulting with the student president whenever an important decision had to be made. He also gave students recognition for accomplishments made in the program.

The principal at another successful school provided more tangible support by securing a large grant from a foundation to enable staff to study other *MicroSociety* programs around the country. And another principal helped the program by reaching out to principals at other *MicroSociety* schools and building learning networks for teachers in the same strands. This kind of interschool networking would have been difficult for the teachers to do on their own without the active assistance of the principal.

Verbal support of the principal was less important than actions. In one case, a principal expressed support for the program, but a teacher complained that the principal "never fully understood what the program was about." A consultant who worked with the school agreed that the principal, though she was "genuinely interested in the idea," was "not a real Micro principal at heart." For instance, when a group of older students were harassing some younger students, the principal had a meeting with the parents rather than have the students deal with it. This action undermined the program in a subtle but important way.

Other research on school change also has documented the importance of active support by the principal. For instance, Firestone and Corbett (1988) found that competing projects, initiatives, and mandates can be a significant problem for innovative programs. One task of a school's leadership is to buffer the staff from these as much as possible. Principals also support change efforts through obtaining resources, providing encouragement and recognition, adapting standard operating procedures, monitoring the improvement effort, and handling disturbances (Heller & Firestone, 1995). Although others in the school can perform these critical leadership functions, the principal usually takes the lead.

Research has shown that principal support is especially important in school change efforts. Portin et al. (2003) found that without strong, active support by the principal, the KEYS initiative simply could not be sustained in a school. And at Central Park East, an important factor contributing to the school's success was the principal's supportive leadership. In concrete, tangible ways, such as taking over a class for a teacher so that she could attend a staff development activity or hiring an office aid to take over routine administrative duties of teachers, such as taking attendance, the principal supported the teachers' efforts (Bensman, 2000).

Although the principal's support was vital for an effective *MicroSociety* program, it sometimes could be a two-edged sword. Without sufficient political support and tangible assistance from the principal, the program would flounder. Yet if principals provided too much support and became too involved, they could reduce teacher commitment to the program. When principals are too actively supportive, teachers may come to see the *MicroSociety* program as the "principal's program." Thus principals should provide political backing, help teachers secure resources and solve problems, and offer encouragement, while also acting in ways that make the teachers and students feel that it is *their* program.

GUIDELINE 16: EMOTIONALLY INTELLIGENT LEADERSHIP

One other success factor that was important for programs once they became operational was the emotional intelligence of people in key leadership positions. By "emotional intelligence," I mean the ability to perceive, understand, and manage one's own emotions and those of others. Emotional intelligence enables people to cope with difficult situations effectively and handle interpersonal relationships with aplomb (Cherniss & Goleman, 2001; Goleman, Boyatzis, & McKee, 2002). Ultimately, it was emotional intelligence that enabled the principals, coordinators, and teacher leaders in the most successful *MicroSociety* schools to create the conditions necessary for effective implementation.

Principals at successful *MicroSociety* schools displayed many of the characteristics that have come to be associated with effective leadership of change efforts. For example, the original principal at City Magnet School in Lowell was described by those who worked with him as "a powerful and positive presence." An administrator in the system said that the principal "massaged" the staff to "help them break boundaries." One of the original teachers described him as "a spark. He kept things going." Still another teacher said that the first principal at Lowell "never saw the glass half empty. He always said, 'You can!' not, 'You can't.'" A teacher told a story about how she was feeling "kind of down" one day, and when the principal saw her, he started doing somersaults to cheer her up. It worked.

The principal at City Magnet also was open to other points of view. As one teacher put it in describing what it was like to work under him, "It was nice to know that your opinion was respected." However, while the principal often was positive and supportive, he also could be tough when necessary. For instance, one of his teachers described how the principal sometimes would "confront the superintendent" on the school's behalf.

The principals at the most successful *MicroSociety* schools tended to have similar qualities. At one of those schools, the principal was described as "very people oriented." She genuinely liked people and tended to see only the most positive aspects of a person. The principal was tolerant and understanding even of those whom others found "difficult." Even in private, she seldom spoke ill of a person. This principal also reportedly gave "lots of strokes to everyone." She even placed a "cheer box" in the school library, which she used to give teachers strokes. The principal also was available to listen to teachers whenever they needed to vent. And she was able to create a nonjudgmental and nondefensive atmosphere with her teachers. They knew that if they disagreed or said something critical, it would not be held against them (though they also knew that the principal would not necessarily change her mind!).

This principal also could use many different leadership styles, depending on what was most needed at any given time. She provided clear direction but also was flexible. She had strong convictions but also listened to and respected others. She was emotional and intuitive, but she also could be analytical and shrewd. She was well organized but not overly compulsive. (These qualities made her excellent at leading meetings. She was able to combine a high degree of structure, while also allowing a high degree of participation on the part of teachers, students, and parents.)

The principals at the most successful schools also were unusually conscientious and committed. At one school, for example, the principal put an enormous amount of time into her job every day. She typically woke at 4:30 a.m. and was at school soon after that. She then would work until 7:00 p.m. or later.

The principals at the most successful schools also demonstrated an unusual degree of initiative. A particularly good example was the principal who, shortly after she had come to the school, noticed that a student had not been picked up by a parent or guardian after school. The principal went out into the community herself to try to locate the child's parent. At one point during her search, she went into some apartment houses and discovered that some children were living in multifamily units with a communal bathroom. The sight would have moved almost anyone, but this principal was not just moved. She acted. She set up an after-school homework program to give students in her school a quiet place to study.

These qualities of effective *MicroSociety* principals are similar to those that have been noted in previous research on the role of leadership in school change, but the attempt to identify a definitive list of specific leadership skills or behaviors that best promote school improvement has often been difficult. According to Louis et al. (1999, p. 267), research on leadership and change, while emphasizing the importance of the principal, has not identified any "one best way" to foster change. In addition, some writers have argued that a "skills-based" approach to leadership misses much of the essence of effective leaders. As one writer put it,

> The leading of any work group is a matter of a whole person in a whole environment interacting in concrete ways with other whole persons in the immediacy and unpredictability of the moment. . . . Leadership cannot be reduced to a list. (Evans, 1996, p. 163)

In response to these difficulties, researchers increasingly have come to focus on a collection of personal qualities that they call "transformational leadership" (Bass, 2002). This new approach "focuses on the role of the principal as setting vision, organizing resources, and creating positive pressures for change" (Louis et al., 1999, p. 267). It emphasizes the role of "strong presence and character" or "identity and personal commitment" in effective leadership (Louis et al., 1999, p. 265). Many researchers believe that such leadership helps develop teacher commitment to change, which is a fundamental task for any successful change effort.

While the most effective change agents do seem to use transformational leadership, there is still something missing. As Evans (1996) put it, "It is easy to embrace transformation . . . but it is quite something else to figure out how to become transformational" (p. 176).

A new and more promising approach focuses on the *emotional* aspects of the change process and the role of leadership in dealing with these aspects. Educational researchers increasingly are tuning into the emotional dynamics that play such a prominent role in any change effort, for better or worse. For instance, Evans has noted that for meaningful change to occur, staff must be emotionally engaged. It is not enough for them simply to go through the motions. Thus "the leadership that counts is the kind that touches people deeply. It taps their emotions, appeals to their values, and responds to their connections with other people" (Sergiovanni, 1992, p. 120).

While emotion is vital for driving the change process, it also can become an impediment. Change "provokes loss, challenges competence, creates confusion, and causes conflict" (Evans, 1996, p. 21). Even the prospect of change can stir up feelings of fear, resentment, and anger, not to mention loss and ambivalence. As Firestone and Corbett (1988) noted, "Implementation is in large part a learning process. Even with innovations that seem clear, people experience substantial ambiguity—along with feelings of confusion, anger, and exhaustion—when they begin using new practices" (p. 330). School improvement "is not just complicated but inherently chaotic and unpredictable" (Louis et al., 1999, p. 256).

Also, schools are not "change-friendly." There is little time for reflection; resources for innovation are limited; superintendents change jobs frequently; and in urban schools, staff turnover is high as well. People do not respond to this reality like robots. They experience a range of emotions that often impede rather than help bring about positive change.

Schools can generate a mix of emotional reactions even without engaging in change, and these emotions can make school improvement even more difficult. In fact, according to Evans (1996), one reason that change does not occur is that administrators who are supposed to lead the process are often stressed out as a result of the mounting pressures directed at them for managing schools as they are: "Together, the legal and bureaucratic requirements have created a glut of paperwork and a preoccupation with procedure that have expanded administrators' workload and shriveled their room to maneuver. . . . The imbalance between resources and demands has never been greater" (p. 153).

Thus school change is always a highly emotional process, and the most effective leaders will be those who excel in the awareness and management of the emotional aspects of change. Leaders need to manage the emotions that are stirred up by the chaos and unpredictability of change. They need to be aware of the underlying emotional sources of resistance in others, and they need to be adept at handling those sources. Rather than avoid conflict because of the discomfort it causes, they need to be able to confront it constructively.

Leaders also need to be able to generate the enthusiasm and hope that are critical for success. As Louis et al. (1999) have argued, "School improvement strategies should unleash positive emotions and inner resources among educators who might make reform work" (p. 265). Emotionally intelligent leaders know how to unleash those positive emotions and inner resources.

It is emotional intelligence that enables principals to become "transformational leaders." Without a certain awareness and understanding of one's own emotional life and the emotional lives of others and without an ability to manage and express emotions effectively, one cannot be an effective transformational leader.

Emotional intelligence also provides the foundation for other traits associated with effective leadership. For instance, in order to persist in the face of setbacks, leaders need to be able to short-circuit the discouragement that can lead them to give up. To effectively manage the chaos and confusion that often accompany change efforts, leaders need to be able to avoid becoming overwhelmed with anxiety. They must be adept at managing their stress and the stress of others. To handle conflict and resistance effectively, leaders need to be able to manage the fear and anger that are often at the root of such reactions. To create a positive, supportive environment, leaders need to be able to sense how others are feeling and what will make them feel good about what they are doing. All of these aspects of effective leadership require emotional intelligence.

Emotional intelligence allows a principal to be a confident, trusting leader who shares responsibility, rather than an anxious, controlling one. Emotional intelligence also enables leaders to adopt a range of different leadership styles, to be democratic and consultative when such a style will be most effective, and to be more directive when that is necessary.

Emotional intelligence also helps leaders to implement many of the other implementation guidelines. For instance, to create a positive problem-solving climate, principals need to manage their own anxiety in the face of uncertainty and threat. They also need to be able to persist in the face of opposition. A good example was the principal at one of the more success-ful schools. She was undaunted by obstacles that would have made most others give up. A telling incident occurred early in her tenure as principal when she mobilized the entire community to drive out a group of drug pushers who had set up shop across the street from the school.

Another implementation guideline suggests that for the *MicroSociety* program to work well, the teachers need to be able to "let go," to allow the students to take control of their own society. But this is risky. To be able to take that risk, teachers need to work in a school where the principal is able to "let go" with the teachers, to encourage them to take the initiative. This means that the principal needs to be able to communicate to the teachers, both verbally and nonverbally, that if they fail, it will be okay. Only admin-istrators who are able to manage their own anxiety effectively can provide this sort of environment.

Yet another guideline relates to teacher empowerment, and emotional intelligence in a principal is important here as well. In one successful *MicroSociety* school, for example, several of the staff reported that when a teacher came up with a new idea, the principal almost always supported it. The principal was able to respond positively because she did not view teacher initiative as threatening. She seemed to be confident that whatever problems might ensue from such initiative, she would be able to handle them. This quality helped promote the teachers' sense of ownership for the program. It also encouraged them to experiment and take risks.

The principal is not the only source of leadership in a *MicroSociety* program. In fact, in many of the more successful schools, the principals intentionally remained in the background and encouraged the *MicroSociety* program coordinator to take the lead. As a result, the coordinator's emo-tional intelligence also was important for the program's success. For ins-tance, we have seen how the coordinators have a particularly difficult role when it comes to motivating and directing the teachers because they are peers. To perform that role effectively requires great skill and sensitivity in managing one's own emotions and those of others. A teacher at one school, in discussing the resistance that the coordinator had encountered from some of the other teachers, said, "She tried to respond patiently and calmly, but she was frustrated. She wanted to get them to buy into the idea, and they wouldn't." Unfortunately, the coordinator's difficulty in managing her own emotional reactions to resistance at this school alienated her from the rest of the staff and further undermined teacher support for the program.

At another school, however, the coordinator accepted dissent with more equanimity. In her words, she was able to be "philosophical" about it when she encountered opposition and criticism. As a result, the resistance never became as fierce at this school, and the program flourished. Emotional intelligence enables coordinators to respond more effectively to resistance, which ultimately contributes to a more positive problem-solving climate.

Whenever I encountered a coordinator who had difficulty in managing his or her emotions and relationships with other teachers, I wondered how that person came to assume the coordinator position. In some of these cases, the coordinator was self-selected. He or she was the teacher who initially discovered the program and became its first and most enthusiastic advocate. When the program was established, it seemed natural for that person to become the coordinator. In other cases, the principal chose the coordinator. When I asked the principal in one school why she had selected the coordinator, the principal said she chose the coordinator because the coordinator was "a superb teacher." While teaching ability would seem to be an important criterion, equally important are a person's emotional intelligence and the quality of his or her relations with the other staff.

Thus in selecting leaders for the *MicroSociety* program, emotional intelligence should be one of the most important considerations. Then once a person is in a leadership role, training efforts should be directed toward helping that person to develop even greater emotional and social competence.

CONCLUSION

No school will follow all the guidelines that I have presented in this and previous chapters, and school change efforts probably can flourish without some of them. However, the chances for success diminish considerably if a school neglects to follow the implementation guidelines that I have set forth. For instance, a school that lacks the capacity to generate and utilize a variety of resources for the program probably will never develop a very effective program. Similarly, if none of the individuals in leadership positions have the emotional intelligence necessary for effective stewardship, the program probably will falter.

In the next section of the book, I present three case studies that illustrate in greater depth how different schools grappled with the problems all *MicroSociety* schools encounter. These case studies show how one school created a vibrant and lasting program by following the implementation guidelines, while another failed to do so because the program's implementers ignored most of the guidelines. The outcome in the third school was mixed: Initially, the program seemed to thrive, but eventually it was discontinued. A close study of the reform process in this third school suggested that while some of the guidelines were followed, others were not, and the result was an exciting program that ultimately could not be sustained.

III

Case Studies in Implementation

7

A Successful Replication: Mesquite Elementary School

The staff at MicroSociety, Inc. (MSI), considered most of the schools I studied to be "successful." However, they regarded Mesquite Elementary School as perhaps the most successful of all. (The name of the school is fictitious, as are the names of all the individuals mentioned in this chapter.) More than one staff member at MSI referred to it as their "flagship" school.

Mesquite stands out as a success for several reasons. First, quantitative data suggest that the *MicroSociety®* program at Mesquite has had a positive impact academically. Before the staff began the *MicroSociety* program, the school's test scores were low. During the 1991–1992 academic year, the year before the school implemented the *MicroSociety* program, the students tested at the 62nd and 60th percentiles in math and reading and in the 35th percentile in writing. After 2 years of doing the program, the reading scores had gone up to the 75th percentile, and writing had gone up to the 70th percentile. After 4 years, the math scores had risen to the 92nd percentile, reading to the 83rd percentile, and writing to the 95th percentile. The scores remained high for the next 4 years, never falling below the 88th percentile.

Second, the *MicroSociety* program at Mesquite has endured. It began in the spring of 1993, and it was still going strong 10 years later. This sustainability is especially impressive given that the school board fired the superintendent who supported the program during the first 3 years of its existence and replaced him with someone who was less friendly toward the program and the school's principal. The program has survived for many years even in this inhospitable climate.

Third, the school has been able to sustain a high level of implementation for an extended period. Until the year 2001, when the school scaled back the program to 4 days a week, the program ran 5 days a week for almost the entire academic year. (At the end of the 2001 school year, the teachers voted to cut back to 4 days per week because the state extended the school day the year before, and, as a result, the teachers lost some planning time.) This fact is significant because many schools have found it difficult to sustain this level of implementation. Some schools do not start until well into the fall and then run the program only 3 days a week. In addition, the *MicroSociety* program has survived a change in the principalship and a principal who was not particularly supportive. In 2002, the original principal retired, and her replacement, an educator who was much more of a traditionalist, was much less enthusiastic about the program. However, the program was so popular in the district—and it had been so skillfully implemented—that the program survived longer than this new principal. The new principal left after only a year, and her replacement was a former assistant principal at the school who was a knowledgeable supporter of the *MicroSociety* program.

There also has been an unusually high level of teacher commitment to the program. Like other schools, the Mesquite teachers initially struggled with the problem of covering the regular curriculum when they had an hour less each day in class. Eventually, they decided that the *MicroSociety* program was so important that they would *voluntarily* work longer. They received permission from the district to add 45 minutes to the day so that they could add Micro without taking time away from other teaching. Moreover, the teachers agreed to work the extra time *without any increase in pay*.

In addition to being unusually committed to the *MicroSociety* program, the teachers at Mesquite appear to understand the true essence of the program better than do teachers at many other *MicroSociety* schools. The most important element of the program is that the school allows the students *to run their own society*. Many teachers in *MicroSociety* schools are unable or unwilling to do this. However, as I observed the application phase of the program in action at Mesquite, I noticed that the teacher presence was less prominent than in most other programs I had observed. In every venture, the students seemed to know what they were doing. One of the teachers confirmed this observation when he said, "By the spring, the kids are pretty much running things on their own."

I saw and heard of many examples of how students take the lead in this *MicroSociety*. For instance, one of the ventures, called "Technology," originally did computer cleaning, Web page design, videotaping, and digital photography. According to the teacher who facilitated this venture, they had a problem making enough money one year. "So we sat down to figure out what we might do to make more. The kids came up with the idea of taking pictures that the other kids could put on Christmas tree ornaments. That was what kept us from going bankrupt." The students saved the enterprise themselves.

Equally important, the program seems to have had a positive impact on the students' behavior. Many of the teachers, parents, and administrators spontaneously commented on this aspect. For instance, one teacher who was familiar with other schools in the district said, "This school is different from the others. You see it in the physical appearance of the building and the kids. The kids take more ownership here. They seem better behaved. They say 'Hi' to you here. Kids in other schools barely even look at you." He went on to say that the difference is primarily due to the *MicroSociety* program. "People here work together more as a result of Micro. For instance, in Micro, the older kids work with the younger ones. Teachers work with kids from different classes and grades. The kids see *all* adults as authorities because they work with several different adults in Micro." The assistant principal, who had worked in several other schools in the district before coming to Mesquite, mentioned that her niece, who attended the school, had been "obstinate and aggressive" in the past but this changed when she began to participate in the *MicroSociety* program.

What was especially impressive about the Mesquite *MicroSociety* program is its impact on the rest of the school day. In at least some instances, it actually has led to a change in the teacher-student relationship and the "behavioral regularities" of the classroom. Jane Thomas, a sixth-grade teacher who has been at the school since the mid-1980s, said that she was a "pretty traditional teacher" before the *MicroSociety* program was introduced to the school. She described her role as a "commander-in-chief," which meant that she made all the decisions. However, because of her participation in the program, she has come to see her role as more of a "facilitator." Jane said that at first, the change in her role was restricted to the application period, "But then the children started taking more initiative in class. I tried initially to remain traditional in the classroom, but I felt a tension in being different ways in Micro and in class." Eventually, she adopted the same kind of facilitative role in the classroom that she used during the application period. For instance, she begins each day by asking the children, "What do you need to do today?" When they respond, she then asks, "What do you need in order to accomplish that?"

Classroom observations suggested that many of the other teachers also seem to have embraced more of a facilitator role in their teaching. In a sixth-grade class, students were busy working on different projects on their own or in small groups. The teacher pointed out the class "menu" through which the students are given a choice of activities to work on for that period. The students had asked for this menu arrangement themselves. This class seemed to be a good example of the student's independence and critical thinking that many adults at the school thought had resulted from participation in the *MicroSociety* program.

Thus it seems reasonable to conclude that the *MicroSociety* program at Mesquite is relatively successful. What was it in the way the school implemented the program that contributed to such a successful outcome?

BEFORE-THE-BEGINNING: PROVIDING A FAVORABLE CONTEXT

Some of the most important ingredients for success were in place even before anyone had thought about bringing the *MicroSociety* program to the school. (See Table 7.1 for a summary of the factors in the "before-the-beginning" stage that contributed to the program's success at Mesquite.) On the surface, Mesquite does not seem very different from other urban schools serving a socially and economically disadvantaged population. Built around 1960, the school is located in a large city in the southwestern region of the United States. Almost all of the 580 students are from disadvantaged backgrounds: 89% are in the free or reduced lunch program. Ninety-four percent of the students are Latino, with 3% African American and 3% Anglo.

Table 7.1   Factors in the "Before-the-Beginning" Period That Contributed to the *MicroSociety*® Program's Success at Mesquite School

- Stable neighborhood
- History of stability and high morale in school's leadership and staff
- History of parent involvement in the school
- Zeitgeist favored child-centered innovation
- Local superintendent favored innovation and created mechanism to encourage it
- New principal had a mandate to bring about change
- Program seemed to meet a specific need and priority of the school

However, not all poor urban areas are alike. Although Mesquite is located in a relatively poor neighborhood, it has been a stable neighborhood. Most of the dwellings are homes owned by the occupants, and many of the families have been living there for several decades. The parents of many of the children who attend the school lived in the neighborhood when they were children and went to the school themselves. The grandparents still live there, and the children often go home to their grandparents' houses after school.

The school itself also has had a long history of stability. Between 1960 and 1990, there had been only two principals. Many of the teachers also had been at the school for several years. In addition, morale reportedly was high. In fact, teachers in the area regarded Mesquite as one of the best places to teach. According to one veteran staff member, a teacher who wanted to teach at the school "had to know someone" in order to secure a position there, assuming there was an opening.

The school also had a history of parent involvement prior to the introduction of the *MicroSociety* program. As noted above, many of the parents had gone to the school themselves as children, and their parents, the grandparents of the current students, still lived in the neighborhood and often had the time and interest to participate in school activities. The previous principal had capitalized on this interest by developing an active program for parents. By 1990, the parents had become so much a part of the school that when they were not involved in the selection of a new principal, they protested loudly. This history of parent involvement was important, for it eventually would provide a strong base of support for the *MicroSociety* program.

Changes occurring at the national, state, and local levels also contributed to a favorable context for implementation. Nationally, the "restructuring" movement was popular in education around 1990. It provided the impetus for local control and teacher participation, as well as innovation. Another important part of the zeitgeist when the program began was a renewed interest in engaging students and making learning interesting. For example, many schools at that time were eliminating basal readers and going to "whole language" and "literature-based reading" programs.

Changes on the state and local levels also favored innovation. The state commissioner of education had been calling for educational reform for some time. Then the local school board instituted site-based management, which allowed individual schools much more autonomy. This autonomy gave each school considerable control over its own spending, which made it easier for a school to implement new practices. The school board also hired a new superintendent who was described by one informant as "pro-child and a visionary." He provided a strong impetus for innovation in the form of a $3 million grant program. He invited the schools in the district to apply for the money and said, "Be as creative as you can be." There was no cap on what an individual school could receive.

However, not everything in the before-the-beginning context was favorable for the creation of a *MicroSociety* program at Mesquite. Many teachers in the school, as well as the previous principal, were not receptive to reform. One teacher said that until 1990, well-informed people regarded the school as a "good, *traditional* school." When the previous principal retired in 1990, after serving for 20 years in the position, the new principal brought with her a mandate for change. Although the new principal proceeded slowly and cautiously, she nevertheless encountered stiff resistance to any kind of change. When the district's Title 1 coordinator visited the school in the middle of that first year, she reportedly said that she did not think the school would change much because the teachers were "so set in their ways."

Nevertheless, the new principal, with the support of the superintendent and the state, was beginning to introduce changes. During her first 2 years at the school, she was able to implement Levin's "Accelerated Schools" philosophy (Levin, 1987). Also, as some of the veterans left, due to retirement or distaste for the changes they saw coming, the principal hired new teachers who were more open to change and shared her more progressive educational philosophy.

Although the school did not have a tradition of child-centered approaches to education, there was an aspect of the culture that did favor the establishment of a *MicroSociety* program. The parents and teachers had long valued exposing the children to a wider world than the barrio in which they lived. The assistant principal was especially keen about providing the school's disadvantaged students with experiences that more privileged children enjoyed. As a result, the staff devoted considerable time and energy to planning field trips for the children each year. When the teachers first discovered the *MicroSociety* program, they saw it as serving the same function: It helped children to "make connections to the real world." Thus while Mesquite was not particularly receptive to change in general, the *MicroSociety* program seemed to meet an important, specific need identified by both teachers and parents, and this contributed to an environment that was compatible with the *MicroSociety* concept.

INTRODUCING THE PROGRAM TO THE SCHOOL

The way in which the *MicroSociety* program was introduced to the school also helped make it a success. Table 7.2 summarizes the positive aspects in the way the program was introduced that helped it become successful.

One of the most important factors involved the role of teachers in initiating the program. In all the schools I studied, the principals allowed the

Table 7.2   Introducing the Program to the School: Factors That Contributed to Successful Implementation at Mesquite

---

- Idea originated with teachers, not principal
- Teachers had meaningful voice in adoption decision
- Principal supported program once adopted by teachers and assisted its development
- There were ample time and resources for planning and staff development before the program began
- Several teachers visited more than one existing program and attended the national summer training conference before the program became operational
- Staff reached out to inform, interest, and involve the parents before the program began
- Teachers who were supportive of the program and also respected by peers were chosen for the management team
- School acquired extensive assistance from a committed consultant with expertise in business and economics
- Teachers conducted a brief and limited but realistic "trial run," followed by a period of further planning and retooling

---

teachers to vote on whether the school would adopt the *MicroSociety* program. However, at Mesquite, the teachers played a greater role in the introduction of the program than they did at any other school. The principal was supportive, but the idea did not originate with her. It originated with a group composed mainly of teachers.

The superintendent set the stage when he established the grants program to encourage innovation. The principal went to the teachers and suggested that they form groups to develop proposals. Several groups formed and began to work on various ideas. One group, which consisted of the reading and writing teachers and the assistant principal, began to meet after school to discuss various options. During one meeting, they began to talk about all of the field trips that the parents helped organize for the children, and one of them said, "Wouldn't it be great if we could develop something here at the school that would serve the same educational purpose as these field trips?" At that point, another group member remembered seeing an article in *Time Magazine* about the *MicroSociety* program. The group became intrigued, and they tracked down the article and read it. The more they learned about the concept, the more excited they became about it. They decided to make the *MicroSociety* program the focus of their proposal, and they took it to the principal.

The principal also found the concept appealing. However, the school had recently adopted the Accelerated Schools philosophy, and part of that approach required that every teacher approve the idea before implementation. When the group presented their proposal to the rest of the faculty, there was much discussion. The other teachers asked probing questions. After a lengthy consideration of what the program would involve, the vote was positive.

Thus the *MicroSociety* program, though supported by the principal, did not *come from* the principal. It came from a group of two teachers and the assistant principal, and the principal did not become a strong advocate for the program until the rest of the teachers approved it. Even then, the principal's role was secondary. A group of teachers, with the support of the assistant principal, continued to be the driving force for the effort. The superintendent and principal set the stage for the innovation; they did not introduce it or take the lead at any point.

The central office liked the proposal that the school submitted. In fact, they awarded $197,000 for it, which was more money than any other school in the district received. Much of the money went into building a special structure on the school grounds for the *MicroSociety* marketplace. However, there also was a considerable amount of money available for planning time and staff development prior to starting the program.

Erecting a special building to house the *MicroSociety* marketplace has proven to be an especially wise decision on the part of the program's leadership. Very few schools erect such a structure for the program, and it is not necessary for the establishment of an exciting and viable *MicroSociety* program. However, the planning team at Mesquite believed that investing a large amount of money in a physical structure designed specifically for the *MicroSociety* program would help sustain the program. Central office personnel at the time tried to get the planning team to eliminate the building from the design, but they stood their ground. In retrospect, the program coordinator believes that the building has been one of the most important forces for sustainability.

The principal continued to play a relatively minor role as the program took shape. However, she supported the effort in subtle but important ways. For example, the plan called for a "management team" to oversee development and direction of the program. The principal knew the staff, and she knew what kinds of teachers would be most useful as members of the team. Therefore she helped the new coordinator and her partner to select teachers who would be supportive of the program but who also had the respect of veterans who were more traditional.

It took almost a full year for the new building to be constructed. Although the complications and delays in the building process were frustrating, they may have been a blessing in disguise because they provided the management team ample time to study and plan. During the months that they were waiting to get started, the management committee had time to "talk a lot and visit different places," in the words of one of the charter members. One of those places they visited was the original *MicroSociety* school in Massachusetts. The principal took a group that included the *Micro-Society* program coordinator, two classroom teachers, the parent coordinator, and a fifth-grade student. However, the Lowell school was not the only *MicroSociety* program that they visited. Staff members from the school also were able to visit other *MicroSociety* programs at schools located in nearby states. In addition, in July of 1993, the principal, the Micro coordinator, and the strand leaders attended the first annual *MicroSociety* program training conference.

These visits to other *MicroSociety* schools and to the summer conference proved to be important once the program became operational. One of the veterans recalled that when they encountered difficulties during the first year or two of full implementation, what kept many of the teachers from giving up was "all the research on other Micro schools" they had done before starting. It convinced them that the *MicroSociety* program could work and that the impact on students could be very positive.

The extended planning period also gave the leadership team time to broaden the base of support for the program. In addition to gaining support from the teachers, the principal and coordinator generated interest in the parents and students. One way they did so was to include the coordinator of the parent program in the Massachusetts trip so that she could see what a *MicroSociety* program looked like. They also arranged for the parent coordinator to take along her daughter, a fifth grader at the school. The student took a video camera with her. When they returned, she went around to all the classrooms and made a presentation on the program, illustrating her points with the video. (The student presentations helped demonstrate the central role that students would play in the new program.)

The principal and parent coordinator also increased parent support by sending out a survey to all the parents in order to seek their input and identify how the program might meet some of their own needs. In addition, the principal sent out newsletters and invited the parents to attend informational meetings at the school. These efforts, along with sending the parent coordinator to Massachusetts, helped gain the support of the entire community for the program.

As the management team reached out for help in the local community, one of the most fateful events involved the local Junior Achievement organization. After one meeting with the head of the local Junior Achievement, it became clear to him that the school needed more help than he could provide through his organization. Fortunately, he knew of a former manager at a large corporation who had recently left the company to start his own management-consulting firm. Originally trained as an engineer, Ronald Olivas had moved into marketing after a few years. Eventually, he worked his way up into a management position. Altogether, he had spent 18 years in the corporate world.

When the president of Junior Achievement asked Ronald whether he would be willing to help Mesquite, Ronald agreed with enthusiasm. According to Ronald, he became "enamored with the Micro concept" as soon as he heard about it. He also grew up in a nearby neighborhood and saw this as a way to "give back" to his community. He believed that he could use the management tools he had learned in the corporate world to help the staff at Mesquite develop an effective *MicroSociety* program. He arranged to spend 2 weeks during the coming summer working with the management team.

Rather than begin with a full-scale implementation of the program, the staff decided to start with just two of the six strands. As part of this initial experience with this program, they organized a "constitutional convention," which led to the adoption of the *MicroSociety*'s constitution before the program became fully operational. They also began with what was in effect a time-limited pilot because the construction workers did not complete the new building until the late spring of 1994. This gave the staff only about 6 weeks to do a full-scale application phase of the program. Although they had not planned to begin with a pilot run, the delays in construction made it happen naturally. The staff also decided to scale back the initial pilot run by limiting it to just the fifth and sixth grades.

Those first 6 weeks of Micro turned out to be a difficult but rich learning experience. The teachers became aware that creating a *MicroSociety* program was an even more complex undertaking than they had anticipated and that they had much to learn. The management team eagerly looked forward to retooling the program during the summer.

After the pilot experience, the management team was especially eager to learn whatever they could from Ronald during the summer, and he was eager to teach them. According to one of the team members, those 2 weeks were intense: "It was like a mini-MBA." During that time, Ronald pushed the teachers to develop a "5-year master plan" for the program. Several staff members, including the principal and program coordinator, also went to the national training conference again that summer. By the time fall came, the management team was ready to try again. They began the year with confidence and enthusiasm.

The way in which the *MicroSociety* program began at Mesquite thus helped establish the program on a sound foundation. The idea originally came not from the principal, but from a group of teachers. The principal supported the program, but only after all the teachers had a chance to learn about the idea and agreed to do it together. There were ample resources and time set aside for planning and staff development prior to starting, and it was particularly fortuitous that the school secured the help of a

Table 7.3   Managing the Program: Factors Contributing to Successful
Implementation

- Stable, cohesive, and active management team
- Committed, energetic, and interpersonally sensitive coordinator
- Knowledgeable and committed external consultant who devotes several
  days to the program each year
- Meaningful participation of teachers in decision making
- Additional planning time and staff development for several years after the
  program began
  - Planning time, training, and team building for students as well as
    teachers

- Effective resource development and utilization
  - Creative scheduling and staffing to make best use of teachers as
    resources
  - High level of parent involvement in program and effective utilization
    of parents as resources
  - Extensive use of community partners

- Strong and skillful support of the principal
- A positive organizational climate
- Principal's skill in managing her own emotions and the emotions of others

---

consultant who knew how to run a business venture and felt a special
commitment to the local community. The school started the program on a
limited basis and then conducted a brief pilot run of the full-scale version.
Then the management team spent much of the next 3 months making
changes based on what they learned from it. Meanwhile, the principal and
program coordinator worked to secure strong support from the parents
and community partners, such as Junior Achievement.

MAKING IT WORK: THE MANAGEMENT
TEAM, COORDINATOR, AND CONSULTANT

Once the program became operational, several other factors contributed to
its success. These success factors are summarized in Table 7.3.

One of the more important factors is the management subsystem.
Throughout the first 10 years of the program's history, there has been
a committed, energetic, and interpersonally sensitive coordinator; a stable,
cohesive management team; and a knowledgeable external consultant who
contributes considerable amounts of time to the program every year.

The Management Team

Along with the program coordinator, the management team at Mesquite plays an active role in providing leadership for the program, and the team seems to function particularly well. One reason is stability: The team consists of five teachers, three of whom are charter members and still on the team 10 years after the program began. (Originally, all the team members were teachers, but one of the charter members eventually left the classroom to become the school librarian. She remained on the team after making the change.) A fourth teacher joined the team after the first year and has remained ever since. (The team keeps one position open for a teacher who serves a year and then rotates off so that another teacher can serve.)

The management team developed into a strong and cohesive group during the year prior to the launching of the *MicroSociety* program. They met for 2 hours every week during that year, and they traveled together to visit different programs. One of the members felt that spending so much time together helped them work together more effectively once the program began.

Another factor that adds to the team's strength and credibility is its diversity in viewpoints. The first three members of the team were all strong advocates of the *MicroSociety* program. However, after the first year, the principal and coordinator asked one of the more skeptical teachers to join the team. She was a strong and respected voice among the more traditional teachers, and the principal and coordinator believed that adding her to the management team would provide a valuable perspective. It was a risk because the skeptical teacher could have become a divisive and disruptive element on the team. However, adding this teacher seems to have worked well. She has continued to be a critical voice, but she also reportedly is one of the hardest workers and strongest advocates for the program. Her presence on the team may reduce internal harmony to some extent, but it also helps to solidify support for the program among the rest of the staff.

The management team helps sustain the program by providing much logistical support for the other teachers. During the summer, the team pulls together all the material for the different ventures so that the teacher facilitators do not have the burden of this task when they return in the fall. This material includes the training material for each venture and all the forms for the Internal Revenue Service (IRS), bank, court, and so on. In many other programs, the coordinator does all of this work alone, or it falls on the teachers, adding still further to their burdens.

The management team at Mesquite also facilitates a venture. This unusual practice came about because some teachers reportedly complained that the management team "didn't know what it was like to run a company."

The management team responded by starting a company, which they now facilitate along with their other responsibilities. Thus in a number of ways, the management team has provided sure and effective leadership for the *MicroSociety* program at Mesquite.

The *MicroSociety* Program Coordinator

The coordinator plays a crucial role in any *MicroSociety* program, and at Mesquite, she has been an important factor in the program's success. Maria Gonzales was part of the group that wrote the original grant proposal, and she has been one of the program's strongest advocates in the school. Since the beginning, she has helped establish and sustain the program in numerous ways. According to one of her coworkers, Maria's commitment has been especially important. He described her as "a real bulldog." He went on to say, "You really need someone with that kind of persistence and attention to detail." Although her commitment to the program is obvious to everyone, people described Maria as "nonthreatening." In addition, her energy level is "nothing short of amazing." These personal qualities have been critical for the program's success.

Maria recognized from the beginning that it would be crucial for the program to have an active cadre of community partners. Therefore she made the development of such partnerships a major part of her role. This decision proved to be particularly critical when the first principal left after several years and a new principal who was much less supportive took over. Maria mobilized an influential group of community partners from the local business community, and they convinced the superintendent that the program was too vital to be scrapped.

The External Consultant

One of the most unique and important aspects of the Mesquite program has been the continuing contribution of the external consultant. Ronald Olivas helped the management team get started during the first summer, and he has continued to be involved with the program ever since. He has helped the program in a number of ways.

First, he has provided basic knowledge about business and management. Second, he has given the teachers "a lot of validation," as one of them put it. He also has helped the management team and coordinator to maintain a sense of perspective. For instance, he helped them cope with resistance from some teachers by getting them to "see teachers as part of the customer set rather than just get frustrated by their resistance."

The external consultant has been particularly helpful with the ongoing evaluation of the program. After the first year or two, he suggested that the management team survey the teachers, students, parents, and community partners every spring in order to identify problems and areas for improvement. Ronald takes the surveys, analyzes the data, and then meets with the management team during the summer to go over the surveys and use them to plan improvements. According to one team member, Ronald helps them to focus on things in the surveys that "we don't see ourselves when we look at the data."

The consultant, along with the program coordinator, also has helped the program develop connections with community partners. For instance, he has arranged for business people from the community to come in each year and review the students' business plans. He also arranged for the local chamber of commerce to have one of their meetings at the school, which resulted in more community partnerships.

Ronald also has encouraged the staff to move in new directions that they would not necessarily choose on their own. As the principal put it, "He has continually challenged the group to raise the bar." For instance, Ronald was the one who suggested to the teachers that they teach the students how to develop business plans. He also pushed the school to sponsor one of the national *MicroSociety* training conferences that occur each summer, which greatly enhanced its visibility and prestige. More recently, he has encouraged the management team to give more thought to the issue of sustainability.

Ronald's success as a consultant to the program was due in part to his background and training in corporate management. However, his personal qualities were just as important. He had not only grown up in a nearby neighborhood but also understood that as a businessperson, he was very much an outsider in the culture of the school. At one point, he commented that when he first began working with the staff, many of the teachers were thinking, "What are we getting ourselves into?" He said that he learned that "you need to put things in educator terms" when working with the teachers.

MAINTAINING TEACHER COMMITMENT THROUGH DECISION MAKING, PLANNING, AND TRAINING

Although the management team, coordinator, and external consultant play important roles in directing Mesquite's *MicroSociety* program, teachers also play a significant role. In fact, the entire teaching staff must approve all important decisions. For instance, when some of the teachers complained that they did not have enough preparation time and wanted the application period to go from 5 days a week to 4, the issue went to a staff meeting, where the entire staff considered it. After much discussion, some of which was quite passionate, the teachers approved the change, and it went into effect, even though the management team and coordinator opposed it.

Giving the teachers such a significant role in decision making has increased their commitment to the program. For instance, at the end of the first year of operation, the teachers felt especially burdened. After considering a number of options, the staff and principal agreed to deal with the problem by dismissing the children an hour earlier in order to give the teachers more time to plan. However, after trying this for a year, the teachers found that this did not give them enough instructional time, so the next year, they decided on a different solution: They would extend the school day for the older students. Because they had been so involved in the problem-solving process and felt that this solution was *their* solution, they were willing to put in the extra time without any extra pay.

Another factor that contributes to teacher commitment is the amount of planning time and staff development that they have to devote to the *MicroSociety* program. The continuing availability of planning time and staff development was especially important during the first few years of operation because the teachers quickly discovered that the program is a more complex undertaking than they had imagined. In fact, despite all of the planning and outside help they received prior to starting, the teachers still found it difficult to implement the program. One teacher said, "When we began to implement Micro, I just couldn't get it. It was very overwhelming at the beginning." Another teacher said, "There was lots of griping and complaining at first from people who didn't understand how Micro worked" (Grote, 2002). Only after additional planning time, staff development, and trial-and-error learning did the teachers gradually begin to understand the intricacies of the program and the best ways to implement it.

Mesquite has sent several teachers to the national conference every year, and after 9 years, about half of them have attended. The principal expects the teachers to present while they are at the conference, and then when they come back in the fall, they share what they learned from other teachers. There also is a staff development session devoted to the *MicroSociety* program after school one day each month. In addition, the management team set aside 2 days in the summer of 2001 to meet with the rest of the teachers in order to "reflect on the Micro program." Any teacher who wanted to participate could receive compensation for doing so.

Mesquite also has given considerable thought and effort to training for students. Rather than just throw them into the application phase of the *MicroSociety* program without any training, the Mesquite program sets aside 8 weeks at the beginning of the year for the students to learn their new jobs. They use some of this time for "team building" as students in each venture get to know each other and develop into a well-functioning team. The students also develop business plans and go to the bank to secure loans for their businesses during this start-up period. The new student presidents and CEOs receive training through a "leadership academy," and all of the student leaders, along with the teacher facilitators, attend monthly meetings during the remainder of the year. According to one teacher, these training meetings encourage the student presidents to take more responsibility, and as a result, the teachers are less likely to feel that they have to "do it all."

Adequate time for planning and training is especially important for the successful implementation of school reform models such as the *MicroSociety* program. Mesquite is unusual among *MicroSociety* schools in providing teachers and students with so much time for planning and staff development once the program became operational.

SEEKING OUT AND USING RESOURCES

The way in which the staff has utilized various resources within the school and the larger community also has contributed to the success of the Mesquite *MicroSociety* program. One common problem that many *MicroSociety* programs face is that the teachers feel stretched to the limits as they try to oversee 20 to 30 students in a complex venture. This strain invariably undermines teacher commitment to the program.

To address this problem, Mesquite has modified its daily schedule. As at other schools, the application phase at Mesquite takes place at the end of the day, from 2:45 until 3:30. The younger students (Grades K–3) earn Micro money in their own classrooms and then have an opportunity to spend it in the schoolwide *MicroSociety* marketplace twice a month. If they are not scheduled to go to the marketplace, they are dismissed at 2:45. The early dismissal of the K–3 students means that all of the K–3 teachers are available to help in the application phase along with the other teachers. This arrangement enables the school to almost double the teacher-student ratio during Micro time. As a result, the ventures are relatively small (12 to 15 students), and each one has at least two facilitators. The consequence is that teachers experience less strain and feel a greater sense of efficacy.

The *MicroSociety* program at Mesquite also has effectively utilized parents as resources. Once the parent coordinator and her daughter visited the original schoolwide *MicroSociety* program at Lowell, the parent coordinator became a strong advocate for the program, and she developed a number of mechanisms for involving the parents.

For instance, a group of parents known as "Micro Moms" work in the ventures and agencies and receive "wages" in Micro money. To make it easier for the Micro Moms to work in Micro after school, the parent coordinator began another program called "Mini Micro," which provides a scaled-down version of the program for younger students (K–3), who would not normally remain at school for the extra hour when the application phase of the program occurred. The Mini Micro made it possible for parents with younger children to participate in Micro with their older children.

The Micro Moms are not the only parents who participate in the program. Because the application phase begins just as most of the younger children are dismissed for the day, it is relatively easy for their parents or grandparents, who usually come to pick them up at school, to remain another 45 minutes while their children go to the marketplace to spend their Micro money. Many of the parents even join their children. According to the parent coordinator, the parents are encouraged to do this, and they enjoy it. "It is like going shopping together."

The parent coordinator's personal qualities play an important role in securing a high level of parent involvement. She displays great insight and sensitivity in the way she goes about working with the parents. For instance, during our interview, the parent coordinator said, "Parents don't like to come if there's nothing for them to do. So I spend a lot of time making sure that they have something to do. Also, you need to make sure they're appreciated."

Parent involvement and support for the program eventually became an important political asset. The superintendent was a strong supporter of the *MicroSociety* program when it began, but after 3 years, the school board fired him. The new superintendent and board were much less supportive of the program. However, by that time the parents were solidly behind the program. Their support provided political protection for the program and helped prevent the board and superintendent from discontinuing it.

The leadership at Mesquite, especially the program coordinator, also has shown great ingenuity and initiative in the way they have worked with community partners in the *MicroSociety* program. For instance, when the school first established the IRS, they arranged for an agent who worked for the federal IRS to show the teacher facilitators how to set up a viable tax collection service. The local police department has been even more involved. One of their officers comes to the school almost every week during the year to help train the *MicroSociety*'s crimestoppers. The local bank not only provided training and guidance in the beginning but also prints the checkbooks and money used in the program free of charge. In addition, other community partners provide money for food when there is a special celebration. But perhaps most important was the quiet influence that some of the more prominent community partners brought to bear when a new principal took over. Their political support for the program helped to sustain it during a difficult transitional period.

Thus the staff at Mesquite seems to be especially adept at creatively seeking out and tapping resources within the community, and this is another factor that contributes to the program's success there.

A SUPPORTIVE PRINCIPAL
AND ORGANIZATIONAL CLIMATE

During the *MicroSociety* program's first decade of existence, there was just one principal at Mesquite. And although she tried to remain in the background so that the teachers perceived the *MicroSociety* program as *their* program, she made a significant contribution to the program's success through her continuing support for it. The program coordinator, who had become familiar with many other *MicroSociety* programs around the country, said that the strength of the first principal's support for the program at Mesquite "sets it apart" from other programs. Many other informants agreed that the principal, Teresa Lopez, was a crucial factor in the program's success.

However, the principal always insisted that others take the lead. As she put it, "I initially saw my role as encourager, cheerleader, and gatekeeper. Now I am merely a supporter." The program coordinator confirmed that the principal gave her "a lot of autonomy." During the first 4 years of the program, the principal's role was especially limited because the assistant principal provided more active support for the program within the school. In fact, the principal played such a limited role that the program coordinator said she "hardly knew the principal" during that initial period.

Nevertheless, the principal's support for the program and the organizational climate she created within the school were vital components in the program's success. One way that the principal supported the program was through her vigorous advocacy on its behalf. For instance, once the teachers voted to adopt the program, the principal put all of her authority behind it. It became one of the few "nonnegotiables" at the school. Even when the school district began to put more emphasis on testing and there was pressure to abandon the program in order to spend more time preparing the students for the tests, Teresa, in the words of one teacher, "held her ground." In fact, at the end of the first year, when the students' achievement test results dropped, Teresa went to the superintendent and argued strongly for giving the program at least 3 years before looking at the scores. She pointed out to him that "the literature shows that test scores always drop initially whenever a change is instituted."

Teresa also aided the program by helping to create a positive, supportive climate at the school. As one teacher said, "The administration is supportive, helpful, and positive. If you want something, they try to get it for you. If you make a mistake, they are positive about it. They say, 'That's okay. It's a learning experience.'" In this school, teachers seem to get along particularly well, and relations between teachers and parents are positive as well. As one person noted, there is a sense that "we're a team." Teresa played a significant role in creating such a climate.

In addition to helping create a general tone of supportiveness and a sense of community within the school, Teresa was particularly receptive to teacher input. In fact, she actively encouraged it. At one point, she declared, "I want the teachers to be the decision makers, not me." According to the teachers, she succeeded. One teacher said, "If we have ideas, the administration sits and listens." Another teacher said that when the teachers decided that they needed to reduce the application phase from 5 days to 4 days a week in order to have more time for planning, the principal said, "You've got it," even though the principal did not necessarily agree with the decision.

Although Teresa valued teacher involvement in decision making, she did not adopt a laissez-faire leadership style. At one point, she said, "I've always worked with the staff to be reflective about the decisions that they make. They need to take ownership of these decisions. But they also need to make decisions thoughtfully, based on what is best for the kids." She went on to say, "I try to hold teachers accountable for the expectations they set for themselves."

Teresa also established clear expectations and limits. I have already noted that once the teachers voted to adopt the *MicroSociety* program, it became a "nonnegotiable." During my visit to the school, I heard the term "nonnegotiable" used several times by teachers and administrators as they discussed various aspects of the school. It suggested that Teresa managed to be clear about limits and expectations.

The teachers also reported that Teresa pushed them to achieve. It began when the teachers were hired. When Teresa interviewed candidates for teaching positions at Mesquite, they were "told up front that they will be working longer and harder than other schools in the district" (Grote, 2002, pp. 155–156). Teresa also said to them, "If you're not willing to make the personal commitment, don't take the job." Teachers confirmed that Teresa and her assistant principal had "very high expectations for teachers" and that "they do push you."

Even though Teresa held the teachers to high standards and expected more of them than did many other principals in the district, the teachers did not complain. One said that the high standards were all right because Teresa "gives us what we need" to achieve them. In addition, a number of high-quality teachers in the district wanted to teach at Mesquite during Teresa's tenure but could not do so because turnover was so low.

Teresa also has contributed to a positive organizational climate through her ability to articulate a vision that motivated and inspired the staff. Although Teresa often tried to let others take the lead, she made it clear what her values and beliefs were, and she inspired others with her words and actions. The assistant principal said that Teresa "constantly verbalizes her commitments and vision." At the same time, Teresa was aware of how others were responding and was careful not to push too much. As one informant put it, "Teresa brings a nice balance of maturity and perspective. For instance, she will ask, 'Are we moving too fast?'"

Another reason that the *MicroSociety* program at Mesquite has flourished is that the staff has been continuously committed to their own learning. Moreover, this commitment is not restricted just to the *MicroSociety* program. It is part of the school's culture, and Teresa, as principal, had much to do with making it so. At one point, Teresa said, "For kids to be excited about learning and being in school, teachers need to feel that way." While Teresa was principal at Mesquite, the teachers had 4 regular staff development days each year. In addition, the teachers said that any time they wanted a day off to attend a staff development program on their own, Teresa would support it.

One important way in which the school culture at Mesquite promotes learning at all levels concerns the way the staff views problems and conflicts. At the very beginning of our first interview, the program coordinator said, "The most critical thing in running Micro is the way you deal with problems." Later, the assistant principal observed that Mesquite is different from other schools at which she has worked in that "conflict is viewed as positive. People are encouraged to disagree as long as they do so respectfully." Conflict is tolerated, even encouraged, because it provides a way of identifying and resolving problems that might be undermining the educational mission of the school.

Part of the positive problem-solving climate at Mesquite involves a tolerance for risk taking and failure. One teacher, a member of the Micro management team, said, "In order for teachers to be able to give kids more control, they have to be able to take risks." She then said that for teachers to be able to do that, "Administrators have to provide the environment for it. They have to say, 'If you fail, it's ok.'" According to this teacher and others with whom I spoke, Teresa as principal succeeded in conveying that message to the teachers. She encouraged everyone to "think outside the box."

The strong, positive leadership provided by Teresa was especially impressive because her own superiors were always supportive. She did have a supportive superintendent for the first few years of her tenure at the school, but then a more conservative board fired him and replaced him with an unsupportive individual. The next several years were difficult ones for Teresa. Nevertheless, she continued to support the *MicroSociety* program and other progressive innovations, while maintaining a positive organizational climate for teachers, parents, and students. What enabled her to do this?

THE PRINCIPAL'S SOCIAL CAPITAL AND EMOTIONAL INTELLIGENCE

One reason that Teresa was able to maintain continuous support for the program and a positive climate in the school was her long history in the system. She had been born and raised in the community, and she had always lived there. She taught in the district for 19 years before becoming an administrator. This long history of involvement provided her with the knowledge and connections that she was able to use to sustain her school during difficult times. She had acquired powerful friends and a reputation for being honest, committed, and effective. This kind of "social capital" is useful for the principal of any school.

Equally important were Teresa's personal qualities, particularly a set of competencies that relate to "emotional intelligence," or the ability to manage one's emotions and those of others. The principal's emotional intelligence was especially important in the way she managed the emotional turbulence that accompanied the implementation process.

For example, when Teresa came to the school, most of the staff had taught there for several years, and her predecessor, who had been the principal there for 20 years, had hired them. According to one teacher who was there at the time, "Some of those teachers initially gave her hell." What was telling about this transitional time was the way in which Teresa handled the resistant teachers—and her own emotions.

In response to the staff's initial resistance, Teresa moved slowly and remained positive. As one veteran who witnessed the process commented, "Teresa came in with ideas about change, but she was careful, slow, and deliberate about how she went about it. She just talked to teachers during that first year. The only change she made on her own was to have the school painted."

The teachers were not the only source of resistance when Teresa became the principal. The parents also were suspicious, in part because they had played no role in her selection. The powerful parent coordinator even tried to resign in protest the first year. Nevertheless, Teresa soothed her and got her to agree to stay on. Eventually, the parent coordinator became one of Teresa's strongest supporters.

The principal has demonstrated her resilience more recently as the school has had to deal with the new emphasis on standards and testing. Even though the new emphasis is at odds with the more progressive approach that the school has adopted, the principal has stayed the course. With her unflagging support, the staff has not abandoned the innovative practices they adopted over the previous 10 years. Instead, they have managed to help their students perform well on the standard tests and have adequately complied with the new mandates, while continuing much as before.

Another aspect of Teresa's emotional intelligence that has played an important role in her effectiveness is her awareness of how her own feelings and actions create a tone for the whole school. At one point, she said that she always tries to be "upbeat and positive when she walks into the school" because she knows how that will affect others.

Another personal quality that has helped the principal respond so effectively to resistance is her optimistic outlook. She said that she dealt with recalcitrant teachers by reminding herself, "If I want the teachers to believe that all children can learn, I have to model this by acting as though all teachers can learn." Another informant confirmed that Teresa had enormous "faith in every teacher. She always finds positive qualities in them."

Thus during the first decade of the *MicroSociety* program's existence, the principal at Mesquite used a number of social and emotional competencies to create an organizational culture that was particularly supportive for the *MicroSociety* program. The "emotional intelligence" of the school's principal was an especially important factor in the program's success at Mesquite.

CONCLUSION

In this chapter, I have shown how several factors were important for the successful implementation of the *MicroSociety* program at Mesquite Elementary School. First, there was a long history of stability within the school, with little turnover among teachers or principals. Stability also characterized the neighborhood in which the school was located. All of this stability contributed to high morale among the teachers. There also was a history of parent involvement. In addition, the state and the local district superintendent also provided autonomy and incentives for implementing new programs. Finally, the strong value placed on student field trips made the *MicroSociety* program appear to be a good fit with an important aspect of the school's culture.

Second, the school introduced the program in a way that minimized resistance. The idea originally came from teachers, not the principal, which enhanced teacher buy-in. The principal insisted that all the teachers have an opportunity to learn about the program and discuss it before they voted on whether to adopt it. Moreover, the initial expectations and time perspective were realistic: The principal was prepared to wait for at least 3 years before seeing any positive impact on the school. In addition, there was adequate time set aside initially for planning: After almost a year of study and planning, there was a 6-week pilot run, followed by a summer of retooling.

Once the school had established the program, other factors contributed to its success. The program benefited from a stable and effective management team, an energetic and skillful coordinator, and a knowledgeable external consultant who provided ongoing training, guidance, and support. The principal and the first assistant principal consistently provided resources that gave the management group time for planning and problem solving. There also was considerable time set aside for staff development for all the teachers. More than half of the teachers attended at least one of the annual summer training conferences. In addition, students and their parents played meaningful roles in the program, and the school invested considerable time and effort into developing many active community partners.

Finally, an "emotionally intelligent" principal and program coordinator provided a high degree of support. In the case of the principal, this support was provided directly, through her advocacy and logistical support, and indirectly, by creating a school culture that encouraged innovation, risk taking, commitment, and reflection.

8

Wellfleet Elementary School: Everything That Can Go Wrong . . .

It often is difficult to clearly assign "success" or "failure" to a particular school's efforts to implement the *MicroSociety*® program. Most schools fall somewhere on a continuum. In fact, a given school may be more successful in one aspect of implementation and less successful in others. However, in the last chapter, we saw a school that stood out as successful in most respects. And in this chapter, we consider a school that represents the opposite. In almost no way could Wellfleet Elementary School's *Micro-Society* program be considered a successful implementation. After a little more than 3 difficult, conflictual years, in which teachers and students struggled to figure out how to make the program work, the principal finally discontinued it. Although Wellfleet represents a failure in implementation, it provides a valuable learning experience for those who would like to be more successful in implementing school change.

THE SCHOOL AND ITS HISTORY WITH THE PROGRAM

Wellfleet was an old K–8 elementary school located in a poor, deteriorating section of a large midwestern city. There were 550 students and

42 teachers at the school. The student population was 85% black, 13% Latino, Asian, and other minority groups, and 2% white when the *MicroSociety* program was implemented. The teaching staff was about 50% minority. Although many of the children came from chaotic family situations and teachers complained about discipline, the school was clean and orderly.

The principal, a white male, came to the school as principal in 1987, 5 years before they adopted the *MicroSociety* program. He had taught in several schools in the district during the previous 15 years. There had been site-based management at the school since 1989, and the mayor had just taken over the school system after years of conflict over the poor perfor-mance of the schools.

Wellfleet was viewed as a problem school within a problem district. In fact, it had been designated a "remediation school" a year or two before it adopted the *MicroSociety* program because of poor student performance on standardized achievement tests. Only 6% of the students tested at or above grade level in reading when the school implemented the program.

The principal and staff began to discuss the *MicroSociety* program dur-ing the 1991–1992 school year, and the faculty and school council voted to adopt the program near the end of that year. They tried the program on a small scale during the summer session of 1992. In the fall of 1992, they began it on a regular basis with the upper grades (4–8). The lower grades (1–3) were not added until the spring of 1995. (The lower-grades program was classroom based, with each class doing a venture picked by the teacher.)

The program was discontinued at the end of the fall 1995 term. Accord-ing to the principal, he ended the program because student test scores did not go up after an initial rise during the first year and few teachers "ever got the spark." The first coordinator of the program agreed, saying that the biggest problem was "lack of acceptance by the teachers." The principal conducted a survey of the teachers before terminating the program, and he stated that the results showed that they were "overwhelmingly against" the program.

One reason that so many teachers opposed the program was the additional amount of work that it represented for them. A first-grade teacher, for example, complained about all of the paperwork associated with the program—payroll forms, tax forms, attendance forms—and said that she spent "as much time planning for that 1 hour as for the rest of the day."

Although most teachers seemed to experience a significant increase in their workload as a result of implementing the program, there was some evidence that a few did not. The coordinator said that while some teachers spent the whole summer planning for the program, others "spent only a day." One of the resource teachers on the coordinating committee complained that one teacher in his strand sometimes would not even show up for her venture. The principal thought that many of the teachers saw the *MicroSociety* program as an opportunity for "a free period," rather than another thing to teach. He said, "Some teachers worked hard, but others saw it as a chance to relax. They didn't realize they were supposed to still teach."

Another problem that teachers mentioned was that they could not see how to tie the program into the regular curriculum. One of the teachers, a supporter of the program, said that it was easy to link Micro with math and reading in some jobs but it was difficult to do so with others. For instance, students who did piecework in the manufacturing venture had little opportunity to use math or reading skills. This teacher believed that the linking problem was a major source of teacher resistance to the program. If the teachers had been more able to link the program to the curriculum, they would have seen it as part of the curriculum and part of the day, rather than another add-on.

Student behavior also was a significant problem associated with the *MicroSociety* program at Wellfleet. In fact, Wellfleet was the only school I studied in which student behavior was a significant problem. In the more successful programs, student discipline problems greatly diminished during the application period as the students became engrossed in their ventures and policed themselves through their own law enforcement agency and court system. But at Wellfleet, some students used the application period as an opportunity to act out. One of the aides said, "The students would go to court when they did something wrong, but it wouldn't matter to them, even though they'd get fined. If they lost money at court, they'd win it back gambling. It was like playtime for them. Even the Micro police got out of control." Even if students stayed out of trouble, they often did not participate in a meaningful way. According to one teacher, too many students saw the program as just "free time" and used the application period to "goof off."

As the teachers became more frustrated with the problems they encountered, conflict and resistance among the staff escalated. The staff became increasingly polarized between those who supported the program and those who opposed it. And as the conflict increased, those who opposed the program began to withhold their support. The science resource teacher, a supporter of the program, complained that "some teachers didn't hold up their end." For instance, the teachers were supposed to teach the students certain skills that they needed in the *MicroSociety* program, such as how to write a check. However, few of the teachers did so. Some teachers did not even show up for their ventures. The coordinator complained that many of the teachers "argued" with her and "refused to listen."

Even though the Wellfleet *MicroSociety* program ultimately failed, there were some bright spots. A teacher who was glad the program had been eliminated conceded that some students who were attendance problems began to show up at school more often. Also, there were some good ventures that taught students useful skills, such as the sewing and construction businesses. Student behavior was less of a problem in these ventures. In one such venture, the teacher said that even a special education student with a diagnosis of "behavior disorder" did fine. And one of the teachers who complained loudly about student discipline admitted that it was not a problem in his venture during the first 2 years. He believed there were no problems then because he was working with a teacher who was "very good" and made the venture (a business that made and sold banners, posters, and cards) interesting and successful.

Although most teachers apparently wanted to end the program, a few were more enthusiastic about it. One teacher commented that many of the students really enjoyed participating in the program and that it was important to have students enjoy being in school. This same teacher also thought that she saw big gains in self-esteem in some students and that the program had a positive impact on her relations with the students. As a result of the *MicroSociety* program, those relationships had become "more low-key, friendly, like we are in this together."

Despite these positive aspects, the problems mounted over time, and the program seemed to spin out of control. As a result, the management team spent more and more time trying to "fix" things. By the last year, they were meeting two or three times per week just to deal with all the problems.

WHAT WENT WRONG? THE BEFORE-THE-BEGINNING PHASE

The *MicroSociety* program at Wellfleet failed in part because the school did not provide particularly fertile soil for an innovation like *MicroSociety*. The factors in the "before-the-beginning" phase that contributed to the program's demise are summarized in Table 8.1.

One of the biggest problems was the relationship between the principal and the staff. Although most of the staff I interviewed were circumspect, several did suggest that the principal was not particularly liked or respected. I became aware of the staff's lack of respect for the principal early on, when I called the school and asked to speak to him in order to arrange my visit. It was about 2:45 p.m., and the person who answered the phone said, "He's not here. He's never here after 2:30." The tone of disapproval in the person's voice was clear. Another teacher talked about how

Table 8.1   Factors in the Before-the-Beginning Phase That Contributed to the Failure of the *MicroSociety*® Program at Wellfleet Elementary School

- Conflict and lack of respect between principal and staff and among the staff
- Program did not seem particularly compatible with any of the school's previous emphases or current needs
- School was on probation for previous record of failure, which created a high degree of anxiety and impatience
- No history of strong parent involvement or community partnerships at the school

poor leadership and lack of support from the administration had long plagued the school.

Relations among the staff also did not seem to be particularly strong or positive prior to introduction of the *MicroSociety* program. Although I heard few complaints about staff relations, there was no indication that relations among the faculty were particularly warm or that there was a strong sense of community within the staff. The dominant theme in discussions of faculty relations was divisiveness rather than harmony.

In addition, I found no evidence that the *MicroSociety* program built on what the school had been doing previously. In fact, the program was selected precisely because it was seen as something radically different from what they had been doing. There also had not been any previous history of community partnerships at the school. And there was no indication that there had been much parent involvement in the school (outside of the school-based management team mandated by the district). Parent and community involvement just did not seem to have been a priority of the principal or staff prior to introduction of the *MicroSociety* program.

Many staff did not believe that the *MicroSociety* program addressed the school's most pressing needs. In fact, they saw it as interfering with what the school most needed to do. Because the school had already been designated a "remediation school," the teachers felt great pressure to teach the skills that the students needed to perform better on the tests. (The students' test scores were published in the newspaper every year for all to see.) Most staff did not see the program as addressing this need—at least not in a very direct way. Thus they felt it took time away from the "really important" work of preparing the students for the next round of tests. The fact that the school day was already rather short (9:00 a.m. to 2:30 p.m.) contributed to the teachers' sense of urgency and impatience with the program.

Table 8.2   Introducing the Program to the School: Factors That Contributed to the Failure at Wellfleet

- Idea for the program came from the principal, who tried to "sell it" to the staff
- Teachers knew little about the program when asked to vote on adoption
- Only the upper-grade teachers were given the opportunity to vote on adoption
- Initially, teachers were assigned to *MicroSociety* ventures rather than having a choice or being encouraged to develop ventures that were particularly appealing to them
- Teachers had no training prior to implementation, and there was only 1 day of planning time
- Expectations that the program would lead to rapid, sustained increases in achievement test scores were unrealistic

Other, more successful schools that I studied eventually felt a similar conflict between spending time on the *MicroSociety* program and spending time "on the tests." However, at Wellfleet, the pressure to have students perform well on tests was much more intense and existed to a much higher degree even before the program was introduced. Thus in a number of ways, the climate at Wellfleet was not conducive to the creation of an innovative educational reform such as the *MicroSociety* program.

SOWING THE SEEDS OF TROUBLE: INTRODUCING THE PROGRAM TO THE SCHOOL

Even though Wellfleet did not provide a very receptive environment, the *MicroSociety* program might have succeeded if it had been introduced to the school in ways that encouraged commitment and support on the part of teachers and parents. Unfortunately, the program's introduction to the school further increased resistance. The factors associated with its introduction that most contributed to failure are summarized in Table 8.2.

Generating teacher ownership for school change is crucial, and much depends on the way in which it is introduced to the school. At Wellfleet, the teachers played a more limited role in the adoption of the program than was the case in most of the other schools I studied. Although the teachers ultimately were given the opportunity to vote on whether to participate, and most voted in favor of adopting the program, the way in which it was introduced to them made many teachers feel that the *MicroSociety* program was really "the principal's program."

At Wellfleet, it was the principal who first presented the *MicroSociety* program to the staff and urged them to adopt it. The principal initially learned about the *MicroSociety* program at a meeting in the summer of 1991. He brought the idea to his faculty that September and reportedly said to them, "We're doing it by the book and failing. We need to do it by another book—George Richmond's book." He then distributed copies of the book to all the teachers and asked them to read it. During the next few months, the principal and assistant principal visited two existing programs at schools in other states, but no teachers visited a *MicroSociety* program before they were asked to vote on whether to adopt the program.

Thus when it came time for the teachers to vote, most saw the program as the principal's pet project. According to the assistant principal, "The principal imposed it on the teachers. He said, 'This is what we're going to do.'" A teacher concurred: "There didn't seem to be anything done to get commitment. It was a top-down issue for some people." Another teacher acknowledged that the teachers had been allowed to vote on whether to adopt the program but that, in her words, they "really didn't know anything about it" when they voted.

Initially, only the upper grades were involved in the program. When the school implemented the program in the lower grades, the teachers had even less say about it. A first-grade teacher reported that when she was hired, she was told that the program was just for the upper grades and that she would "not have to do it." The next year, she and the rest of the primary teachers were required to implement it.

The teachers' sense of ownership for the program was further diluted in the way they were assigned to ventures and agencies. Initially, the teachers had no choice about the venture to which they were assigned. After the first year, a few teachers were allowed some choice but many continued to be assigned to ventures. One teacher worked in three different ventures over the course of the program, and he had no voice in choosing any of them.

In addition to the lack of meaningful teacher involvement in the adoption process, the program suffered from a lack of adequate planning and staff development prior to full implementation of the program. As a result, the initial experience was chaotic. As one teacher put it, "We were trying to figure out how to do it while the kids were watching us!" There was virtually no training for the teachers prior to implementation of the program. The only preparation the teachers had was reading George Richmond's book. No teacher visited another school that had adopted the program. Only the principal and coordinator had observed a live *MicroSociety* program, and neither of them did much to share their knowledge with the other teachers. One teacher said, "It was all kind of vague when it was introduced to us. We were given the money but not told what to do."

There also was very little time set aside for planning prior to implementation of the program. According to a teacher who served on the management team, the team met together in a local restaurant for just one day to plan the program before launching it. The school did conduct a pilot run, but it proved to be of limited value because they did it during the summer session, which was a relatively small and unstructured program that combined recreation and remedial academics. Only 3 out of 40 teachers participated in the summer program. When the program was implemented for the rest of the school in the fall, the summer program experience proved of limited value in providing direction.

One final problem with the introduction of the program to the school was the staff's unrealistic expectations. The school adopted the program in large part to raise student test score performance. Apparently, the principal expected that the program would lead to a rapid rise in test scores, and initially it seemed to be doing so. After the first year, the scores leveled off, and there was no further improvement after the second or third year. At that point, the principal became disillusioned with the program and decided to terminate it. He replaced it with a commercial program designed to teach students test-taking skills.

In summary, the way in which the program was introduced contributed to its demise. Teachers played a minor role in the decision to adopt the program. They were not even allowed to choose their own ventures initially. There also was little time spent on planning or staff development before the teachers had to implement the program. Also, the initial goals and time perspective were unrealistic. Even if the faculty had been more committed, it is unlikely that the principal's goals of large increases in student test scores within 2 or 3 years could have been met.

BECOMING OPERATIONAL: TRYING TO COPE WITH CHAOS

Once the program was up and running, the teachers began to encounter a variety of challenges. In this respect, the Wellfleet experience was no different from any other school. However, at Wellfleet, the structures and processes that were created for dealing with those challenges became another source of difficulty. The factors that impeded development of the program once it became operational are summarized in Table 8.3.

The first factor that impeded effective implementation involved decision making. The school created an elaborate structure that was complex, hierarchical, and ineffective. The teachers were organized into strands, and each strand had a strand leader. If a teacher had a problem or issue that

Table 8.3   Factors That Contributed to the Program's Demise at Wellfleet
Once It Became Operational

- A cumbersome, top-down decision-making structure
- Most teachers on the management team were not committed to the program and did not have a high degree of credibility among the other teachers
- Teachers were unable to learn from colleagues who were more knowledgeable about the program
- Turnover and inconsistency in the coordinator position
- Coordinator felt she did not know enough to be helpful to other teachers
- Ineffective utilization of resources
- Little involvement by parents or community partners
- Teachers did not effectively utilize students as resources
- Widespread, dysfunctional conflict and low morale impeded organizational learning and problem solving
- Ineffective leadership and lack of support from the principal

needed to be resolved, it usually would be discussed first in a strand meeting. However, the strands had no authority to make even the smallest decisions. So the strand leader inevitably would have to take the issue to the "board of directors."

The special teachers (science, fine arts, library, and gym) along with the coordinator comprised the board of directors. The directors were not chosen based on personal qualities, knowledge of the program, or even interest in the program. They became the management team for the program because they had an extra planning period, which they all shared. Only one of the four directors was at all enthusiastic about the program, according to one of the teachers. Without enthusiasm at that level, it was hard to get it at other levels.

Although the board of directors in theory was the decision-making body for the program, in practice, they too had little power to make decisions. Almost all decisions had to be reviewed and approved by the principal. However, the principal never met with the board. As a result, the coordinator was constantly taking issues from the board to the principal and back again. Communication thus was always delayed and indirect. And the principal eventually vetoed many of the board's suggestions and requests.

The board was particularly frustrated over the issue of money. They repeatedly asked the principal how much money there was for the program, and he would say, "It's hard to say." He finally told them that each strand could have $600.

The coordinator often felt caught between the principal and board of directors. The board of directors, similarly, felt caught between the teachers and the principal. The teachers were particularly frustrated. They experienced this arrangement as hierarchical and disempowering. One of them complained that "all the important decisions were made by the board of directors" rather than by the students or faculty. He rightly pointed out that this was inconsistent with the *MicroSociety* concept.

As the teachers became more frustrated with the board's apparent intransigence, the board's influence further diminished. It became increasingly difficult for the board of directors to get the teachers to listen when the board came up with what they thought were helpful ideas.

Although the school did little in the way of staff development before the program began, once it became operational, some staff development did occur. During the first year, a principal from an established *MicroSociety* school came and did a daylong inservice with the teachers. At the end of the second year, some business people came in and taught the teachers how to price items properly. In addition, the strand leaders went to the summer conference after the first year of operation, and eight more teachers went the next year.

Thus after 2 years of operation, there was considerable expertise within the faculty. Fourteen teachers had attended the summer conference. The principal had attended the conference several times and was viewed by MicroSociety, Inc. (MSI), staff as someone who really understood what the program was "all about."

Unfortunately, the school did not seem able to make use of this growing expertise. The principal believed that the teachers who attended the conference "got the spark," but "it didn't rub off." A teacher agreed that those who attended the summer conference returned "very excited," but then they became discouraged after a couple of months. And the teachers who did not attend the summer conference were not able to get the guidance they needed from those who did. As one of the teachers put it, "We could have asked them questions when they returned from the conference, but for some reason that didn't work out." She went on to say that even though some of her colleagues had considerable knowledge and expertise, she did not go to any of them for help. In addition, although time was set aside during staff development days for the teachers to raise questions, she and many of her colleagues "didn't know what to ask."

The coordinators also seemed unable to help the teachers learn what they needed in order to implement the program effectively. (There were two different coordinators during the program's brief existence. The first one resigned after the first year because she became the school's assistant principal. Another teacher then took on the role.) Although the coordinators had attended the summer conference, they did not feel that they learned what was most important for establishing the program. One of the coordinators said that she was hampered because she did not have any business background. She wished that she had been given more of that.

Thus even though the school invested in staff development once the program became operational, many of the teachers in the program continued to struggle as they tried to figure out on their own what they were supposed to be doing. As one teacher lamented, "I never could get a handle on basic time management and organizational problems, because I had no guidelines." Many of the other teachers made similar comments. Much of the time they felt lost and overwhelmed.

Resources were another problem. Actually, Wellfleet's *MicroSociety* program seemed relatively rich in resources compared to many others. The real problem seemed to be the way in which those resources were utilized. It was never clear how much money was available for the *MicroSociety* program, but the school did have a large federal grant that provided considerable sums of money each year for the program. The school also was able to secure other kinds of resources. The coordinator indicated that the principal was "good at digging up money," and an aide said that she and the principal had gone around to "a lot of big companies" and had received "lots of donations for the store."

Nevertheless, the program seemed to be resource starved much of the time. Virtually all of the money set aside for supplies was used up early in the year. Teachers complained that they had to use their own money to purchase supplies for their ventures. Much of the federal grant money went into salaries for the coordinator and aides, but not all of their time was available for the *MicroSociety* program because the principal used them for other administrative tasks as well.

The school did make use of nonprofessional personnel. The lunchroom staff, the janitor, the security person, and the school-community person all participated. However, even with these extra staff working in the program, the ventures seemed to have too many students and too few staff. One teacher said that initially he had 40 students in his venture.

The teachers also received little help from outside the school. There was less parent involvement in this *MicroSociety* program than in some of the more successful programs. Also, the school did not have a very active group of community partners. One teacher said that they initially had "some contact with local businesses" but the businesses "seemed to lose interest." She was not sure why.

The most important human resource in any *MicroSociety* program is the students themselves, and Wellfleet struggled more than most to utilize its students effectively. Many teachers reported that they had trouble finding enough meaningful work for the students to do. A first-grade teacher who put out the paper said that out of 25 students, only 8 really worked on the paper.

There was some indication that over time, a few teachers learned how to use students more effectively as resources. A teacher who developed a successful sewing business told how she put responsibility for solving problems on the students, which was one of the most important factors in making the venture work so well. Another teacher who initially was overwhelmed said that the program went better the second year because she found a third grader who could help her with the forms and other administrative tasks. Unfortunately, these examples were the exception rather than the rule. Most teachers struggled largely on their own, perpetuating the traditional teacher-student relationship in their *MicroSociety* agencies and ventures.

The *MicroSociety* program at Wellfleet thus demonstrates that a school with some of the ingredients necessary for success may fail if it cannot use those ingredients effectively. There was a principal who believed in the program and was knowledgeable about it. Also, many staff attended the summer conference, and there seemed to be relatively ample resources. However, the school was unable to effectively utilize the information and resources that were available, because of weak leadership and a negative organizational climate.

THE ORGANIZATIONAL CONTEXT: WEAK LEADERSHIP AND A NEGATIVE CLIMATE

The way in which the staff dealt with problems was both a cause and symptom of a highly dysfunctional organization that lacked the capacity for effective organizational learning and problem solving. When the staff came together to discuss problems and make decisions, the meetings often would become "bitch sessions" with "nothing positive coming out of them." When there were disagreements among the staff, they were not settled. They would be debated for a while and then the issue would be dropped.

The situation seems to have worsened over time. One teacher said that there began to be "a lot dissension" by the end of the first year. Then the staff became divided and polarized into two camps: those who liked the program and those who did not. At that point, people would just complain at strand meetings. The coordinating committee members could not get people to listen to ideas. One of the coordinators complained that the staff "just argued and refused to listen." Eventually, the whole planning structure broke down. Some teachers would not even attend the strand meetings.

Some of the directors even missed board of directors meetings. Finally, the primary teachers just stopped attending meetings and stopped doing the application phase, saying they did not want to do it anymore.

Leadership often plays a significant role in shaping an organization's climate, and that seemed to be the case at Wellfleet. Many of the problems encountered in implementing the program ultimately could be traced to the nature of leadership in the program and in the school generally.

The problem was not lack of support on the part of the principal. The principal was in favor of the program initially. In fact, he was the one who brought it to the school and convinced the teachers to adopt it. However, he did not provide the program and the teachers with the *kind* of support that they needed to make it a success.

Strong, involved leadership at the top is not absolutely necessary for success. Support, guidance, and direction can come from other sources, such as the coordinator or even respected and influential teachers. But when the principal is the one who initiates the program, the principal needs to provide more of the inspiration and direction necessary for effective implementation, at least initially. Especially during the first year or two, when the workload is so heavy and the teachers are experiencing as much failure as success, they need firm and supportive leadership to keep them going. Such leadership was missing at Wellfleet.

The principal's lack of support was apparent on the most basic levels. He rarely walked around to observe during the application phase, and he did not attend board of director meetings. The teachers came to resent this lack of involvement. According to one of the teachers, "The principal wanted the teachers to do everything themselves. He wanted the program to be up and running, but he was always too busy to become involved himself. Even when the teachers asked him to get involved with the elections or the marketplace, he refused."

One of the coordinators told a story that illustrated the principal's lack of engagement. When some students stole a large amount of money from the bank, the staff was upset and unsure about how to handle it. The coordinator went to the principal to ask him what he thought they should do about it, and "he just laughed. He thought the whole thing was just a joke."

The principal hurt the program not only by failing to provide enough advice, guidance, and encouragement. He also hurt it by not using his authority to deal with problems. One of the teachers said that she felt that she did not have a boss, that she could do anything she wanted, and that there were no consequences for doing a good or bad job. Rather than finding this liberating, she experienced it as neglect and became increasingly unmotivated.

The principal was aware that some teachers were not fulfilling their obligations. The board of directors reported to him that few teachers were teaching their students skills they needed to function effectively in the *Micro-Society* program, and he himself complained that some of the teachers did not realize they were "still supposed to be teaching during Micro time." But the principal refused to intervene. The coordinator complained that if she had problems with a teacher and went to the principal for help, he would say, "Oh, just talk to her in a nice way." He would never discuss the situation directly with the teacher. He did not put his authority behind implementation of the program. This lack of firm leadership fueled the divisiveness among the faculty and increased teacher resistance to the program.

The principal was aware of the staff's criticism that he was not involved and supportive enough. In his own defense, he said, "My job was not to run Micro. That was the coordinator's job." However, there were several problems with relying on the coordinator for all of the necessary support and direction. First, the coordinator was a peer of the teachers. She did not have the formal authority that the principal had, and there was no way he could delegate it to her. This put her in a difficult position. Without strong support and backing from the principal, her position became even more difficult.

Second, the first coordinator became the vice principal after the first year of the program, and another staff member took over the coordinator position. Thus during its relatively brief existence, the program had two different coordinators. This lack of consistency further weakened the coordinator's ability to function effectively.

Another problem was that the second person who took on the coordinator role lacked some of the competencies necessary for the role. Several teachers said that the second coordinator might have known much about the program but had a hard time communicating it. When she tried to tell the staff what she wanted, she often became "lost and confused." As one teacher put it, "She's the kind of person who can't get her point across. Then she gets upset with people if they don't understand it the first time."

When I talked to the second coordinator, she said that she had "tried to intervene" but that there were just too many problems. She became overwhelmed. A teacher displayed considerable empathy when she said, "The coordinator felt everyone was yelling at her. The teachers didn't have solutions to problems. They wanted her to know what to do. But she didn't seem to know herself."

Part of the problem with the second coordinator's lack of leadership ability may have been related to the way in which the position was filled. The second coordinator was one of four people who applied for the job when it opened up. According to one teacher (a supporter of the program who was generally sympathetic toward the coordinator), the coordinator was selected for the job because of "who she was" rather than because of ability.

In addition to lacking some key leadership competencies, the second coordinator was hampered by the sheer amount of work she had to do. A teacher commented that "lots of jobs were thrown on the coordinator" and that the *MicroSociety* program seemed to be low in priority. For instance, shortly after she became coordinator of the program, the principal gave her responsibility for implementing a major new initiative imposed by the central office. At that point, the stress became almost unbearable. The coordinator said, "It was horrible. I thought between my other responsibilities and Micro, I'd drop dead from stress, and teachers would quit."

The principal contributed to the program's demise in a less direct way as well. He seemed to lack some of the critical social and emotional competencies necessary for leading a troubled urban school, and this lack contributed to the dysfunctional organizational climate that made implementation so difficult.

One problem with the principal's performance was that he was so disorganized. Many staff mentioned this problem in interviews, and I observed it directly when I first met with the principal. I discovered that the principal had lost the material I had sent him prior to my visit, and he had no idea why I was there. He then joked about the mess in his office. (He had a very large table in the middle of his large office; and the table, along with every other surface, including much of the floor, was covered with stacks of paper in disarray.) During our interview, he spent an inordinate amount of time talking about all sorts of unrelated topics; it was extremely difficult to keep him on task.

In addition to his lack of organization, the principal suggested in his comments and behavior that he was not particularly engaged in his job. I never saw him out of the office the whole time I was at the school, even at the end of the school day. He acknowledged that he could "not take things too seriously." He also made asides such as, "I would have liked a job at that other school because it's just one story and they have air conditioning." Referring to another principal in the system, he said, "She got smart, she retired." Then he launched into a long discourse on how principals are not paid enough.

Although the principal's dominant style was "laissez-faire," at times he would act in arbitrary authoritarian ways. For instance, he terminated the *MicroSociety* program without any discussion or warning: He merely sent a memo to the staff stating, "This will be the last week of the Micro program. We will no longer have it after this week."

Thus a major factor in the *MicroSociety* program's demise at Wellfleet seemed to be the principal's leadership. He failed to provide the kind of active support that the teachers needed in order to implement the program effectively. Part of his approach seems to have been dictated by a conception of leadership that emphasizes autonomy for teachers, while minimizing the importance of support for them. But part of the principal's lack of engagement seemed to be a more general, lackadaisical approach to his work. Effective leadership, especially in a large urban school dealing with the sorts of problems that Wellfleet faced, requires considerable dedication on the part of the principal. To provide the teachers with the kind of support they need to succeed—whether it is in the *MicroSociety* program or any other aspect of the school—principals must be committed. They must work hard and spend many hours on the job. This principal clearly was not willing to do so. He preferred to spend his time sitting in his disorganized office talking with whoever was around to listen. And when school ended at 2:30, he usually was "out of there."

Although it is easy in this case to blame much of the failure on the principal, I think that to some extent, the principal's inadequacies were symptomatic of the stress that he encountered in this highly dysfunctional system. As I listened to him talk about himself and his school, I had the feeling that he was struggling to cope with overwhelming stress and anxiety—his own as well as his staff's. He seemed to see himself as the captain of a sinking ship who had done everything he could to save himself and his crew and who had reached the conclusion that the situation was hopeless. His erratic behavior in part represented his way of dealing with those feelings. His cynicism and gallows humor seemed to function as a psychological defense mechanism.

As noted above, the school had been designated a "remediation school." The principal was not clear how much time he had to turn the situation around, and he did not receive much help from the central office in doing so. But he knew that unless he succeeded in turning the situation around soon, the school would be closed.

The pressure on the principal increased further when the mayor took over the school system. The new administration emphasized accountability and performance standards even more. Then the central office announced that all schools in the district had to develop two performance-based assessment tests for each educational goal set by the state.

Dealing with such a demanding situation requires a high degree of emotional intelligence. To be effective, a principal must be able to manage his or her own emotional reactions as well as those of the staff. With greater emotional and social competence, the principal at Wellfleet may have been able to create a more positive organizational climate, and the implementation of the program would have been more successful.

However, the principal's lack of emotional intelligence was only one of several problems that ultimately led to the demise of the *MicroSociety* program at Wellfleet. The history of this failed attempt to implement the program illustrates how important it is for those who embrace the *MicroSociety* concept to be skilled in managing change. Wellfleet provides a vivid example of what can happen when a school ignores many of the guidelines that are important for effective implementation.

9

The Challenge of Sustainability: Montgomery Middle School

Initially, the *MicroSociety®* program at Montgomery Middle School looked like a great success. The teachers implemented the program in the fall of 1994, and within a short period of time, there was a dramatic improvement in the school climate. Daily student attendance rates went from 75% to more than 95%. Suspensions decreased from 444 to 3 per year. Vandalism also declined: There had been 20 to 30 windows broken the year before the program began, but by the second year of its existence, there were only 3 broken windows.

There also was evidence that the *MicroSociety* program was helping the teachers to teach traditional subjects better. For instance, one teacher said, "Sixth graders had a hard time understanding South American revolutions until they connected it with their experiences in Micro." Teachers and staff also came to know each other better and to appreciate each other more. There was less concern about territoriality. For the first time in many years, teachers requested to come to Montgomery Middle to teach.

The program at Montgomery Middle became a showcase for the entire movement. The national office viewed it as one of the great successes because of its innovative businesses and practices. The First Lady of the United States even paid it a visit. At its peak, the *MicroSociety* program at Montgomery Middle included more than 150 businesses.

However, the program ultimately could not be sustained. The *MicroSociety* program continued at Montgomery for 7 years, but in 2000, a new principal decided to end it after conducting a survey of the staff. A closer examination of the school and the way in which it implemented the program suggests some of the factors that contributed to its eventual demise.

THE SCHOOL AND ITS COMMUNITY

Montgomery Middle School is more than 100 years old. About a third of the students are from minority groups, and 71% are on free or reduced lunch. Almost 30% are classified for special education. The school is located in a small midwestern city (population 75,000), which is highly segregated by race and social class. There are four middle schools, two located in poor, ethnically diverse neighborhoods and two located in more affluent, white neighborhoods. Montgomery Middle School is located in one of the poor neighborhoods. In 1990, the county led the state in a variety of negative social indicators, such as teenage pregnancy, juvenile crime, and substance abuse. Montgomery Middle's neighborhood contributed more than its share to these statistics.

The school is located in two buildings. The main building, an old brick structure, houses 600 students, including all of Grades 7 and 8. Due to overcrowding, half of the sixth graders (130 students) were moved to an annex, about 3 miles away, 2 years before the *MicroSociety* program was adopted. At the time the *MicroSociety* program was introduced to the school, most of the 72 teachers were "traditional" in their teaching philosophies and practices.

In the late 1980s, the state began putting pressure on the district to reduce concentrations of minority students in certain schools. The district resisted this pressure until the state threatened to take them to court. Even then, the district managed to avoid actually changing the composition of the schools. Instead, they agreed to set aside about $250,000 per year to support school-based initiatives that encouraged greater mixing of students along socioeconomic status (SES) and racial lines.

However, the community continued to be highly polarized around issues relating to desegregation. For instance, in the late 1980s, a small

Table 9.1   Factors in the "Before-the-Beginning" Phase That Affected the Implementation of the *MicroSociety*® Program at Montgomery Middle School

---

- Positive factors:
  - A new principal had been appointed with a mandate to innovate
  - Desegregation funding provided additional resources for implementing a new program
  - Recent adoption of site-based management helped build capacity in the staff and provided a supportive structure
  - The new program helped address a pressing problem (segregation) in the school and district

- Negative factors:
  - Deep-seated conflicts and factions among the staff
  - History of weak leadership with high turnover
  - High turnover within staff
  - History of conflict in larger community over desegregation policies

group of teachers and administrators received authorization and funding from the school board to develop a plan for magnet schools. But the plan never was implemented. A well-organized faction in the community fought successfully against it because they saw magnet schools as a threat to "neighborhood schools."

Like many schools serving a large, disadvantaged population, Montgomery Middle had gone through difficult times prior to adoption of the *MicroSociety* program. Teacher and administrator turnover had been high. Principals came and went every 2 years or so. Student achievement, attendance, and vandalism all had been problems.

In this crisis-like climate, relations among teachers were mixed. To some extent, the teachers felt they had to band together just to survive, and they did so. However, there were deep divisions within the faculty that went back many years. As one of the teachers put it, "The faculty was very cliquey." The divisions had become sharper in the early 1980s when the district shifted from a junior high to middle school model and the sixth-grade teachers were transferred from the elementary schools to the middle school. There continued to be strong splits between the "subject-oriented" teachers who tended to be found in the seventh and eighth grades and the "child-oriented" teachers, who were concentrated in the sixth grade.

However, in 1993, things began to change for the better at Montgomery Middle. Dr. Bill Nelson became the new principal, with a mandate to bring about change. The superintendent and school board did not particularly care how he did it, as long as the situation improved.

In some ways, the appointment of a new principal with a mandate for change was not surprising. Even though the district is located in a conservative midwestern community, it had a reputation for being innovative. A few years before the new principal was appointed, the district had adopted site-based management as a philosophy, and a number of staff, including the new principal, had been trained as part of this initiative. The school board and central office hoped that this decentralization would encourage individual schools to try innovative approaches to education, and some had done so. It appeared that now Montgomery Middle would as well.

In sum, the "prehistory" of the *MicroSociety* program at Montgomery Middle was mixed. On one hand, a new principal with a mandate to innovate provided the kind of climate that fosters adoption of a new educational practice such as the *MicroSociety* concept. Also, the desegregation problem resulted in money becoming available for an innovation that might make the school more of a magnet for middle-class students in the district. On the other hand, the deep-seated conflicts among the staff, along with a history of weak and changing leadership, would prove to be a liability when it came to sustaining a viable *MicroSociety* program. (The factors in the "before-the-beginning" phase that most influenced the program's subsequent development are summarized in Table 9.1.)

INTRODUCING THE PROGRAM TO THE SCHOOL: THE PRINCIPAL TAKES THE LEAD

The new principal at Montgomery Middle started the process of adopting the *MicroSociety* program. During his first year at the school, he heard about the *MicroSociety* program from the then-assistant principal. The principal later said that the idea appealed to him because it seemed to fit with many of his priorities: establishing a true middle school concept based on grade-level teams, promoting cooperative learning strategies, and adopting mainstreaming and inclusion for special education students. The concept also fit with his educational beliefs. At one point he said, "In order to change kids' behavior, you need to empower them." The *MicroSociety* program also appealed to the principal because of his earlier career experiences: Before he went into education, he had received a degree in economics and then worked for a finance company. This experience showed him that "many people cannot handle finances responsibly." When he became a teacher, he created a business in his class for the students to run. For many reasons, then, the principal was intrigued with the *MicroSociety* program when he first heard about it.

Although the program looked good on paper, the principal wanted more information. He arranged for himself and two of his staff to visit an

established *MicroSociety* school. One of the staff members was a guidance
counselor. The other was Janet Duncan, a teacher with more than 20 years
of experience and a reputation for being dedicated and innovative. The
three of them visited the original *MicroSociety* school in Lowell. Janet was
especially impressed. When they returned, they described what they saw
to the rest of the faculty.

As was the case in many other schools that adopted the program, the
teachers were given the opportunity to vote on whether they would participate, but not right away. In addition to the presentation from those
who visited Lowell, the teachers saw a video on the program. There also
were some informal discussions. Then a few months passed. Finally, the
teachers participated in a workshop on "resistance to change." At the end
of the workshop, the principal asked them to vote on whether they wanted
to go ahead and adopt the *MicroSociety* program. All but one teacher voted
to go along with the program.

Although the teachers did vote to adopt the program, several of those
I interviewed 3 years later said that they really were not sold on the program when they voted. They went along because they felt that "it was
coming anyway" and they wanted to appear supportive. Janet Duncan
had assumed the leadership role at that point, and many of the teachers
liked and respected her. Their vote for the program was more a vote of
support for her than for the *MicroSociety* program. Some teachers still
had misgivings, and many others believed that they had not had enough
information about the program to make a really informed decision. They
believed that had they known then what they later knew about the program, the vote would have been different.

Once the teachers voted to adopt the program, there was relatively
little planning or staff development prior to full implementation. The vote
occurred late in the school year. When summer came, 10 teachers assembled to write an initial "curriculum" for the program. Two of the teachers
assumed leadership within the group. One was Janet Duncan. The other
was Mary Pierce, who, like Janet, was an experienced and respected
teacher with a reputation for being child oriented. Both Janet and Mary
attended the national summer conference that year, and they used what
they learned there to write the curriculum. However, they felt that none of
the programs they had studied was a suitable model, because all had been
elementary schools.

The teachers spent about a week writing the curriculum, which was
meant to teach both the students and teachers about the program in the
fall. The faculty did teach the curriculum during the early fall, and then
they started the program around Thanksgiving. At that point, no other
teachers had attended a summer conference or observed a *MicroSociety*
program in another school. There also was no pilot run. The entire school

began the program after Thanksgiving and continued with it until nearly the end of the school year in May.

Even though the teachers had voted to adopt the program, many felt little sense of ownership for it. Unfortunately, the way in which the teachers initially were assigned to ventures did little to increase their sense of commitment. At Wellfleet, the teachers had had little choice about which ventures they would oversee, and their interests were often ignored in the assignment process. (See Chapter 8.) At Montgomery Middle, there was more consultation, but many teachers still ended up in ventures that were not personally interesting or meaningful to them. Initially, Mary Pierce, who became the coordinator of the program, gave teachers an interest questionnaire to fill out. In some instances, Mary also would consult with the teachers. She then assigned teachers to activity areas based on their responses. (She continued to use this procedure in each of the subsequent 2 years.)

The success of this matching procedure was mixed. The teachers who were more committed and interested in the program gave the process some thought. If they were unhappy with their initial assignments, they sought out Mary and discussed alternatives. Consequently, the matches tended to be good ones. But in other cases, the teachers had a more passive attitude that prevented good matches from being made. Several of the teachers I interviewed suggested that they were not very invested in the program, but they wanted to be supportive to a colleague whom they liked and respected. And so they went along with whatever they were given. These matches tended to be less than ideal, and that fact tended to make these lukewarm teachers even less enthusiastic about the program.

Another factor that complicated the matching process was the coordinator's desire to give students a strong voice in deciding what ventures they would create. Thus outside of the government and bank jobs, students were encouraged to think about a business that *they* would like to start. Then, the coordinator would put students who had similar businesses (e.g., food-related or craft-related) together in a classroom with a teacher. Consequently, teacher interests often had to be ignored in making assignments to ventures.

Although there were several problems in the way the program was introduced to the school, the effects were somewhat mitigated by the fact that the principal encouraged the staff to have realistic expectations and a long-term perspective. Unlike the Wellfleet case, the *MicroSociety* program at Montgomery Middle was not implemented primarily in order to raise student test scores. The main motive had to do with gaining more control over student behavior. Student discipline, absenteeism, and vandalism rates, rather than test scores, would determine success. The school board did want to see improvement in test scores, but the principal saw this as a separate issue. He said, "The way to raise test scores is to take apart the tests and make sure that you are teaching students the material that is covered by the tests." The *MicroSociety* program might help to reinforce some of the learning, and it could help many students to develop good planning and problem-solving skills. But the principal believed its main contribution to raising performance on standardized tests was to get the students to come to school every day and to behave well enough in the classroom so that the teachers could teach them what they needed. Thus while the *MicroSociety* program eventually should help improve student achievement, the effect would be a long-term one. The program was not viewed as a "quick fix" for improving test scores.

The principal also encouraged the staff to adopt a longer time perspective. He repeatedly stated that "7 years is necessary for change to work." He made it clear that the *MicroSociety* program would have considerable time to become established and prove its worth. This longer time perspective proved to be important. One group of teachers said that it was not until the third year that they began to feel comfortable with the program.

The *MicroSociety* program did fit a pressing need within the district, which was to address the segregation issue in some way. Also, the program was congruent with some of the things that the board valued. The board reportedly liked the program because it was "innovative," and there had been a strong push to encourage schools to come up with their own innovative programs. The *MicroSociety* program also appealed to some of the conservative values that were especially strong in this community, such as teaching kids about business and "the real world."

Thus the way in which the *MicroSociety* program initially was implemented both helped and hindered the development of a viable program. The principal's strong support of the program, based on his personal values and experiences, was clearly a plus. And the way in which two of the teachers assumed leadership for the program early on helped to dilute the perception that this would just be the "principal's program." Also helpful was the principal's insistence that the program would have ample time to prove itself and that ultimately it would be judged on the basis of student behavior rather than increases in test scores (a more realistic expectation). However, the teachers had little real understanding of the program before they were asked to adopt it. As a result, most of them did not have a true sense of ownership for it. Also, when the teachers implemented the program, only one teacher had firsthand knowledge of what an actual *Micro-Society* school looked like, and only two had attended a summer conference. Finally, there was no real pilot or "trial run" before full implementation. These facilitating and inhibiting factors are summarized in Table 9.2.

Table 9.2   Factors in the Way the Program Was Introduced That Affected Its Subsequent Development at Montgomery Middle School

---

- Positive factors:
  - New principal found the concept to be appealing because it fit well with his educational values and priorities
  - Two highly respected, experienced teachers with a strong belief in the program assumed leadership
  - Principal's expectations for the new program were modest, and his time perspective for change was realistic

- Negative factors:
  - Many teachers voted to adopt the program without much information about it or strong conviction
  - Little planning or staff development prior to full implementation
  - Many teachers were not particularly invested in their initial ventures

BECOMING OPERATIONAL: THE TEACHERS CONFRONT REALITY

Once the program became operational, there continued to be aspects of it that contributed to success along with negative factors that ultimately contributed to its demise. These positive and negative factors are summarized in Table 9.3.

Although almost all the teachers initially had voted to adopt the program, many began to rethink the wisdom of their votes once the *Micro-Society* program was up and running. The first year was highly demanding and stressful. Many teachers found that the program initially required much extra work. One teacher said that she spent more time preparing for her venture (the bank) than for all her classes.

However, not all teachers experienced additional work demands. Some who were less committed to the program managed to "get by" without spending much time on it. A teacher who worked in manufacturing, for instance, described her role there as "just babysitting." This lack of engagement on the part of some teachers became a source of conflict and added stress. Teachers who were committed to the program and who worked hard on its behalf resented those who did not pull their weight.

Even more problematic were the teachers who did not follow the rules. For instance, some teachers allowed students to leave their activity areas during Micro time without wearing the required badge. The coordinator also complained that it was hard to get some teachers to turn in their attendance sheets. A few teachers reportedly did not even follow the Micro constitution.

Table 9.3   Factors That Affected the Program's Survival Once It Became
Operational at Montgomery Middle School

- Positive factors:
  - Principal was responsive to teacher concerns
  - Teachers liked and respected the principal and coordinator
  - Coordinator was committed, knowledgeable, and creative
  - Coordinator and principal had high level of "emotional intelligence" (i.e., they managed themselves and others well)
  - Effective partnership between coordinator and a fellow teacher
  - Principal allowed coordinator to assume the leadership role while continuing to provide active support in various ways
  - Principal created a positive organizational climate within the school

- Negative factors:
  - Teacher resistance
  - Continuing conflicts over the "middle school" and "junior high" models
  - Lack of engagement on part of older students
  - Inadequate resources
  - Many teachers found it difficult to give up control and let the students run the ventures
  - Insufficient training and planning time
  - Lack of teacher participation in decision making
  - After 6 years, the first principal left, and he was replaced by someone who was not a strong supporter of the program

Some teachers also were frustrated because they felt they had less time in class to cover the regular curriculum. Initially, the application period consumed two periods a day. Although the principal was able to change the schedule so that the teachers lost only a few minutes from each period, many felt the loss keenly. An art teacher, for instance, complained that those few minutes had a discernible effect on the number of projects that his students could do during the year, as well as on the quality.

All of this stress took its toll. One teacher said that he became so frustrated with the program during the first year that he "kicked a file cabinet so hard that now one of the drawers won't open."

After the first year, however, the situation improved. The principal agreed to cut back the program from two periods to one. Also, the teachers learned from experience and gradually worked out some of the problems that created extra effort and frustration. By the third year, the *MicroSociety* program was running much more smoothly. However, it continued to require considerable time and effort for many of the teachers, and teacher dissent continued, albeit at a low level. The program got caught up in the ongoing conflict between "middle school" and "junior high" models. The teachers who continued to cling to the junior high model viewed the program as "more of a four through six program." These dissenters pointed to the lack of interest among the eighth graders as proof that the *MicroSociety* program was inappropriate for older kids.

Many eighth graders still were interested in the *MicroSociety* program, and sometimes the same students who lacked interest with one teacher were enthusiastic when working with another. However, in general, it did seem to be the case that over time, some eighth graders became less engaged in the program. One teacher said that the oldest students gave away their Micro money because "they aren't interested in any of the stuff that they can buy with them." On more than one occasion, some of the teachers tried to pull the eighth graders out of the program.

I spoke to a number of eighth graders who said they still liked the program. But some also conceded that it "wasn't as good as it had been" when they were in sixth and seventh grade. However, their reasons were different from those suggested by the teachers. The students said that the program was better the first year because they'd had two periods for Micro each day rather than one. Also, they complained about the limit on the amount of money they could withdraw from the bank on any given day. (It was not clear who imposed this limit or why it was imposed.)

Even though the coordinator and principal dealt with teacher dissent skillfully, it did not go away. A few of the strongest dissidents were allowed to engage in alternative activities during the application period. And the coordinator continued to try to find better matches for the less supportive teachers who remained in the program. There were many enthusiastic supporters of the program, and the esteem that the teachers had for the coordinator and principal muted their resistance to some extent. But clearly, the lack of teacher commitment was a problem, one that hampered effective implementation of the program. Ultimately, that dissent and resistance contributed to the program's demise.

THE PROBLEM OF RESOURCES

One source of teacher resistance was philosophical. However, limited resources also contributed to dissent. The Montgomery Middle School *MicroSociety* program was not well funded. The school received only $12,000 per year in additional funding for the program. Consequently, the coordinator could not be paid for her time. She continued to teach a full load and received no extra money for serving as coordinator of the program. (Despite this, she was one of the most dedicated and effective coordinators I observed.)

The lack of funding would not have been such a significant problem if the staff had been more successful in securing additional human resources. However, relatively few adults other than the teachers worked with the program. Virtually no parents were involved, and nonprofessional staff at the school did not participate either.

A group of six teachers that I interviewed agreed that the biggest problem with the program was "not enough adults." One of the students said that he did not like the program at first because "there was no one to help me get a business started." Another teacher confirmed that students sometimes had to wait 2 weeks at the beginning of the year before a teacher could get to them in order to help them develop an idea for a business.

Montgomery Middle did reach out to the community in effective and creative ways, which brought in some additional resources. The principal was particularly helpful in arranging links with various groups in the community. A good example of his skill in cultivating community resources was the bike shop, a venture set up for students classified as "behavior disordered." In this venture, the students would earn Micro money by repairing broken bikes. But where would they get the bikes? It soon became apparent that there were not enough broken bikes within the school's own population to provide the bike shop with the volume it needed. The principal came up with the solution. He contacted the police department and talked them into donating a large number of the stolen bikes that they recovered each year and that went unclaimed. The students in the bike shop then repaired the bikes and sold them in the *MicroSociety* marketplace.

The "mini-mall" concept was an interesting example of a "community partnership" developed within the school system itself. The mini-mall was a version of the *MicroSociety* marketplace that was held on a regular basis at several of the elementary schools in the district. A bus would take a group of Montgomery Middle students and teachers to an elementary school, and the students would quickly set up a marketplace in the elementary school's gym or other large space. Then a group of the elementary students would come in with Micro money to spend on the objects sold in the marketplace. The elementary students earned Micro money for good attendance, completing their work and turning it on time, and so on. Mini-malls occurred every 2 weeks at four different elementary schools. The program was popular among elementary school teachers and principals because it gave them a new incentive for controlling their students' behavior. One elementary principal reported that the mini-mall reduced suspensions by 70% in his school because it was such a good incentive for the students. The elementary students loved the products, and they provided a good market for the

MicroSociety ventures. (Unfortunately, the mini-malls were a drain on the program's limited funding due to the transportation costs.)

The *MicroSociety* program at Montgomery Middle used community resources in other ways as well. Each activity area had 1 day set aside each marking period for either a guest speaker or a field trip related to that activity. For instance, the students who worked in the beauty shop went on a field trip to the local beauty college. The students who ran the *Micro-Society* program's radio station visited an adult radio station in town.

Montgomery Middle's success was more mixed when it came to utilizing the students themselves as a resource for running the program. A few of the teachers were able to give up control over the process enough so that the students truly ran their own society. When teachers were able to let the students take more responsibility, the students became resources for each other and a single teacher could facilitate a relatively large number of student ventures. For instance, one teacher who supervised several different ventures simultaneously said that she was able to do so by "teaching the kids what they needed in order to run things and then letting them do it."

However, many other teachers had not grasped this essential aspect of the program. As a result, they quickly became overburdened. Their ventures were often less rewarding for them and their students because they did not know how to give up control and empower the students. For instance, one of the teachers, who was in charge of unemployment, complained that she did not have enough time to provide guidance and coaching to each student. As a result, weeks went by before a student in unemployment received the kind of support he or she needed to find a rewarding and productive job. When I asked this teacher about using successful students as coaches for the less successful ones rather than trying to do it all herself, she said she had "never thought of doing that." She did employ four students to help out, but she used them only as runners.

There were many other examples of how teachers were either unable or unwilling to give up control and truly empower students in the program. For instance, at one point, I observed some students trying to sell the same piece of property twice. A teacher intervened and stopped it "so that they wouldn't have to go to court." While the teacher's intervention "solved" the "problem," having the students go to court might have been a good learning experience for all involved, including the teacher.

INSUFFICIENT TRAINING
AND PLANNING TIME

The reluctance of many teachers to empower the students was related in part to their educational philosophies and previous experience. However, lack of training also seemed to be a contributing factor. Because there was so little funding for the program, Montgomery Middle could not provide much staff development for teachers. In fact, after 3 years of operation, no teachers other than Janet and Mary had attended a summer conference or observed in another school that had adopted the program. Also, while there were a few days set aside each year for staff development at the school, the teachers often had to use the time to explore topics unrelated to the *MicroSociety* program.

The coordinator provided some guidance and direction for the teachers. The teachers spoke highly of her patience, warmth, and positive outlook. She also was viewed by all as someone who really understood the *MicroSociety* concept and who could be very helpful in showing other teachers how to use it effectively. There also was the *MicroSociety* program committee, which met twice a month. Teachers could go to their meetings with a problem or question, and often the committee would come up with a helpful idea. However, teachers would have to do this on their own time, and many chose not to do so. Unlike some of the other schools I studied, Montgomery Middle had no funding available for extra planning time. Teachers had to do all the planning for the *MicroSociety* program on their own.

The situation was better in some ways at the annex because there was only one team there and they had a common planning period. This meant that they met each day together for 40 minutes and usually spent part of the time discussing their *MicroSociety* program. On the other hand, their isolation meant that they had less contact with the *MicroSociety* program coordinator. As a result, they had even less guidance than other teachers had in implementing the program.

LACK OF TEACHER VOICE IN DECISION MAKING

When the program was introduced to the school, teachers were given the opportunity to vote on whether it would be adopted. They voted, but they did not feel empowered. This pattern continued once the program became operational.

Both the principal and the coordinator recognized the importance of giving teachers some say over the operation of the program. The principal had been involved in site-based management early on, and he had participated in much of the training. He respected differences of opinion, even valued them. Nevertheless, many teachers did not feel that they had much influence over the program.

Formally, the teachers were empowered through the management team. The team met twice each month and was made up of a representative from each team (i.e., two from each grade level). The coordinator led the meetings, and the principal regularly attended. But the committee served mainly as a problem-solving vehicle. When it came to actual decision making, it seemed that the coordinator ultimately made many of the most important decisions, in consultation with the principal and one other teacher. Although the faculty viewed the coordinator and principal as relatively open and flexible, many teachers felt that if there was a disagreement, it was the leaders who prevailed. As a result, teachers often did not use the channels that were open to them when they disagreed with a policy or had a suggestion for change. Some teachers even forgot that such channels existed. One said, "If people have a complaint, there is no place to raise it." The teachers' sense of powerlessness was reflected in comments such as, "We feel they keep adding things that make it more complicated."

Thus even though there were opportunities for teacher input and the leadership seemed to welcome it, the large size of the faculty, as well as Mary and Janet's central role in developing the program, ultimately restricted how much say the rest of the teachers had when it came to the *MicroSociety* program. There was a sense of resignation and passivity among many of the teachers, which, in this district, seemed to extend beyond the *MicroSociety* program to almost any school-related issue. Because many teachers never developed a sense of ownership for the program, teacher resistance continued to be a problem throughout the program's history.

AN EFFECTIVE COORDINATOR

Despite all of these problems, the program became established and was regarded as a highly innovative and exciting model of what the *Micro-Society* program could be. One important reason for its success was the leadership provided by the coordinator.

Mary Pierce became the coordinator of the *MicroSociety* program shortly after the school decided to implement it. A more logical choice might have been Janet Duncan, who had visited the program at Lowell and had become enthusiastic about it almost immediately. Mary, in fact, had some misgivings about the idea initially. However, she eventually became a convert, and there seemed to be an understanding that Mary would be a better choice as coordinator because she would be more "diplomatic" with the other teachers than would Janet. But in many ways, Mary and Janet could be thought of as the leadership team for the program. They worked closely together and supported each other throughout its history. They were the only two teachers who had attended a summer conference, and they seemed to be equally knowledgeable about and dedicated to the program.

Although Janet's and Mary's enthusiasm and knowledge were important for the program's success, equally vital was their credibility with their colleagues. One of the biggest critics of the program said that the *MicroSociety* program had not become an issue with the teacher's union even though many teachers disliked the program, because of the "respect that the teachers have for Janet and Mary." He indicated that this respect was based on the amount of work they did and the kind of people they were. As he put it, "We know that they are doing it for the kids."

Mary's colleagues also gave her points for being "diplomatic" in her role as coordinator of the program. Although the other teachers thought she had a great deal of power to decide how the program was run, they believed that she was reasonable when they had problems or complaints. They described her as "a good listener" who was effective in helping teachers to come up with solutions to problems. They also appreciated her ability to provide guidance and direction to teachers who sought out her help.

Mary's effectiveness in the role of coordinator had much to do with her "emotional intelligence," that is, the way in which she managed herself and others. For instance, when she talked about a teacher who was having difficulty grasping the essence of the *MicroSociety* program, she added, "But he'll get it eventually." This quiet optimism and faith in people did much to make Mary an effective coordinator. Mary also showed great sensitivity to the feelings of others. She was highly empathic, not only toward all of her students but also toward other teachers who disagreed with her and had very different teaching philosophies.

Although Mary carried a normal teaching load and did not receive any additional pay for her work as coordinator, the teachers thought that she always was available to help them. And she spent an enormous amount of time, along with Janet, in planning for the program. She was able to do so because her own children were grown and she had more than 30 years of experience as a teacher.

THE ORGANIZATIONAL CONTEXT: A SUPPORTIVE PRINCIPAL

One of the most important positive factors in the Montgomery Middle *MicroSociety* program was the support of the principal and the kind of leadership he provided in the school. Although the faculty were divided in their opinions about the *MicroSociety* program, they were unified in their respect and affection for the principal. Many teachers were willing to go along with the program because the principal seemed willing to go along with it.

Once the principal had introduced the program to the teachers, he receded into the background. As Janet and Mary assumed leadership, the principal became much less identified with the program. In fact, there were times when he expressed reservations and even prevented the leadership team from moving ahead with an initiative. In the eyes of the less committed teachers, the *MicroSociety* program was really "Janet and Mary's program" rather than the principal's. However, in his own quiet, low-key way, the principal provided invaluable support to the program.

An especially important type of support that the principal provided was political. He was willing to take on resisters and opponents to the program in order to ensure its survival. At one point, he met with some teachers who were critical of the program and heard them out. Then he told them, "This isn't a 2- or 3-year project. It's a 7-year project." He concluded by indicating that "they might need to find something else" if they "did not like it."

The principal also worked hard to secure community partners. For instance, when the leadership team came up with the idea of mini-malls, the principal worked with the elementary principals in order to implement the idea. He also was the one who went to the local police and arranged for them to send stolen bikes to the school for the "bike shop" business.

The principal also helped in the area of public relations. He played a major role in arranging for one of the state's U.S. senators to visit the school, and he also helped make the subsequent visit of the First Lady a success. When I visited the school to collect data for this study, the principal was the one who met me at the airport. For the next 3 days, he took me out to eat, drove me around the community for various appointments, and did everything he could to make sure that I came away with a positive impression of the program.

Another important way in which the principal contributed was by being a "sounding board" and "problem solver." He regularly attended the *MicroSociety* program team meetings, and although he did not lead them or dominate the discussion, he often offered invaluable ideas and suggestions.

The principal also may have helped the program by providing a brake on the enthusiasm of the strongest advocates. For instance, when the group that visited Lowell returned, they wanted to start the program right away. The principal thought they should go more slowly. Because Janet and Mary assumed leadership for the program and became such powerful advocates for it, the principal was able to assume a more neutral position and represent the interests of the entire faculty, including the dissidents. His reticence sometimes frustrated the leadership team, but it probably helped secure more support for the program than it otherwise would have had among the rest of the teachers.

One could argue, on the other hand, that if the principal had been more of a "cheerleader" and advocate for the program with the faculty, teacher resistance would have been less strong and the program ultimately might have survived the change in principals. I do not think this interpretation is plausible, however, because the teachers already saw the principal as being in favor of the program. If he had assumed more active leadership of it, the dissident teachers would have felt that it was the "principal's program," just as they had at Wellfleet Elementary School (see Chapter 8).

The principal also contributed to the program in a less direct way: by creating an organizational climate within the school that supported innovation. Bill Nelson had come to a school that had had a long history of problematic leadership. None of his three predecessors had lasted more than 2 years in the position, and each seemed to be more unpopular than the last. Bill brought in a positive, supportive, hands-on but low-key style of leadership that gradually won over most of the teachers and students. As one teacher put it, Bill was "a real people person." Many people I interviewed praised the principal for the way he related to both students and faculty. They felt he made both the students and teachers "feel appreciated." One teacher said, "Bill is really concerned about kids. And he is never negative. He is very supportive." The art teacher, who was critical of the program, said that every time he ran into the principal (which was almost every day), the principal had something nice to say to him about his work. "At first I thought it was corny and phony. I still think it's a little corny sometimes, but I realize now that Bill really means what he says." The teacher added that even though he finds it "corny," he enjoys receiving the praise that the principal gives out so freely.

The staff also appreciated the principal's willingness to let others get credit rather than take it all for himself. An example occurred when I attended an awards assembly given to recognize students for their accomplishments in the *MicroSociety* program. On two different occasions, the principal was given an opportunity to speak, and both times he said very little so that he would not upstage the assistant principal, who was leading the assembly, or the *MicroSociety* program coordinator.

The principal, though low-key and nondirective, was highly visible at the school. He spent much time walking the halls, and teachers felt that they could come to him with problems any time. When teachers did bring problems to the principal, he did not become threatened and overreact. He was able to respond to problems constructively. For instance, the coordinator said that whenever a teacher went to the principal with a problem with the *MicroSociety* program, his response was positive and constructive. The coordinator said, "If someone comes with a complaint about Micro, Bill sees it as a problem to be solved. He doesn't say, 'Close Micro!'"

The way in which the principal handled resistance and conflict was especially important for creating a positive organizational climate in the school. When he first came to the school, he did not bring with him any specific ideas for change because he wanted to "see what things were like." When possible, the principal would avoid conflict. However, he also recognized that conflict and resistance are inevitable and that change is difficult. Rather than dread resistance, he saw it as potentially valuable. As he said at one point, "You will have resistance whenever you do something innovative. And that's not bad. The resisters help you to improve it." This attitude enabled him to deal with resistance constructively.

The principal also helped create a positive climate for change by continually encouraging his teachers to try new things and not to worry about failing. He said, "I won't write up a teacher for trying something new and then failing. In fact, I'll praise the teacher for trying."

The principal was described as a "good sounding board" and "nonjudgmental." The teachers felt that he would "listen to everyone." However, the principal did have strong values and beliefs, and he spent much time talking with me about them. He was someone who managed to express strong convictions without making those who disagreed with him feel disrespected. And he would act decisively when those deeply held values were threatened. For instance, when he first came to the school, he found that any student who was adjudicated as delinquent was automatically placed in the "Behavior Disorder Room." He thought this practice was harmful, and he put a stop to it as soon as he heard about it.

What enabled this principal to provide such positive leadership to the school? How did he get to be the way he was? Partly, it was due to training. When the school district decided to adopt site-based management, the principal received much training in how to reach consensus. But even more important than this training were certain personal qualities: a self-awareness and self-confidence that he brought to the job. When Bill Nelson became the principal of Montgomery Middle, he was an experienced educator in his 50s. He had been successful in a variety of roles during his career, including previous stints as principal in another district. He said that he did not worry about failing when he came to Montgomery Middle, even though he was under pressure to turn around a bad situation. He felt confident that he would succeed. And he also felt that if he did fail, he could go on with his life because he had "failed in the past and survived." This self-confidence, along with a belief in others, contributed to an effective leadership style. With Bill as principal, an innovation like the *MicroSociety* program had a better chance of thriving. And thrive it did, but only for a while. After 7 years, it was abruptly terminated.

THE PROGRAM ENDS

Just as a principal played an important role in the creation and initial success of the *MicroSociety* program at Montgomery Middle, so too did a principal play a critical role in the program's demise. After the *MicroSociety* program had been in existence for 5 years, there was a shake-up at the district level, and a new superintendent took over. The next year, Bill Nelson was transferred to one of the high schools and became the principal there. The assistant principal at Montgomery Middle, who had never been as strong a supporter of the program, took over. The program was terminated 1 year after the new principal took over.

It would be a mistake, however, to attribute the *MicroSociety* program's demise totally to a change in principal. The climate of the country also had changed over the 7 years that the *MicroSociety* program was in existence. There was much more concern about student achievement as measured by standardized tests. It is likely that the school board's expectations and priorities changed during this period as well and that the new principal felt more pressure to raise test scores than had the previous principal.

The eventual demise of the program also resulted from factors that existed within the school from the very beginning. For instance, a few parents reportedly protested the decision to terminate the program, but the lack of parent involvement in the program meant that there were few strong advocates for the program among the parents. Similarly, the number of teachers who were willing to advocate actively for retaining the program was limited because of the mixed history of teacher involvement. When the teachers voted to adopt the program, they did not know much about it. Their vote was not based on a real understanding of the program or much enthusiasm for the values and principles on which it was based. The staff then launched the program with little additional training. Resources were scarce, and without adequate training or time for reflection, few of the teachers were able to use those resources effectively.

Thus at Montgomery Middle School, two highly dedicated, effective, and respected teachers along with the principal and a handful of other staff managed to keep the program going despite a number of disadvantages. In fact, it even became a national model due to their efforts. But when the principal left the school, the program could not survive.

IV

Sustaining School Change in an Ever-Changing World

10

Implications for Research, Policy, and Practice

The *MicroSociety*® program represents a promising approach to dealing with many of the problems confronting education today. However, like other school change efforts, the process of implementing the *Micro-Society* program in the schools I studied involved a number of challenges, and the long-term viability of the program ultimately depended on how well those who implemented it were able to address those challenges. An in-depth study of more and less successful *MicroSociety* programs led to a set of guidelines that can help inform any school change effort. In this final chapter, I consider some of the larger implications for research on the sustainability of school change, public policy, and educational practice.

IMPLEMENTING CHANGE VERSUS SUSTAINING IT

There is a difference between implementing a school change and sustaining change over time. Even when reformers are able to overcome the challenges of implementing a new program or educational practice, it may prove impossible to sustain it for more than a few years. As difficult as it was to implement a *MicroSociety* program successfully, it often proved to be even more challenging to sustain it. In two schools that I studied, strong *MicroSociety* programs failed to survive the replacement of the principal. And in another case, many of the staff and parents believed that the program had declined over time, starting with the departure of the first principal who had played a major role in establishing it at the school. Several of the teachers at this school said that in recent years, "much of the excitement had gone out of" the *MicroSociety* program, and they felt as though they were "treading water" or even regressing because they no longer were learning, changing, or growing.

My research on the implementation of *MicroSociety* programs has suggested that many of the factors that contribute to effective implementation also are important for sustaining change over a period of time. However, some lessons have emerged that pertain specifically to the problem of sustainability.

One aspect of the sustainability problem relates to turnover and succession: New teachers who come into a mature program have not been involved in the process of adoption and start-up. As a result, they do not have the same understanding or commitment as the pioneers. The problem was exacerbated in the early *MicroSociety* programs I studied because teachers who joined the staff after the program had been implemented often received only a minimal amount of orientation and training. Consequently, over time, there was a growing cadre of teachers who lacked the enthusiasm and knowledge to sustain the vibrancy of the early years. An obvious solution to this problem is to provide new teachers with better training and orientation.

But the problem of sustainability in school change efforts also seems to be related to *leadership* turnover and succession. It is when the first leader (or the first strong and supportive leader) leaves and is replaced by one who is less committed and effective that the innovation is most threatened. Training may be a possible solution here as well. New principals might not be such a threat to school reforms if they were provided with training that helped them to better understand the concept.

However, the negative impact of leadership succession also suggests that strong and effective leadership, if it continues for too long, may actually undermine the development of a reform like the *MicroSociety* program. In a book on the creation of new settings, Goldenberg (1971) suggested that the first leader of a new setting should serve for only a limited period of time and that the duration of his or her tenure as leader should be known to all from the very beginning. In this way, all of the staff and the next leader can prepare for the change in leadership. Looking at the problem of sustainability in educational change efforts, there seems to be some wisdom in such a practice.

For example, one of the strongest *MicroSociety* programs I studied initially benefited from the strong leadership of the principal, but only for a relatively brief period of time: The principal helped orchestrate adoption of the program and then left after the first year of operation, at which point there already was a strong leadership team made up of four or five teachers. In this case, the brief tenure of the first leader seemed to help make the program less dependent on that leader, which, in turn, helped to make it more sustainable.

On the other hand, weak leadership does not seem to be a promising way of sustaining educational reform in a school. The Wellfleet case (Chapter 8) shows what can happen when the principal intentionally tries to remain less involved from the beginning. Sustainability was not even an issue for this program because it never got off the ground. Thus strong support and guidance from the principal (or some other person in a leadership position in the school) appears to be highly advantageous during the initial start-up period. But if the teachers and students become too dependent on the principal's leadership, long-term sustainability might become more problematic.

Sustainability also seems to be related to the degree of teacher buy-in. Overzealous reform advocates sometimes believe that a new practice should be imposed on teachers even if they are not completely sold on the idea, because "It is so good for kids." However, the Montgomery Middle School case (Chapter 9) suggests that such a view may be misguided. At Montgomery, a dedicated and skillful pair of teachers implemented the program and kept it going for several years despite opposition from a number of other teachers; but when a new principal came in, the opposition prevailed and the program ended. A certain level of teacher buy-in is necessary to implement a school change. However, *an even higher level of teacher buy-in is necessary to sustain it.* Without a high degree of teacher buy-in, it will be difficult to sustain a new program.

The degree of integration with the core curriculum is another factor that seems to affect sustainability. It sometimes was difficult to sustain the early *MicroSociety* programs because they were not well integrated with the rest of the curriculum. For instance, in a math class, a teacher usually will begin with a textbook and a teacher's guide, and much of what the teacher does during the year will be determined by that curriculum. Any of the standard curricula chosen by the teacher (or more likely chosen *for* the teacher) will not have been developed with the *MicroSociety* program in mind. It is possible for teachers to make links between a standard, prepackaged math lesson and the Micro experience, but it requires extra thought and preparation on the part of the teacher. And it takes even more time and effort to throw out the standard lessons and develop alternative ones from scratch.

MicroSociety, Inc., can address this problem by developing curricula and educational materials that link the program to all the traditional subject areas. But then they have to convince *MicroSociety* schools to abandon the curriculum materials they are using and buy the *MicroSociety* program's materials instead. Politically, this would be a difficult task, for such decisions ultimately are made not by the schools, but by the school board and central office staff. (Increasingly, state-level authorities are playing a role in such decisions as well.) And it would be expensive to develop a Micro-related K–12 curriculum in all the basic subjects. The project would be economically feasible only if a large number of school districts agreed to adopt the curriculum.

The Montessori movement may provide an interesting model for those who wish to sustain an innovation such as the *MicroSociety* program. Unlike many other radical educational innovations that have come and gone relatively quickly, the Montessori model has survived for over a century. One reason may be that the movement decided early on to develop a complete curriculum of its own and take control of training and certification for all its teachers and principals. This probably has limited the degree to which Montessori schools have spread, but it also may have helped the model to survive and grow, albeit at a slow pace.

Another aspect of the sustainability problem has to do with the tendency for almost any new practice to become routine over time. Once a new program becomes established, some teachers are tempted to sit back and coast, rather than to think about how to move the program to new levels. In general, it seems hard to sustain a spirit of innovation in almost any school reform effort. Sooner or later, what begins as an adventure becomes simply another part of the routine (Sarason, 1972).

Growing routinization, and the boredom that comes with it, thus represents another threat to sustainability. If it is to survive for an extended period of time, any school change such as the *MicroSociety* program needs to constantly reinvent itself. For instance, after the program has been in existence for a few years, it may be desirable to stop and begin all over again so that a new group of teachers and students have the experience of creating their own society from scratch. This would mean, among other things, throwing out the original constitution and having a new "constitutional convention." Another approach might be to start a second *MicroSociety* program within the school by having a group of teachers and students go off on their own and begin all over again. However it is done, some form of renewal may be necessary in order to sustain *MicroSociety* programs in schools, and the same may be true for other educational innovations.

One final factor that can promote sustainability of school change is good evaluation research. Increasingly in education, schools are being required to

Table 10.1   Guidelines for Enhancing the Sustainability of School Change
Efforts

- Provide adequate training and socialization to new participants (teachers, principals, parents, students) so that they have the same degree of commitment and knowledge as the pioneers.
- Limit the tenure of the first strong leaders and prepare for new leadership to take over so that the reform effort does not become too dependent on one or two individuals.
- Make sure that teacher buy-in is even greater than the level necessary for adoption and implementation.
- Make sure the new practices fit seamlessly with the core curriculum materials and the core curriculum materials reinforce the new practices.
- Find ways to periodically rekindle the spirit of innovation and avoid increasing routinization and boredom.
- Continuously evaluate the impact of the new practices in each school that implements them.

use teaching strategies that are supported by empirical evidence. Thus in order to implement a new practice, reformers need to demonstrate that it has been effective in other contexts in the past. However, in order to sustain a school change, reformers will need to demonstrate that it is effective in that particular school and with that particular population of students (Fishman, 1999). And evaluation needs to be ongoing. Each new study demonstrating the effectiveness of a practice helps provide support for sustaining it. If the flow of positive research stops, support for sustainability may eventually wither. Fortunately, ongoing evaluation (sometimes referred to as "continuous quality improvement") is becoming the norm in many areas of practice, and educators increasingly are touting its virtues for teaching and learning (Fullan, 1993, 2001).

Thus a number of factors seem to be particularly important for the sustainability of school change. These are presented in summary form in Table 10.1.

TWO CENTRAL LESSONS
THAT EMERGE FROM THE STUDY

In this book, I have identified a number of specific factors that help reformers to implement and sustain school change. However, there are two central lessons that stand out. The first lesson is that *every significant educational alternative is based on at least one principle that constitutes its essence.*

Helping teachers and other key actors to understand and enact that essence constitutes one of the greatest challenges in school change.

For people who are most familiar with the *MicroSociety* program and its underlying rationales, the "student empowerment principle" is the *essence* of the innovation (C. King, personal communication, January, 2005). A true *MicroSociety* program empowers students by putting them in charge of their own society. The program is supposed to be run by the students, not the teachers. When problems occur, it is the students who should come up with possible solutions and decide which to implement. Teachers may serve as guides, facilitators, or consultants, but they should not be the bosses.

Most of the benefits of the *MicroSociety* program depend on the student empowerment principle. Students will not become enthusiastic about learning unless they find themselves to be in a responsible and meaningful role in their own society. Only then will learning become compelling. Students also will not struggle to get to school on a bright sunny spring day unless they believe that their *MicroSociety* venture or agency needs them to show up that day. And students will not develop the social and emotional competencies that are so important for success in life unless they are able to practice those competencies in roles that provide realistic social and emotional challenges. It is only when they are truly in charge of their own fates in the *MicroSociety* program that students are likely to have the experiences that provide the best training ground for developing those competencies. The student empowerment principle is the key for realizing many of the educational benefits promised by the *MicroSociety* concept. So central is the student empowerment principle that it probably is the single most reliable indicator of whether a school has really implemented the program effectively (C. King, personal communication, January, 2005).

Unfortunately, the student empowerment principle also is the most difficult aspect of the program for educators to adopt in practice. It goes against everything they have learned about how a "real school" should run. From the time that they themselves are students in elementary school, teachers learn that the teacher is supposed to be in charge. If there is a problem in the classroom, it is the teacher who comes up with a solution and then expects the students to follow it. If there is a crisis, it is the teacher who steps in and resolves it. Once someone becomes a teacher, these early lessons about teacher authority and control are reinforced. In fact, in many schools, *the cardinal sin is for a teacher to lose control of a class.* If their children do not learn, teachers may or may not be reprimanded. If their children are bored, that in itself will probably not get a teacher in trouble. But if the teacher "loses control" of his or her class, there almost always will be serious negative consequences. The notion that "Teacher is boss" is ingrained in the culture of schools (Sarason, 1996).

The *MicroSociety* program in many schools tries to change this basic pattern for only 1 hour each day. In theory, it should extend beyond 1 hour, but most teachers find it difficult to change the way they think of their role even for that 1 hour. It goes against all the years of socialization that they have had, both as students and teachers. It also violates the expectations they have developed for their students: It is inconceivable to many teachers that their students can assume so much responsibility and not have the result be unproductive chaos. Thus in little and not so little ways, even teachers who are highly committed to the *MicroSociety* concept and its underlying principles act in ways that undermine the student empowerment principle. They establish policies and procedures that leave much of the decision making in the hands of the teachers. They jump in whenever there is a problem and come up with a solution themselves rather than help their students grapple with it.

Fortunately, many teachers are able to change. One virtue of the *MicroSociety* program is that sooner or later, situations arise that enable the students to assume more responsibility, and some teachers then begin to see that their students are capable of more than they expected. These are often the most exciting and fateful moments in the life of a *MicroSociety* program. However, in the schools I studied, it proved extremely difficult for most teachers to grasp and then enact the student empowerment principle. In many cases, they seemed never to understand that student empowerment was the essence of the program. Instead, they seemed to think that the important thing was getting a constitution written or erecting realistic storefronts. They confused ends and means.

The student empowerment principle is specific to the *MicroSociety* program, but every significant educational alternative will be based on at least one principle that constitutes its essence. Furthermore, if it is a true alternative, following that basic principle will involve significant changes in the mind-sets of teachers and others. In the *MicroSociety* program, it is the student empowerment principle. In other educational reforms, the basic principles that represent the essence of the innovation are different, but the challenge is the same. Meaningful school change requires a significant change in the mind-sets of teachers and others, and such change is always difficult.

Teachers, parents, school board members, and other key actors are used to thinking about schooling in certain ways, and their habitual ways of thinking make it difficult for many of them to comprehend what a true educational alternative involves. And even if they are able to "get it," changing their usual way of thinking and acting in the classroom will often prove to be extraordinarily difficult. As Tyack and Cuban (1995) noted, innovations that run counter to people's conception of "real school" will be especially difficult to implement. Their analysis of the history of educational reform during the last two centuries suggested that "Both general beliefs in the broader culture about what a 'real school' was and the hold of standard operating procedures on staff and students put a brake on innovators who sought basic changes in classroom instruction" (Tyack & Cuban, 1995, p. 10). Addressing and overcoming these general beliefs about "real school" represents a core challenge for almost any meaningful school change effort. The struggle to implement the *MicroSociety* program's student empowerment principle is not unique in this respect.

Although many factors can help teachers to allow their students to take over in a *MicroSociety* program, the most important ultimately is the way in which the teachers handle their own anxiety and the anxiety of those with whom they work. And this leads to the second central lesson, which concerns the role of emotional intelligence in successful school change.

Emotional intelligence has to do with the way in which people manage emotions. Emotionally intelligent people are good at perceiving how they and others are feeling, understanding why they are feeling the way they do, and then using these insights to handle their emotions in ways that lead to effective action (Goleman, 1995). The *MicroSociety* program is, among other things, a vehicle for helping children to develop greater emotional intelligence. However, an analysis of the implementation process reveals that for the program to work effectively, the teachers and administrators in schools that implement it must possess a high degree of emotional intelligence themselves.

The need for emotional intelligence begins with the teachers. For most teachers, giving up some control and letting their students run things makes them anxious, and this anxiety often prevents them from implementing the student empowerment principle. It is only when teachers become aware of their own anxiety and its sources, see the detrimental effect it is having on the *MicroSociety* program, and then use that insight to manage their anxiety that change becomes possible.

Teachers often are unable or unwilling to let go because of their fear of failure for themselves and their students. The most successful teachers in a *MicroSociety* program seem to be the ones who are not so afraid of failure. They are risk takers. They have confidence not only in their students but also in themselves. Self-confidence, positive expectations, and the ability to take risks are all related to emotional intelligence (Goleman, 1998).

A good example of emotional intelligence in the implementation of a *MicroSociety* program occurred at one of the schools I studied. The upper-grade teachers had implemented the program a year or so earlier, and now it was time for the K–2 teachers to do so. But they were reluctant. One of the teachers, the informal leader of the group, recognized that the underlying problem was fear. She found the idea of implementing the program to be "scary," and she realized that her colleagues felt much the same way. During one meeting, she talked about those feelings and made it easier for the other teachers to do so as well. Finally, after the teachers had an opportunity to explore their feelings about the change, the group leader said, "I think it's time to do it. Let's just hold hands and jump in together." At that point, the teachers decided they could do it, and they implemented the *MicroSociety* program during the next semester.

This example reveals that an important part of the change process involves the way in which teachers manage uncertainty—particularly the anxiety and stress associated with the unknown. Too often teachers avoid uncertainty, or they become overwhelmed with the anxiety associated with it. Or they react with anger rather than anxiety to the tension associated with uncertainty. These dysfunctional ways of handling anxiety are a major impediment to meaningful school change. Emotionally intelligent teachers are able to understand and effectively manage the emotions associated with uncertainty, and thus they are more likely to support the effective implementation of school change efforts.

Emotional intelligence affects school change initiatives in other ways as well. For instance, teachers who are most likely to embrace a new educational alternative and truly understand the underlying essence are those who are interested in changing and growing themselves (Sarason, 1996). They see the proposed change, whether it is the *MicroSociety* program or something else, as a vehicle for doing so. Some teachers will resist a proposed change because it does not connect with what is most meaningful and valued by them. But many teachers resist change because they have become disengaged from teaching and education to such an extent that no innovative program appeals to them. Their primary motive has become to exert minimal effort and just get by.

This characteristic of the resistant teacher, which we often refer to as "burnout," is influenced in part by the external environment. As the research on burnout has repeatedly shown, the climate of the work setting does much to influence the level of burnout (Cherniss, 1995). However, the level of teacher burnout also is influenced by the teachers' own emotional intelligence, that is, how well teachers understand and manage the emotional factors influencing them and the people (students, parents, peers, and administrators) with whom they work. Thus emotional intelligence helps teachers not only to manage anxiety and other emotions that can disrupt the change process but also to sustain their enthusiasm for their own personal change and development, and this, in turn, makes them more willing to embark on school change initiatives.

While emotional intelligence was important for the teachers who were involved in implementing the *MicroSociety* program, it also was vital for those in leadership positions (Cherniss, 1998). The most successful programs were implemented in schools where both the principal and the *MicroSociety* program coordinator were unusually intelligent about how to manage their emotions and the emotions of others. Emotional intelligence also was important for informal leaders in the school, like the teacher who helped her colleagues "take the plunge" in the example above.

Emotionally intelligent leaders are able to understand and manage the anxiety, frustration, and excitement that inevitably accompany attempts to change the basic assumptions and behavioral regularities associated with "real school." They are able to manage their own emotions and, at the same time, help other teachers and administrators in the school manage theirs as well. Leaders, as emotional models, strongly influence the emotional climate of an entire group or organization (Goleman, Boyatzis, & McKee, 2002).

School change has been problematic in part because those who plan change have failed to adequately appreciate and take into account the central role of emotion (Louis, Toole, & Hargreaves, 1999). Previous research on school improvement has identified a number of guidelines and factors associated with effective change; yet positive, sustainable change remains the exception rather than the rule. One reason is that there must be effective change agents to implement those guidelines and strategies, and the critical competencies for effective "change agentry" have to do with the awareness and management of one's own emotions and those of others (Goleman, 1998). There is more to successful school change than simply managing emotions well, but the other ingredients are usually ready at hand if the staff catches the spark and is able to handle their own fears and apprehensions.

Thus sustainable school change requires two things. First, teachers, principals, and other key actors must understand the *essence* of the proposed change. Second, teachers and key leaders in the school must be able to understand and manage their own *emotions* and those of others with whom they work. When these two central elements are in place, the other ingredients necessary for implementing school change usually will follow. But how do we create these two crucial elements in schools?

A FIRST STEP: THE SELECTION AND TRAINING OF EDUCATORS

The traditional approach to helping participants to understand the essence of a school change program is "inservice training." However, Sarason (1996) pointed out more than three decades ago that the typical approach to such training—a few hours of intensive workshops, usually attended by teachers during the summer—is not a particularly effective way of helping teachers to adopt a new mind-set, much less the new skills, that meaningful change usually requires.

The same is true for helping people to become more emotionally intelligent. Such learning involves changing deeply embedded neural pathways, a task that requires months of intensive practice. A few hours in a workshop or seminar is not enough (Cherniss & Adler, 2000; Goleman, 1998).

Unfortunately, this level of training requires a substantial investment of time and money. Is it realistic to expect that public schools will ever make that kind of investment given public attitudes, bureaucratic constraints, underfunding, and the politics of school boards? In some cases, individual schools and school districts have done so, but these tend to be the exceptions. The average public school in the average public school district probably will not be able to make the necessary investment (Berends, Bodilly, & Kirby, 2002).

A more realistic alternative, especially for developing higher levels of emotional intelligence in educators, is to focus on preservice training. Colleges and universities do possess the resources necessary for more intensive professional development in their leadership training and teacher training programs. They have students who undergo hundreds of hours of instruction as part of a degree program. They also are able to evaluate candidates for degree programs and exclude those who seem unfit for practice. And they receive a substantial amount of steady funding dedicated to such selection and instruction. The question is whether they will use those opportunities and resources to select and train for emotional intelligence.

It is clear that teacher preparation programs and administrative leadership programs in universities could do more to select and train their students in those aspects of emotional intelligence that are so important for school change, such as self-awareness, empathy, and skill in managing one's own emotions and the emotions of others. Professional training programs in fields such as psychology and social work always have made social and emotional learning a priority. MBA programs and medical schools increasingly are doing so as well (Boyatzis, 1994; Cherniss & Adler, 2000; Kramer, Ber, & Moore, 1989). The field of education also could select and train its practitioners for the social and emotional competencies that are associated with effective teaching *and* implementation of reforms such as the *MicroSociety* program.

THE ROLE OF THE EXTERNAL ENVIRONMENT

In this book, I have focused primarily on what goes on within the school itself. In doing so, I may have underestimated the extent to which the success of a *MicroSociety* program depends on forces beyond the walls of the school. Politics and priorities in the district office, the school board, and federal and state bureaucracies can impose limits on what even the most skillful and dedicated staff can do within a particular school.

For instance, in the case of the *MicroSociety* program, it is hard for individual teachers and schools to embrace the student empowerment principle, because they are part of a larger system dominated by a top-down, hierarchical power structure. It is a system that also is highly bureaucratic, with a growing emphasis on standardized curricula and rigid accountability mechanisms. Is it realistic to expect that teachers and principals can "empower" students when they themselves increasingly find their degree of autonomy and discretion constrained (Sarason, 1997)?

The situation has only worsened in recent years with the passage of the federal No Child Left Behind legislation. This act has put even more emphasis on standards and accountability in education. On the surface, increased accountability may seem to be a good thing for public education. However, educational reforms such as the *MicroSociety* program tend to be undermined by such an emphasis. Many teachers, for instance, who might otherwise support the *MicroSociety* program feel that it gets in the way of their efforts to prepare their students to "pass the tests." And many principals wonder whether it is possible to follow the standard curriculum and still have the kind of freedom that would allow their schools to continue with the *MicroSociety* program.

In addition, the new accountability standards are likely to lead to expectations for rapid improvement in student achievement. As we saw in the Wellfleet case (Chapter 8), if such improvement does not occur, school reform models such as the *MicroSociety* program are likely to be abandoned in favor of something perceived to be "better" (Berends et al., 2002). Thus the *MicroSociety* program, along with many other kinds of reforms in education, seems to run counter to the current emphasis on testing and standards in education.

Even when the larger system supports innovation, it often does so in a way that makes meaningful, sustained change less likely. As Sarason (1990) has noted, those policymakers and administrators who call for implementation of new programs often do not seem to understand the complexities of the process. Also, they often are under great pressure to make change happen fast. As a result, they do not provide the time and money required for meaningful change to occur. And then they impose multiple, sometimes conflicting, mandates, which further undermines the likelihood that change will occur.

On the other hand, it is all too easy to rationalize failure or inaction on the school level by blaming these larger forces. To some extent, the influence of external forces on a school depends on how well a school's leaders manage their own and others' emotions. Effective school leaders and change agents believe they have enough control over the external environment to make a difference, and this belief often becomes a self-fulfilling prophecy (Sarason, 1996). Also, a high degree of emotional intelligence can provide leaders with the tools they need to work around constraints imposed by others. A good example was the principal who managed to keep the *MicroSociety* program going even after a sympathetic superintendent was fired and replaced by a less supportive one who, with the backing of the school board, tried to do away with the program (Chapter 7). Similarly, there was the first-year teacher in a *MicroSociety* school who said that he saw no conflict between the *MicroSociety* concept and the state-imposed core learning objectives. He said that he reconciled the *MicroSociety* program and the learning objectives by always thinking of the objectives whenever he did Micro. In other words, he constantly looked for ways to make the connections.

These examples point us back to the two central lessons that emerged from my research. When educators really understand the essence of the program and when they possess the emotional and social competencies that allow them to overcome the hopelessness and fatalism that grip many educators when confronted by external obstacles, it often is possible for schools to overcome those obstacles and implement meaningful school change.

Ultimately, however, the larger social and political context will limit the extent to which schools can implement innovative practices such as the *MicroSociety* program. The research on which this book is based, along with countless other studies, has demonstrated that change, if it is to be sustainable, requires considerable time, effort, skill, and commitment. School boards, state legislatures, and the federal government typically do not provide the resources necessary for doing the necessary work of implementation. There is a kind of "wishful thinking" that leads the public and their representatives to believe that significant change is possible without the expenditure of much additional time or money. Reform on the cheap has become a way of life in education, despite an enormous amount of evidence suggesting that it just does not work (Schorr, 1997).

What is required, again, is a change in mind-set. When political leaders, policymakers, educational administrators, and the general public begin to realize that school change requires much more time, effort, and funding than we usually provide, then school change efforts may lead to the kind of sustained improvement that up to now has been so elusive. Until there is a change in mind-set—one that has imprisoned educational policy and practice in this country for decades—school-based change efforts will continue to falter.

CONCLUSION

John Dewey once said, "Education is not preparation for life. Education is life itself." That statement is especially apt for the *MicroSociety* school. For the *MicroSociety* is a community that is run by the students themselves, and as such it provides a powerful vehicle for linking education and life in ways that many educators since Dewey have only dreamed.

However, the *MicroSociety* program is not the only educational innovation that has come along since Dewey's time, and it probably will not be the last. Many other reforms have come and gone during the last century. Whether the *MicroSociety* program proves to be more effective and to have more staying power will depend not only on the dedication and enthusiasm of educators, students, and parents. It also will depend on how effectively the concept is implemented in real schools. And the same is true for virtually any educational reform. Lasting success always depends on how the reform is implemented at the school level.

This book and the research on which it was based point to the critical ingredients for making the implementation of new programs and practices in schools more successful and for sustaining change over time. Ultimately, however, the future of such efforts will depend on the tenacity and skill of those who are responsible for implementing them in schools. The process of translating theory into practice is always the most critical challenge. Those who take it up are the real heroes of educational reform.

Resource A:
A Description
of the Study

SETTINGS

Six schools that had adopted the *MicroSociety*® program were studied most intensively. However, I also conducted hour-long interviews with the principals of five other schools and with a program coordinator and teacher from a sixth. I attended three of the national summer training conferences, during which I participated in several workshops and informally spoke with dozens of teachers and principals from other *MicroSociety* schools. I also led several workshops that focused on organizational problems associated with implementation.

The six schools studied most intensively were chosen in order to represent diversity on a number of dimensions. The first was degree of success in implementation: One school discontinued the program shortly before I visited the school to do the research, while the other five were generally perceived to be successful by most of the staff, parents, central office personnel, and MicroSociety, Inc. (MSI). "Success" can be difficult to operationally define when it comes to educational reform. I was interested primarily in successful implementation: the extent to which the *MicroSociety* program was implemented as it was intended to be (sometimes referred to as the "fidelity" criterion) and the extent to which the staff are committed and satisfied with it.

The second selection criterion was urban versus suburban: Two schools were located in very large cities, two in medium-sized cities, one in a small city, and one in a rural/suburban area. The third selection factor was the student population mix: One school was predominantly African American, two were predominantly Latino American, and the other three had a heterogeneous mix with no racial or ethnic group representing a majority of the population. The fourth consideration was region of the United States: One school was located in the Northeast, two in the Midwest, one in the Southeast, one in the Southwest, and one in the far West. Another selection factor was length of time that the program had been in place: The program had been operational 4 years or less in four of the schools, about 8 years in another school, and 14 years in the last school. The last criterion was type of school: One school was a middle school, and the other schools were elementary schools, with three K–5 and two K–8.

George Richmond and Carolynn King of MSI initially nominated eight schools for the study, all of which they considered to be relatively successful. I interviewed the principals or program coordinators over the phone and chose four case study schools based on the above criteria, plus geographic accessibility. One of the four schools later refused to participate in the study. I then replaced this school with a school that had just discontinued the program so that there would be more diversity on this dimension. Somewhat later, two other schools were added, one because it was a middle school and there were none other in the sample and the other because it had emerged as one of the strongest programs in the country.

INFORMANTS

In each of the case study schools, I interviewed a wide variety of individuals. This usually included the principal, the program coordinator, a cross section of teachers, the school secretary, paraprofessional staff, at least one staff member from the central office, several parents and community partners, and a number of students. In some instances, I also interviewed teachers and principals who had been key figures in the past but were no longer at the school. Interviews lasted from 30 minutes to 1 hour, and key people such as principals and program coordinators usually were interviewed two or more times. I also interviewed two university-based consultants and one private management consultant who were familiar with one or more of the schools. Information also came from several conversations that I had during the course of the project with George Richmond, Carolynn King, and Lew Gantwerk, a friend and colleague who has consulted to MSI for several years.

The teachers I interviewed were selected to represent wide diversity in grade taught, attitude toward program, age and length of time teaching in the school, race, ethnicity, and gender. The principals usually selected the initial group of people to be interviewed. I tried to confirm that the selected people met the criteria by showing the list to at least two other informants and asking whether the people selected for interviews included the mix I desired. In every case, my informants stated that the principals' selections met the criteria and did not seem to represent a bias. However, in several instances, I asked to interview others based on my growing understanding of the setting. For instance, in one school that was 50% African American, the principal selected three parents for interviews, all of whom were white. I asked whether I could interview an African American parent, and the principal arranged for me to do so. In another instance, I discovered that the teacher with the most seniority and considerable influence in the school had not been selected. I asked to have her added to the list, and the principal readily agreed. (The principal had not included this teacher initially because she believed the teacher would not be interested in participating. The teacher, as the principal had predicted, was reluctant, but she eventually agreed to participate.)

DATA COLLECTION PROCEDURES

I spent 2 to 5 days in each school. Data came from multiple sources: individual and group interviews, observation of one or more *MicroSociety* sessions, observation of classrooms during periods of the day when the *MicroSociety* was not in operation, observation in nonclassroom settings such as the cafeteria, playground, halls, media center or library, main office, and teachers' lounge, observation of faculty planning meetings, and study of archival materials (which included minutes of faculty planning meetings, principal's notes, grant proposals, newspaper articles, etc.).

I tried to conduct interviews in a private location within the school. On a few occasions, I interviewed two or more teachers together. I interviewed students individually and in groups of varying sizes. The interviews were tape-recorded, but I also took notes during the interviews. In addition, I kept detailed field notes in which I recorded observations and reflections.

I told people in the schools that I was interested in writing a book on the *MicroSociety* program. I also explained that my primary interest was in learning about the implementation process so that those who wanted to adopt the program in the future would have some guidance. I encouraged informants, therefore, to tell me about the problems and difficulties they had encountered, as well as the achievements. I also said that I was especially interested in the strategies they had used to overcome obstacles.

THE RESEARCH RELATIONSHIP

The issue of trust came up early in the project. George and Carolynn wanted the *MicroSociety* program to thrive. Thus they took a risk in allowing me such open access to schools that were implementing the program.

I assured them that they would be able to read the book and any papers that I would eventually write, which helped to allay some of their concern. However, they surely realized that once they read a draft and gave me feedback, their influence over what would appear in print would be limited. One factor that helped me to gain their trust was Lew Gantwerk. George and Carolynn had worked closely with Lew for several years and had great trust and confidence in him; thus his endorsement of me and the project made George and Carolynn more willing to allow me access.

Trust, however, was an issue at the school level as well. Two of the schools were leery about being identified in written reports. I told the principals that they could review the draft of the book that I hoped to eventually write in order to ensure that there was nothing that would harm their schools' reputations. This method of ensuring confidentiality reassured the principals. Having the endorsement and support of George and Carolynn also helped me to gain access to the schools and the trust and confidence of most informants.

My own views about the *MicroSociety* program undoubtedly affected the results as well. In the beginning, the *MicroSociety* program intrigued me, and it seemed to incorporate many of my own educational values. But I tried to retain as much of a neutral and disinterested stance as possible. Over time, however, my views toward the program became even more positive, and I became less concerned about remaining neutral. I hope that as one who was sympathetic toward the program, I was better able to do my job, which was to learn how best to implement it.

At this point, my view is that the *MicroSociety* program is a valuable approach to making schools more interesting and productive places for both teachers and children. But like any innovation, the effectiveness of the program depends on how it is implemented. Also, it is not a panacea, and it is not for everyone. For some children and teachers, other approaches may well be more appropriate. However, one of the strengths of the program is that it can accommodate so many different interests and learning styles. It can be as varied as society itself in the opportunities that it provides for exploration, learning, and growth.

DATA ANALYSIS AND HYPOTHESIS GENERATION

At the end of each visit to the first few schools, I wrote a memorandum summarizing what I had observed and learned. I shared the memorandum with George, Carolynn, and Lew. I usually spoke with Carolynn about the memorandum, which often led to new information and insights.

After I had studied two schools, I began to develop an initial set of hypotheses about the implementation factors that were most important. When I had finished collecting data in all the schools, I went back to each case looking for data that both confirmed and disconfirmed each hypothesis. Finally, I examined the literature on implementation to see how the findings fit other views.

These procedures incorporated the guidelines for increasing reliability and internal validity put forth by Eisenhardt (1989): multiple perspectives and a divergent approach to verification in which one looks for disconfirmation as well as confirmation from the data. The other validation procedure, which has been incorporated to a limited degree in this paper, is to support any propositions included in written reports with ample examples from the data.

Resource B: The Implementation Guidelines

CREATING A FAVORABLE CONTEXT FOR THE PROGRAM

Guideline 1: The relationships among teachers and principal in the school should be positive. If they are characterized by mistrust and conflict, then efforts should be directed toward improving those relationships before attempting to implement change.

Guideline 2: There should be a good fit between the proposed change and the school's priorities and values.

Guideline 3: There should be a history of parent involvement and community partnerships at the school.

Guideline 4: The principal should support the idea.

INTRODUCING THE PROGRAM TO THE SCHOOL IN A WAY THAT GAINS NECESSARY BUY-IN

Guideline 5: Give teachers a meaningful voice in the adoption and planning process.

Guideline 6: Before the program begins, there should be a planning period that includes effective staff development and a "pilot run."

Guideline 7: Implementers should secure additional funding for the program.

Guideline 8: Teachers should be matched to ventures and agencies in a way that leads to a good fit.

Guideline 9: The program should be based on realistic goals and time perspectives.

KEEPING THE PROGRAM RUNNING

Guideline 10: Look for ways to increase student responsibility and autonomy. Avoid having teachers take over for the students, especially when problems occur.

Guideline 11: There should be at least one staff member whose role is to seek out and utilize additional resources on an ongoing basis.

Guideline 12: Create a culture in which experimentation and learning from experience are highly valued. Don't become preoccupied with making things run smoothly. Keep in mind that in dealing with problems, it's the process that counts, not the solution.

Guideline 13: Once the program becomes operational, continue to set aside time for planning, group problem solving, team building, and training.

Guideline 14: Create an open and flexible decision-making structure for the program in which teachers have a meaningful voice. Minimize the "nonnegotiables," and make it clear what they are.

LEADERSHIP: THE CRITICAL INGREDIENT

Guideline 15: The principal should be a strong advocate for the program, within the school and beyond.

Guideline 16: Select people for leadership positions who are "emotionally intelligent," and help leaders develop greater emotional intelligence over time.

References

Arete, C. (2002). *Microsociety: The impacts*. New York: Arete Corporation.

Bass, B. M. (2002). Cognitive, social, and emotional intelligence of transformational leaders. In R. E. Riggio, S. E. Murphy, & F. J. Pirozzolo (Eds.), *Multiple intelligences and leadership* (pp. 105–118). Mahwah, NJ: Erlbaum.

Bensman, D. (2000). *Central Park East and its graduates*. New York: Teachers College Press.

Berends, M., Bodilly, S. J., & Kirby, S. N. (2002). *Facing the challenges of whole-school reform: New American Schools after a decade*. Santa Monica, CA: RAND.

Berends, M., Bodilly, S., & Kirby, S. N. (2003). New American Schools: District and school leadership for whole school reform. In J. Murphy & A. Datnow (Eds.), *Leadership lessons from comprehensive school reforms* (pp. 109–132). Thousand Oaks, CA: Corwin.

Berman, P., & McLaughlin, M. W. (1976). Implementation of educational innovation. *Educational Forum, 40*, 345–370.

Boyatzis, R. E. (1994). Stimulating self-directed learning through the managerial assessment and development course. *Journal of Management Education, 18*, 304–323.

Cherniss, C. (1995). *Beyond burnout: Helping teachers, nurses, therapists, and lawyers overcome stress and disillusionment*. New York: Routledge.

Cherniss, C. (1998). Social and emotional learning for leaders. *Educational Leadership, 55*(7), 26–28.

Cherniss, C., & Adler, M. (2000). *Promoting emotional intelligence in organizations*. Alexandria, VA: ASCD.

Cherniss, C., & Goleman, D. (2001). *The emotionally intelligent workplace*. San Francisco: Jossey-Bass.

Dow, P. B. (1991). *Schoolhouse politics: Lessons from the Sputnik era*. Cambridge, MA: Harvard University Press.

Eisenhardt, K. M. (1989). Building theories from case study research. *Academy of Management Review, 14*, 532–550.

Elmore, R. F. (1996). Getting to scale with good educational practice. *Harvard Educational Review, 66*(1), 1–26.

Evans, R. (1996). *The human side of school change*. San Francisco: Jossey-Bass.

Finnan, C., & Meza, J. Jr. (2003). The accelerated schools project: Can a leader change the culture and embed reform? In J. Murphy & A. Datnow (Eds.),

Leadership lessons from comprehensive school reform (pp. 83–108). Thousand Oaks, CA: Corwin.

Firestone, W. A., & Corbett, H. D. (1988). Planned organizational change. In N. Boyan (Ed.), *Handbook of research on educational administration* (pp. 321–341). White Plains, NY: Longman.

Fishman, D. B. (1999). *The case for pragmatic psychology.* New York: New York University Press.

Fullan, M. (1993). *Change forces: Probing the depths of educational reform.* London: Falmer.

Fullan, M. (2001). *The new meaning of educational change.* New York: Teachers College Press.

Goldenberg, I. I. (1971). *Build me a mountain: Youth, poverty, and the creation of settings.* Cambridge: MIT Press.

Goleman, D. (1995). *Emotional intelligence.* New York: Bantam.

Goleman, D. (1998). *Working with emotional intelligence.* New York: Bantam.

Goleman, D., Boyatzis, R., & McKee, A. (2002). *Primal leadership: Realizing the power of emotional intelligence.* Boston: Harvard Business School Press.

Grote, J. (2002). *Case study of a MicroSociety school.* Unpublished thesis, Illinois State University, Normal, IL.

Hargreaves, A., & Fink, D. (2003). Sustaining leadership. *Phi Delta Kappan, 84,* 693–700.

Haynes, N. M., Emmons, C. L., Gebreyesus, S., & Ben-Avie, M. (1996). The school development program evaluation process. In J. P. Comer, N. M. Haynes, E. T. Joyner, & M. Ben-Avie (Eds.), *Rallying the whole village: The Comer process for reforming education* (pp. 123–146). New York: Teachers College Press.

Heller, M. F., & Firestone, W. A. (1995). Who's in charge here? Sources of leadership for change in eight schools. *Elementary School Journal, 96,* 65–86.

Kramer, D., Ber, R., & Moore, M. (1989). Increasing empathy among medical students. *Medical Education, 23,* 168–173.

Kutzik, D. M. (2003). *Capitalizing on MicroSociety: How students profit from real-world learning.* Philadelphia: MicroSociety, Inc.

Levin, H. M. (1987). Accelerated schools for disadvantaged students. *Educational Leadership, 44*(3), 19–21.

Levine, M., & Levine, A. (1973, June 22–24). *Change in organizational settings: A diagnostic framework.* Paper presented at the NIMH Continuing Education Seminar on Emergency Mental Health Services, Washington, DC.

Louis, K. S., Toole, J., & Hargreaves, A. (1999). Rethinking school improvement. In J. Murphy & K. S. Louis (Eds.), *Handbook of research in educational administration* (2nd ed., pp. 251–276). San Francisco: Jossey-Bass.

Mayhew, K. C., & Edwards, A. C. (1966). *The Dewey school.* New York: Atherton.

McLaughlin, M. W. (1990). The RAND change agent study revisited: Macro perspectives and micro realities. *Educational Researcher, 19*(9), 11–16.

Muncey, D. E., & McQuillan, P. J. (1996). *Reform and resistance in schools: An ethnographic view of the coalition of essential schools.* New Haven, CT: Yale University Press.

Olson, L., & Jerald, C. D. (1998). Barriers to success. *Education Week, 17,* 9–23.

Poole, M. (199). *MicroSociety* program in Sioux City: "To make a good school even better." *Middle Matters, 4*(3), 1.

Portin, B. S., Beck, L. G., Knapp, M. S., & Murphy, J. (Eds.). (2003). *Self-reflective renewal in schools.* Westport, CT: Praeger.

Purkey, S. C., & Smith, M. S. (1983). Effective schools: A review. *Elementary School Journal, 83,* 427–452.

Retallic, J., & Fink, D. (2002). Framing leadership: Contributions and impediments to educational change. *International Journal of Leadership in Education, 5*(2), 91–104.

Richmond, G. (1973). *The Microsociety school: A real world in miniature.* New York: Harper & Row.

Richmond, G. H., & Richmond, C. K. (1996). *The MicroSociety handbook.* Philadelphia: MicroSociety, Inc.

Sarason, S. B. (1972). *The creation of settings and the future societies.* San Francisco: Jossey-Bass.

Sarason, S. B. (1990). *The predictable failure of educational reform.* San Francisco: Jossey-Bass.

Sarason, S. B. (1996). *Revisiting "the culture of the school and the problem of change."* New York: Teachers College Press.

Sarason, S. B. (1997). *How schools might be governed and why.* New York: Teachers College Press.

Sarason, S. B. (1998). *Charter schools: Another flawed educational reform?* New York: Teachers College Press.

Sarason, S. B. (2002). *Educational reform: A self-scrutinizing memoir.* New York: Teachers College Press.

Sarason, S. B., & Lorentz, E. M. (1989). *The challenge of the resource exchange network.* San Francisco: Jossey-Bass.

Schorr, L. B. (1997). *Common purpose: Strengthening families and neighborhoods to rebuild America.* New York: Anchor Books Doubleday.

Schwebel, M. (2003). *Remaking America's three school systems.* Lanham, MD: Scarecrow.

Senge, P. (1990). *The fifth discipline.* New York: Doubleday/Currency.

Sergiovanni, T. J. (1992). *Moral leadership: Getting to the heart of school reform.* San Francisco: Jossey-Bass.

Slavin, R. E., & Madden, N. A. (Eds.). (2001). *Success for all: Research and reform in elementary education.* Mahwah, NJ: Erlbaum.

Traub, J. (2002, November 10). Success for some. *The New York Times,* "Education Life" section, pp. 25–31.

Tyack, D., & Cuban, L. (1995). *Tinkering toward utopia: A century of public school reform.* Cambridge, MA: Harvard University Press.

Weinstein, R. S. (2002). *Reaching higher: The power of expectations in schooling.* Cambridge, MA: Harvard University Press.

Index

Accelerated Schools, xvii, 60, 76, 116–117
Accountability, xviii, 32, 40, 43, 186
Adler, M., 185
Adult roles, 15–16
Annie E. Casey Foundation, 10
ARCO Chemical, 10
Arete, C., 18, 19, 21
Attendance, 19
Authority structure, 94–97, 128, 147–148

Banks, 13, 16, 85–86, 127
Bass, B. M., 105
Beck, L. G., 40, 57, 100, 102
"Before-the-Beginning" factors, 114–116, 138–140, 155
Behavior problems, 34–37, 43, 113, 137–138
Ben-Avie, M., 24, 40, 85, 100
Bensman, D., 90, 102
Berends, M., xvii, xix, 24, 26, 27, 28, 38, 40, 51, 65, 71, 77, 100, 185, 186
Berman, P., 53, 60
Ber, R., 185
Bodily, S. J., xvii, xix, 24, 26, 27, 28, 38, 40, 51, 65, 71, 77, 100, 185, 186
Boredom, 178
Boyatzis, R., 103, 184, 185
Burnout, 183
Businesses, 5, 13, 16

Central Park East, 90, 102
Challenges:
    behavior problems, 34–37, 43, 113, 137–138
    core curriculum integration, 30–34, 43, 177–178
    emotional intelligence, 182–185
    external environment, 185–187
    funding issues, 162–165
    implementation issues, 39–40, 43, 140–146, 156–160
    routinization, 178

staff conflicts, 37–39, 43
student responsibility, 180–182
sustainability, 40–42, 43, 160–162, 175–188
workload demands, 25–30, 43, 136–137, 160–161
See also Commitment; Leadership
Change, impact of, 105–106, 115–116
Cherniss, C., 70, 103, 183, 184, 185
Clement G. McDonough City Magnet School (Massachusetts)
    academic impact, 17
    funding, 71–72
    goals and expectations, 75
    origins, xx, 9
    parent involvement, 54–56
    planning process, 87–88
    positive staff relationships, 49
    principal support, 103
    as prototype, 65–66
    teacher participation, 60–61
Clinchy, Evans, 52
Coalition of Essential Schools, xvii, 30–31, 38, 43, 60, 96
Comer, James, xvii, 24, 85, 100
Commitment:
    challenges, 24–25, 42–43
    coordinators, 26
    decision making, 124–126
    implementation guidelines, 59–65
    interpersonal conflicts, 37–39
    Mesquite Elementary School, 112, 116–121, 124–126
    problem-solving climate, 87–90
    sustainability, 160–162, 177
    union-management conflicts, 50–51
Community involvement:
    implementation guidelines, 53–56, 195
    importance, 16, 85–86
    Mesquite Elementary School, 119–120, 123–124, 127–128

Montgomery Middle School, 163–164
sustainability, 43
Wellfleet Elementary School, 139, 145
Comprehensive School Reform
    Demonstration (CSRD) Act (1998), xvii
Conflict management, 37–39
Constitutions, 14, 178
Consultants, 67–68, 123–124
Coordinators:
    authority structure, 94–96
    commitment issues, 26
    core curriculum integration, 33–34
    emotional intelligence, 107–108, 167
    funding issues, 72
    goals and expectations, 76
    interpersonal conflicts, 38
    Montgomery Middle School, 158,
        162–163, 165, 166–167
    parent involvement, 119, 126–127
    personal qualities, 167
    planning process, 66
    problem-solving climate, 88–90
    program coordinator, 118–119, 123, 127
    training activities, 67–68
    venture matching process, 158
    Wellfleet Elementary School, 143–149
Corbett, H. D., xvi, xviii, 51, 70, 71, 96–97,
    102, 105
Core Knowledge, xvii
Court system, 6, 14–15, 16
Credit unions, 86
Crimestoppers, 6, 14, 16, 85, 127
Cuban, L., xviii, 181–182

Data analysis, 192–193
Data collection procedures, 191
Decision making:
    implementation guidelines, 94–97, 196
    Mesquite Elementary School,
        124–126, 129
    Montgomery Middle School, 165–166
    student responsibility, 80, 92
    Wellfleet Elementary School, 142–143
Desegregation efforts, 52, 54–55, 72, 75,
    154–155
Dewey, John, xviii, 188
Dewey School, xviii
Discipline, 19, 34–37
Dow, P. B., xvi, 54
Duncan, Janet, 157, 166–168

Economic system, 13–14
Edwards, A. C., xviii
Effective schools movement, xvi

Eisenhardt, K. M., 193
Elmore, R. F., xviii, 68
Emmons, C. L., 24, 40, 85, 100
Emotional intelligence:
    coordinators, 107–108, 167
    implementation guidelines, 103–108, 196
    importance, xxii
    leadership, 103–108, 131–132, 150–151
    sustainability, 182–185
Empowerment
    See Student empowerment; Teachers
Enthusiasm issues, 41–42, 43, 136–143, 162
Evaluation procedures, 178–179
Evans, R., xvi, 60, 104, 105–106
Expectations, goals and, 74–77, 129, 142,
    158–159, 196
Experimentation, 87–90, 196
External environment, 185–187

Facilitators, 72
Failure factors, 135–151, 154–171
Fink, D., 41, 100
Finnan, C., 41
Firestone, W. A., xvi, xviii, 51, 70, 71,
    96–97, 102, 105
Fishman, D. B., 179
Ford Foundation, 43
Fullan, M., xvi, 54, 70, 85, 87, 99, 179
Funding issues, 27, 71–73, 82–83,
    162–165, 195

Gantwerk, Lew, xx, 192
Gebreyesus, S., 24, 40, 85, 100
Goals and expectations, 74–77, 129, 142,
    158–159, 196
Goldenberg, I. I., 176
Goleman, D., 103, 182, 184, 185
Gonzales, Maria, 123
Goodness of fit, 51–53, 195
Grote, J., 39, 125, 129

Hargreaves, A., xvi, xviii, 41, 99, 104,
    105, 106, 184
Haynes, N. M., 24, 40, 85, 100
Heller, M. F., 102
Hirsch, E. D., Jr., xvii

IBM, 10
Implementation guidelines:
    community involvement, 53–56, 195
    emotional intelligence, xxii, 103–108,
        150–151, 182–185
    funding issues, 71–73, 82–83,
        162–165, 195

goals and expectations, 74–77, 129, 142, 158–159, 196
goodness of fit, 51–53, 195
leadership, 99–108, 196
organizational learning, 87–90, 196
parent involvement, 53–56, 195
participation principle, 59–65, 140–142, 156–160, 195
planning process, 65–71, 90–94, 195
positive staff relationships, 48–51, 195
principal support, 56–57, 195, 196
resource development, 82–87, 196
staff development, 65–71, 91–94, 196
student responsibility, 79–82, 92, 180–182
venture matching process, 73–74, 141, 158, 196
See also Mesquite Elementary School; Montgomery Middle School; Wellfleet Elementary School
Informants, 190–191
Inservice training, 184–185
Interpersonal conflicts, 37–39, 43, 88–89, 137

Jennings, Peter, 9
Jerald, C. D., xv
Junior Achievement, 119–120

King, Carolynn, xx, 9, 10–11, 180, 190–192
Kirby, S. N., xvii, xix, 24, 26, 27, 28, 38, 40, 51, 65, 71, 77, 100, 185, 186
Knapp, M. S., 40, 57, 100, 102
Kramer, D., 185
Kutzik, D. M., 24, 32

Laws, 6, 14, 16
Leadership:
  authority structure, 95–96
  challenges, 33, 41, 43
  emotional intelligence, xxii, 103–108, 150–151, 184–185, 196
  implementation guidelines, 99–108, 196
  importance, 99–100
  management subsystem, 121–124
  personal qualities, 104–106, 129–132, 170
  sustainability, 176–177
  training activities, 125–126
  weak leadership, 138–139, 146–151, 176–177
Legislatures, 6–7, 14, 16
Levine, A., 70, 72
Levine, M., 70, 72
Levin, Henry, xvii, 60, 76, 116
Lopez, Teresa, 128–131
Lorentz, E. M., 87

Louis, K. S., xvi, xviii, 99, 104, 105, 106, 184
Lowell, Massachusetts, xx, 9, 51–52
  See also Clement G. McDonough City Magnet School (Massachusetts)

"MacNeil-Lehrer News Hour," 9
Madden, N. A., 68, 76
Magnet schools, 9, 17, 40, 52–53, 155
  See also Clement G. McDonough City Magnet School (Massachusetts)
Management team, 122–123
Mayhew, K. C., xviii
McKee, A., 103, 184
McLaughlin, M. W., xviii, 53, 60
McQuillan, P. J., 26, 31, 38, 43, 60, 65, 96
Mesquite Elementary School, 111–133
Methodology, 189–193
Meza, J., Jr., 41
Micro Moms, 126–127
MicroSociety® program:
  academic impact, 17–19, 21, 113–114
  adult roles, 15–16
  basic elements, 12–16
  benefits, xi–xiii
  challenges, 23–43
  economic system, 13–14
  emotional intelligence, xxii, 103–108, 150–151, 182–185
  external environment, 185–187
  funding issues, 71–73, 82–83, 162–165, 195
  goals and expectations, 74–77, 129, 142, 158–159, 196
  goodness of fit, 51–53, 195
  guiding philosophy, 10–12
  historical background, xix–xx
  implementation, xx–xxii, 9–10, 21, 39–40, 43, 140–146
  Mesquite Elementary School, 111–133
  Montgomery Middle School, 153–171
  nonacademic impact, 19–20
  organizational learning, 87–90, 196
  origins, 7–9
  participation principle, 59–65
  political system, 14–15
  positive staff relationships, 48–51
  resource development, 82–87, 196
  student responsibility, 79–82, 92, 180–182
  sustainability, 40–42, 43, 112, 175–188
  typical day, 3–7
  venture matching process, 73–74, 141, 158, 196

Wellfleet Elementary School, 135–151
See also Community involvement;
     Parent involvement; Planning
     process; Principal support; Staff
     development
MicroSociety, Inc. (MSI), xx–xxi, 9–10,
     73, 178
Mini-malls, 163–164
Montessori model, 178
Montgomery Middle School, 153–171
Moore, M., 185
Morgan Stanley, 10
Muncey, D. E., 26, 31, 38, 43, 60, 65, 96
Murphy, J., 40, 57, 100, 102
Murphy's Law, 76

Neighborhood schools, 155
Nelson, Bill, 155, 167–171
Networking, 102
New American Schools (NAS) Development
     Corporation, xvii, 24, 26, 77, 100
New Math, xvi
No Child Left Behind Act (2001), xviii, 186
Noncertified staff, 86, 145
Northwest Regional Educational
     Laboratory, 10

Olivas, Ronald, 119–120, 123–124
Olson, L., xv
Open classrooms, xvi
Organizational learning, 87–90, 130,
     146–151, 196

Parent involvement:
  impact, 20
  implementation guidelines, 53–56, 195
  importance, 16, 83–85
  Mesquite Elementary School, 115, 119,
     126–127
  Montgomery Middle School, 163
  Wellfleet Elementary School, 139, 145
Participation principle:
  implementation guidelines, 59–65, 195
  importance, xxii
  Mesquite Elementary School, 116–121
  Montgomery Middle School, 156–160,
     165–166
  Wellfleet Elementary School, 140–142
Perfectionism, 76, 81
Pierce, Mary, 157–158, 166–168
Planning process:
  implementation guidelines, 65–71,
     90–94, 195
  Mesquite Elementary School, 117–119, 125

Montgomery Middle School, 157, 165
  Wellfleet Elementary School, 141–142
Political system, 14–15
Poole, M., 20
Portin, B. S., 40, 57, 100, 102
Positive staff relationships, 48–51, 61–62,
     128–131, 195
Preservice training, 185
Principal support:
  authority structure, 95–96, 128, 147–148
  emotional intelligence, 103–108,
     131–132, 150–151, 196
  funding issues, 72
  implementation guidelines, 56–57, 195, 196
  Mesquite Elementary School, 116–118,
     128–132
  Montgomery Middle School, 156–160,
     167–171
  parent involvement, 54–56, 84
  positive staff relationships, 48–51, 61–62,
     128–131, 195
  as program advocate, 100–102, 116–118,
     128–131, 167–171
  school reform, 56–57
  social capital, 131–132
  Wellfleet Elementary School, 138–142,
     146–151
  See also Leadership
Problem-solving climate, 88–93, 125, 130,
     170, 196
Program coordinator
  See Coordinators
Progressive Education, xviii
Purkey, S. C., xvii

RAND Corporation, xix, 38
Resource development:
  implementation guidelines, 82–87, 196
  Mesquite Elementary School, 118–120,
     126–128
  Montgomery Middle School, 162–164
  Wellfleet Elementary School, 145
Restructuring, xvii
Retallic, J., 100
Richmond, C. K., 10–11
  See also King, Carolynn
Richmond, George, x, xix–xx, 7–9, 10–11,
     52, 66, 190–192
Roots and Wings, xvii
Routinization, 178

Sarason, S. B., xvi, 8, 32, 59, 87, 178, 180,
     183, 186–187
School Development Program, xvii, 85, 100

School of choice
See Magnet schools
School reform:
  current issues, ix–xiii
  emotional intelligence, xxii, 103–108,
    150–151, 182–185
  external environment, 185–187
  funding issues, 71–73, 82–83, 162–165, 195
  goals and expectations, 74–77, 129, 142,
    158–159, 196
  goodness of fit, 51–53, 195
  historical background, xv–xviii
  implementation guidelines, 48–57
  implementation issues, xviii–xix, 39–40,
    43, 140–146, 156–160
  organizational learning, 87–90, 196
  participation principle, 59–65
  resource development, 82–87, 196
  student responsibility, 79–82, 92,
    180–182
  sustainability, xix, 40–42, 43, 175–188
  venture matching process, 73–74, 141,
    158, 196
  See also Community involvement;
    Parent involvement; Planning
    process; Principal support; Staff
    development
Schorr, L. B., xviii, 27, 60, 68, 90, 99, 187
Schwebel, M., xix, 60, 64, 70, 76
Senge, P., 87
Sergiovanni, T. J., 105
Shaw, George Bernard, xi
Site selection criteria, 189–190
Sizer, Theodore, xvii, 60
Slavin, Robert, xvii, 68, 76
Smith, M. S., xvii
Social capital, 131–132
Social Development Program, 24
Stable environment, 114–115, 132
Staff conflicts, 37–39, 43
Staff development:
  implementation guidelines, 65–71,
    91–94, 196
  Mesquite Elementary School, 125, 130
  Montgomery Middle School, 165
  Wellfleet Elementary School, 144–145
Standardized tests:
  accountability issues, 32, 40, 43, 186
  background information, xv
  district mandates, 28
  goals and expectations, 142, 158–159
Student empowerment:
  implementation guidelines, 79–82, 92, 196
  importance, 42–43, 180–182

Mesquite Elementary School,
  112–114
Montgomery Middle School, 164
problem-solving climate, 92
training activities, 15
Wellfleet Elementary School,
  145–146
Success factors, 114–133, 161, 179
Success for All, xvii, 60, 68, 76
Sustainability, xix, 40–42, 43, 112,
  175–188

Taxes, 4, 13, 127
Teachable moments, 7, 11, 36
Teachers:
  emotional intelligence, 182–185
  empowerment, 60–61, 94–97, 107,
    116–118, 165–166
  impact on, 19–20
  interpersonal conflicts, 37–39, 43,
    88–89, 137
  positive staff relationships, 48–51,
    61–62, 195
  venture matching process, 73–74, 141,
    158, 196
  workload demands, 25–30, 43, 136–137,
    160–161
  See also Challenges; Commitment;
    Staff development; Student
    empowerment
Teacher supervision, 15–16
Team-building activities, 69, 91,
  125–126, 196
Thomas, Jane, 113–114
Time Magazine, 9
Time perspectives, 74–77
Toole, J., xvi, xviii, 99, 104, 105,
  106, 184
Training activities, 92–93, 125–126, 165,
  184–185, 196
Transformational leadership, 104–106
Traub, J., xvii
Trust, 49, 81, 192
Tyack, D., xviii, 181–182

Union-management relations, 50–51

Venture matching process, 73–74, 141,
  158, 196
Violence, xv

Weinstein, R. S., 20
Wellfleet Elementary School, 135–151
Whole-school reform, xvii, 28, 38, 40–41